DESIGNED

WORDS

FOR

A

DESIGNED

WORLD

DESIGNED WORDS FOR A DESIGNED WORLD

The International Concrete Poetry Movement, 1955–1971

JAMIE HILDER

McGill-Queen's University Press

Montreal & Kingston · London · Chicago

© McGill-Queen's University Press 2016

ISBN 978-0-7735-4733-9 (cloth)
ISBN 978-0-7735-4734-6 (paper)
ISBN 978-0-7735-9920-8 (ePDF)
ISBN 978-0-7735-9921-5 (ePUB)

Legal deposit second quarter 2016
Bibliothèque nationale du Québec

Printed in Canada on acid-free paper that is 100% ancient forest free (100% post-consumer recycled), processed chlorine free

This book has been published with the help of a grant from the Canadian Federation for the Humanities and Social Sciences, through the Awards to Scholarly Publications Program, using funds provided by the Social Sciences and Humanities Research Council of Canada.

McGill-Queen's University Press acknowledges the support of the Canada Council for the Arts for our publishing program. We also acknowledge the financial support of the Government of Canada through the Canada Book Fund for our publishing activities.

Library and Archives Canada Cataloguing in Publication
Hilder, Jamie, 1977–, author
Designed words for a designed world : the international concrete poetry movement, 1955-1971 / Jamie Hilder.

Includes bibliographical references and index.
Issued in print and electronic formats.
ISBN 978-0-7735-4733-9 (cloth).–ISBN 978-0-7735-4734-6 (paper).–
ISBN 978-0-7735-9920-8 (ePUB).–ISBN 978-0-7735-9921-5 (ePUB)

1. Concrete poetry–History and criticism. I. Title.
PN1455.H57 2016   809.1'4   C2016-901804-0   C2016-901805-9

For Helen Jarvis,
with gratitude and affection

CONTENTS

FIGURES

I have made every effort to identify, credit appropriately, and obtain publication rights from copyright holders of illustrations in this book. Notice of any errors or omissions in this regard will be gratefully received and correction made in any subsequent editions.

/ ACKNOWLEDGMENTS

I would like to thank, for their financial support, the Social Sciences and Humanities Research Council of Canada, the Department of English at the University of British Columbia, and the Canada-US Fulbright program, all of whom, in combination, made it possible for me to work. Also, for their tremendous urge to collect, which is matched only by their urge to give, I would like to thank Dr Marvin and Ruth Sackner, who allowed me invaluable access to their Archive of Visual and Concrete Poetry in August of 2008. Their collection forms the vertebrae of this study.

Designed Words is the culmination of years of fascination and confusion that I have been fortunate enough to experience in close proximity to people who regularly fascinate and challenge me. Richard Cavell, through shouts and whispers, asked questions of me to which I still do not know the answers, and I am grateful to him for that and many other gifts. Johanna Drucker continues to embody a pan-disciplinary curiosity that surprises and moves me. Jeff Derksen's lessons transformed the scale of my thinking, and always seem to end up in laughter, my favourite pedagogical tool. Clint Burnham and Peter Dickinson have been my teachers without ever acting like it.

This book was talked through before it was written. To those who helped me speak it, I am thankful. Jonathan Crago, my editor at McGill-Queen's, has earned my deep admiration and respect. Jade Boyd, Stacy Wood, Julia Aoki, Sina Rahmani, Roxanne Panchasi, and Brady Cranfield have all made me smarter just by knowing them. A special thanks goes to Yu-Ting Huang, who knows distance too well; to Ian and Sunja, who occupy some place beyond friendship; and to my neighbour, Andy, who regularly makes my face cramp from laughing.

DESIGNED

WORDS

FOR

A

DESIGNED

WORLD

Figure 1.1
Heinz Gappmayr. "Zeichen"

1 / INTRODUCTION

Concrete poetry had a moment. That is not to say that it has remained there, nor that the poetry has expired. On the contrary, given recent cultural and technological transformations on a global scale, concrete poetry seems more relevant than ever. If we are concerned with how computer technologies have affected our relationship to information and each other, there are poems that address those very issues as they emerged in the 1950s and '60s. If we feel anxious about the role of the nation in an age of global finance, or about environmental degradation resulting from the urbanization of the Earth's population, those anxieties were shared by concrete poets. If we fret about the ability of poetry or art to reach an audience in an increasingly saturated media environment, or about a general scarcity of time in consumerist culture, a close examination of concrete poetry proves that those issues are not new. Concrete poetry had a moment, and that moment is our moment, too.

I want to begin by posing some questions about a poem that many would not immediately recognize as a poem, and some would argue *cannot* be a poem: the Austrian poet Heinz Gappmayr's "Zeichen" (Sign) from 1965 (see fig. 1.1). At first glance, it is a black square. Those familiar with Kazimir Malevich's *Black Square* painting from 1915 might see the poem as derivative, but a black square on paper is different than a black square on canvas, and 1965 in Austria is much different than 1915 in Russia. In addition to its reference to a painting tradition, the work does, in fact, possess literary qualities. Upon closer inspection, a reader can make out fragments of letters leaking out from the top and sides: maybe the top of an uppercase *O*, or an uppercase *M*? Is that part of a lower case *t*, or an *l*? On the left, it looks like an entire lowercase *n* is visible, but could it also be half of an *m*? On the right, where the lines would end – can we even speak of lines? – there is half of a lowercase *s*, or maybe it is part of a different shape that looks like an *s*. Maybe it is not a fragment, but a complete shape designed by Gappmayr to suggest something like a letter, a shape that he attaches to the side of a large, dark, overprinted square.

How are we supposed to *read* this poem? Perhaps it is not the poem that needs reading, but the act of reading itself. What do we expect from ink on pages? What do our habits of looking and comprehending prevent us from seeing, and what do they allow? There are issues of secrecy in the poem, too. Has it been redacted in a way that does not even allow for the remnants of lines, like the redacted passages we are used to seeing in official or confidential documents, where only certain words are blacked out? What are the conditions of secrecy in Europe in 1965? What are the modes of communication? What are the possibilities for art and/or poetry to intervene in people's thinking about information? And how does the poem relate to its technological moment? Is it a misprint, a mechanical glitch that ruined a text? Is the page now a screen, but one that has gone dark, or that is waiting to be turned on or projected upon? Significantly, the putative lack of meaning in the poem allows for more people to understand it. As a *sign*, it becomes meaningful – though differently meaningful – to readers independent of their national languages, and in that way addresses the development of an expanding global audience at a time of rapidly increasing communication networks.

Gappmayr's poem, then, is not a simple derivation of an earlier avant-garde painting. Nor is it an easy or cynical rejection of signification. It operates within its moment, which was characterized by dramatic shifts in technology, nationhood, philosophy, and art. I will return to it in chapter 3 in a discussion of concrete poetry's relationship to mechanical labour, but I want it to function here as an example of what kinds of critical questions concrete poetry requires. There is a footnote in Walter Benjamin's "On Some Motifs in Baudelaire" where he imagines how the appearance of crowds in city streets must have once been a spectacle to behold, rather than the banal scene of potential inconvenience or alienation it often operates as today. He writes that crowds were something that eyes had to adjust to; people's eyes had to learn how to move quickly between faces and bodies to process patterns of dress and movement, and to be able to recognize people they might know or be looking for. The development of these enhanced visual capabilities, Benjamin suggests, forced artists and poets to create new techniques of representation – Impressionism, specifically – to adequately express the shifts in their way of experiencing the world (197). Benjamin's meditation is only a note in his larger study, and is only a suggestion, rather than a developed argument, but his idea contains an impulse that I find particularly helpful in approaching concrete poetry. What is the equivalent of the nineteenth-century crowd for the twentieth-century concrete poet? Is it television? Is it the nuclear bomb? Space exploration? The concrete poets encountered a new kind of crowd, one on the scale of the globe, and created a poetry in response.

Problems at the Beginning

There are problems that emerge in any study of concrete poetry, problems of chronology, category, and scale. To date, the critical methodologies applied to concrete poetry – whether they focus on specific authors, or nations, or relationships to media or visual art – have struggled to present a cohesive understanding of the development of the work within its global context. A brief explanation of where the term came from and how it operates cannot solve these issues, but it will at least serve to establish some signposts. Most histories of the genre point to the 1955 meeting in Ulm, Germany, between Eugen Gomringer, the Bolivian-Swiss secretary to the concrete artist Max Bill, and Décio Pignatari, the Brazilian poet and co-founder (along with the brothers Augusto and Haroldo de Campos) of the Noigandres group, as the initiating moment of the concrete poetry movement (*konkrete poesie* in German, *poesia concreta* in Portuguese). However, the phrase *concrete poetry* appears previously. Öyvind Fahlström, the Swedish[1] artist and writer, used the term in 1953, in his "Hatila Rägulpr pä Fätsklikaben, Manifesto för Concrete Poetry," although his expressed ideas owe more to *musique concrète* than to what would later be understood as concrete poetry. "Concreta" was used to describe Augusto de Campos's "Poetemenos" in *Noigandres 2*, published in 1952 (Gumpel 38). And the Austrian concrete poet Reinhold Döhl pushes the term's beginnings back still further, quoting a 1951 essay by Hans Arp, "Kandinsky, le Poète": "in the year of dada, poems by [Wassily] kandinsky were read for the first time in cabaret voltaire in zürich (...). the dadaists were fervent protagonists of concrete poetry" (Döhl n. pag.; lower case in the original). Arp's usage of "concrete poetry," however, owes more to the sense by which *concrete* had come to refer to techniques in visual art than in literature, specifically the tradition that flows from the publication of Theo van Doesburg's "Manifesto of Concrete Art" in the first and only issue of *Art Concret* in 1930, through to figures such as Max Bill, the painter, sculptor, designer, architect, and critic whose exhibition of concrete art in São Paulo in 1956 had a profound influence on the Brazilian concrete poets. From the very beginning, concrete poetry was slippery, moving between visual art and performance, music and writing, and confounding definition.

Stretching back even further, the American orientalist Ernest Fenollosa uses the term as early as 1906, in his essay "The Chinese Written Character as a Medium for Poetry." He describes the Chinese ideogram for the verb *to be* as an amalgam of symbols that together represent the idea of grabbing the moon with a hand, and comments: "Here the baldest symbol of prosaic analysis is transformed by magic into a splendid flash of concrete poetry" (Fenollosa and Pound 89). This is likely the first time the term *concrete poetry* appears in print, and although it might not describe what is now referred to as "concrete poetry" – what was concrete poetry in 1906 is not the same as concrete poetry in 1955, or 2010 – it is nonetheless significant for the understanding of the visual character of language that would later become central to the International Concrete Poetry Movement. The poetic output of this movement, which operated most productively and energetically during the mid-1950s and '60s, functions as the primary referent of my use of the term *concrete poetry* throughout this study.

The concept of an ideogram as an ideal poetic form continues, though. Although Fenollosa's understanding of the Chinese language has been largely discredited,[2] his essay's role in the development of twentieth-century poetics is immeasurable. Ezra Pound, who edited and annotated Fenollosa's essay before publishing it in 1918, also energetically embraced its ideas. Chinese ideograms appear in various places within *The Cantos*, and Pound's ideas about Imagism exhibit his desire to strip poetry down to an *arrangement* of meaning that operates in much the same way as an ideogram. The essay's influence extends beyond Pound; Charles Olson designated the essay "the damned best piece on language since when," and the Brazilian concrete poet Haroldo de Campos locates in Fenollosa's statement that "relations are more real and more important than the things which they relate" a "structuralist credo before the letter" (Olson 169; Saussy 22). Fenollosa identifies a *material* superiority in the ideogram over the word:

There is little or nothing in a phonetic word to exhibit the
embryonic stages of its growth. It does not bear its metaphor on
its face. [...] In this Chinese shows its advantage. Its etymology
is constantly visible. It retains the creative impulse and process,
visible and at work. After thousands of years the lines of metaphoric
advance are still shown, and in many cases actually retained in the
meaning. (Pound and Fenollosa 55)

This perspective falls within the ideogrammatic fallacy that Tomoyuki
Iino outlines in an essay on the Japanese concrete poet Katsue Kitasono.
Iino counters the Fenollosa-Pound myth of the rational construction of
characters by pointing out that the vast majority of characters have no visual
relationship to the signifier, and that modern readers have no greater concept
of etymology than their English counterparts. A Japanese reader might be
expected to understand the relationship between the kanji character for
corner (角) and its visual source of an ox's horn as much as an English
reader could be expected to know that the etymology for "barbarian" is an
onomatopoetic representation of how foreign language sounded to the ears
of the Greeks: "ba-ba-ba-ba" (Iino 96–7).

However misunderstood, the concept of the Chinese ideogram's potential
to accentuate its *source* made it particularly attractive to poets who meant
to mark a shift in signifying practice around the middle of the twentieth
century. Décio Pignatari's "New Poetry" (1956) holds up the ideogram as an
ideal fusion of form and content: "a general art of language. advertising, the
press, radio, television, cinema. a popular art. the importance of the eye in
this more rapid communication: from neon signs to comic strips. the need for
movement. dynamic structure. the ideogram as basic idea" (86; all lower case
in original). Pignatari witnessed the world changing at an incomprehensible
pace. For him and for the other concrete poets, words in their conventional
modalities could no longer suffice.

So in spite of its possible meanings, historically and categorically
the phrase *concrete poetry* has largely come to refer to the type of poetry
Gomringer and Pignatari and the poets around them were producing,
initially independently from and unaware of each other, in the period leading up to and then following their 1955 meeting. The simultaneity of the
impulses felt by geographically and culturally disparate poets requires an
approach to the work as it is inflected by historical conditions. As both
Gomringer and the Noigandres group would eventually explain in various
manifestos and critical articles, concrete poetry was a movement that sought

to communicate a spatial, rather than a discursive, syntax. This reflects the fact that, from its beginnings, practitioners of concrete poetry aimed for a supranational, supralinguistic poetry, one that would strive for a fusion of form and content by foregrounding the visual character of words and letters over their semantic or phonetic functions. Considering the contemporaneous shifts in communication technology and its effects on everyday life, the poetry's drastic reimagining of language, visuality, and cultural circulation makes sense. In his 1956 introduction to the anthology he and Pignatari planned to publish, but which never came about, Gomringer writes:

> Concrete poetry is founded upon the contemporary scientific-technical view of the world and will come into its own in the synthetic-rationalistic world of tomorrow. If concrete poetry is still considered strange (aesthetically meagre or overly-simplified) this is probably due to a lack of insight into the new directions in which our society is developing in thought and action which in essence contain a new total view of the world. [...]
>
> I am therefore convinced that concrete poetry is in the process of realizing the idea of a universal poetry. (Gomringer, "Concrete Poetry" 68)

This emphasis on the technological imperatives at mid-century, which were to be met by the development of a new poetry, and consequently a new type of reader, distinguishes concrete poetry of the mid-1950s and onward from the work that previously carried the label, and ties it to modernist ideas of progress. The Noigandres group supports these ideas in their major manifesto, the title of which – "Plano-Piloto Para Poesia Concreta" (Pilot Plan for Concrete Poetry [1958]) – carries within it the developmentalist character of its moment, implying that it is only an initial program, the first stage of a permanent poetic revolution:

> Concrete Poetry aims at the least common multiple of language. Hence its tendency to nounising and verbification. [...]
>
> Renouncing the struggle for the "absolute," Concrete Poetry remains in the magnetic field of perennial relativeness. Chronomicro-metering of hazard. Control. Cybernetics. The poem as a mechanism regulating itself: feed-back. [...]

> Concrete Poetry: total responsibility before language. Thorough
> realism. Against a poetry of expression, subjective and hedonistic.
> To create precise problems and to solve them in terms of sensible
> language. A general art of the word. (A. de Campos, H. de Campos,
> and Pignatari 70)

These excerpts redefine the concept of concrete, distinguishing it from those that came before: an updated concrete that accounted for the new organization of everyday life in the postwar west and rapidly modernizing Brazil. It was van Doesburg's frustration with the application of the term *abstract* to his paintings that prompted him to develop his idea of *concrete*, which he used to describe work that was meant only to refer to itself as form: a line, therefore, would never stand in for a greater idea, but would strive to simply be a line. The same goes for a colour. Johanna Drucker explains this concretism as "a search for a universal formal language which had no relation to nature, emotional life or sensory data, and the pursuit of works which were completely void of lyrical, symbolic, or dramatic expression" (Drucker, *Figuring* 116). This is similar to the usage of the term Arp earlier applied to the poetry of Kandinsky, which, like that of Tristan Tzara and Hugo Ball, was non-referential, and strived for a negation of semantic communication.

Conversely, the concrete poets following the examples of Gomringer and the Noigandres Group were engaged in a positive project, a fact that Liselotte Gumpel argues is a result of their development out of a postwar milieu characterized in many ways by the relief of "peace" and the affluence felt in the process of reconstruction. Gumpel attributes the tendency of Dada to engage in nihilistic, destructive negativism to its development in the midst of the First World War, when artists could not help but witness the horror of the technologies of mass killing. Postwar concrete poetry, conversely, "remained curiously positive, to the point of appearing positivistic at times, particularly when the givens of technology were overly stressed. [...] It was this optimism that led the concretists to do positively what Dada had attempted negatively in the way of identifying directly with occurrences in the world of experience" (Gumpel 48–9). Despite the strong connection between concrete poetry and the ideas of the De Stijl group, it is difficult, when reading the second De Stijl manifesto (1920), to recognize any of the concrete poets' attitudes in a statement such as "The organism of contemporary literature feeds on the sentimentality of an enfeebled generation" (quoted in Weaver 124). To begin with, the concrete poets generally favoured metaphors of mechanisms over organisms, and even after witnessing the horrors of the Second World War, they never thought so little of their publics as to insult them as "enfeebled." More often than not they admired their readers, and it was the shift in the organization of everyday life (and perception) that demanded a new type of poetry, not the other way around. Gone was the nihilistic, negative impulse of the avant-gardes of the first half of the twentieth century. In the De Stijl project, there was an urge to destroy the conventional descriptive character of poetry. In concrete poetry, the emphasis is not on destruction but progression, marking the work as leaning out of modernity and into modernization. The poets were not battling something that had become irrelevant, but hoping to keep pace. Witnessing a generation transformed by electronic media and advancements in image-making, the concrete poets adapted traditional conceptions of line and the page in order to interpellate poetry into an aesthetic order that was still fascinated with the possibilities of the "new." In spite of the clear links between concrete poetry and modernist economic and cultural structures, a comprehensive investigation of how the poems operated within an international moment defined and energized by new technologies, and by an emergent sense of the global, has not yet made its way into the popular discussions of the work.

The distinctions between concrete poetry and the literary and artistic experiments that preceded it are valuable for delimiting a type of poetry that often finds itself out of its history, floating as a referent to form only. Such usage severs the work from its explicitly stated concerns and motivations. Recent work by Kenneth Goldsmith argues concrete poetry anticipated our experience of text in the internet age through its emphasis on interfaces and distribution, and in its modularity, but this approach tells us more about how concrete poetry "ended" than how it began. Jesper Olsson does a better job of situating the production of the poetry within its moment in his examination of new media poetry in Sweden in the 1960s, but his work is limited to a single nation, and consequently does not deal with how the technologies functioned across nations and their languages. Similarly, examinations of Brazilian concrete poetry to that nation's concrete art movement and modernization history illustrates important links between various modes of cultural production and infrastructural conditions, but also remain largely within the borders of Brazil. What needs greater attention is exactly how the *international* functioned for the poets, which promises of an emergent global imaginary were embraced, and which met with suspicion. The aim of this study is to emphasize the conditions that made up the International Concrete Poetry Movement, comprised of a group of poets interested in communicating and publishing in modes that foregrounded their geographical and linguistic isolation. While concrete poetry as a form has no necessary relationship to place or time or technology, the *movement* contained internationalism as a constituent factor in the production and distribution of the concrete poets' work.

The World of Now

Concrete poetry went out of its way to announce its temporality. Emmett Williams writes in the introduction to his influential *An Anthology of Concrete Poetry* (1967): "[concrete poetry] was born of the times, as a way of knowing and saying something about the world of *now*, with the techniques and insights of *now*" (vi). One year later, in the introduction to her large-format and full-colour anthology, *Concrete Poetry: A World View*, Mary Ellen Solt echoes Williams while acknowledging the increased commodification and spectacularization of everyday life and its spaces: "the visual poem is a word design in a designed world" (60). Richard Kostelanetz drives home this point in his 1970 anthology *Imaged Words & Worded Images*, which includes, as a "poem," a photograph by John Hinde of London's Piccadilly Circus that looks more like a pop-art collage than a city block.[3] The facades of the buildings are covered with advertisements for everything from Coca-Cola to the Beatles' movie *A Hard Day's Night*, from gin, gum, and cigarettes to travel packages and jewellery. In addition, three double-decker buses act as billboards on wheels (Kostelanetz 9). Now, it might be necessary here to distinguish between concrete poetry and the general display of language in advertising or public spaces. John Hinde is not a concrete poet; he is a photographer who made a career out of making postcard photographs of pleasant, commercialized landscapes. It is only the editorial impulse of Richard Kostelanetz that places Hinde's photograph within the discourse of visual poetry. This is not to denigrate Kostelanetz's decision in anyway. Hinde's artistic production, which is tied to the rise in postcard popularity resulting from increased international tourism, is a commentary on the commercialization of space that the concrete poets often addressed in their style and subject matter, and the presentation of his work as a visual poem instigates a productive confusion. It is through Kostelanetz's editorial proposition that the connections between the explosion of advertising post – World War II and poetry enter the discourse. Concrete poetry emerged from this milieu, and the poems demand readings that take into account cultural shifts that stretch beyond the literary and artistic. Juxtaposing the poems and critical writing of the time against social and technological advances of the mid-twentieth century on a global scale – of which there were many – serves to breath new life into a historically deflated field.

The question that arises from statements like Williams's and Solt's, however, is: when is "now" no longer now? When does "now" become "then"? Kostelanetz's introduction, where he opts to replace the term *concrete poetry* with *word imagery*, is significantly dated 1 January 1970, marking the beginning of a new decade, and the year many feel marks the termination of the International Concrete Poetry Movement. Stephen Scobie argues that the movement's demise can be located in, "ironically, 1967–68, the years of its apparent triumph, with the publication of the three major anthologies edited by Emmett Williams, Stephen Bann, and Mary Ellen Solt. The very definitiveness of these collections 'froze' Concrete Poetry in its historical moment" (Scobie, *Earthquakes* 146). Scobie might be guilty of an Anglo-American bias here, however, as Solt defers the pinnacle to November 1970 and the opening of the massive concrete poetry exhibition, *Concrete Poetry?*, at the Stedelijk Museum in Amsterdam (Solt, "Concrete Steps" 351). This exhibition, which would travel to Stuttgart, Nürnberg, Liverpool, and Oxford in 1971, has a retrospective quality to it. Curator Liesbeth Crommelin's catalogue essay supports Solt's timeline by referencing Nicholas Zurbrugg, who in the spring of 1970 collected and published in his magazine *Stereo Headphones* "a number of sta[t]ements on the death of concrete poetry, as voiced by various well-known poets in this field" (Crommelin n. pag.). Ian Hamilton Finlay refused the invitation to be included in John Sharkey's *Mindplay: An Anthology of British Concrete Poetry* in 1971 because "he found it increasingly impossible [sic] to detect any shared formal criteria by the late '60s. Nor could he find any criteria of quality that linked all of these productions. One had to move on to something else" (Bann "Interview" n. pag.).

While reports of the deaths of forms or movements are generally greatly exaggerated, and strict periodizations of poetic or artistic styles should always be met with skepticism, I remain interested in the possibilities of reading concrete poetry within a particular historical framework. This strategy is not meant to disqualify all concrete poetry produced after 1971 as illegitimate, or to mark all visually based poetry before 1955 as simply precursors to a more developed form. Work that falls outside of the tidy space between Gomringer and Pignatari's 1955 meeting and the closing of the travelling exhibition still deals with similar issues of language and form, but has a necessarily different relationship to its historical context. My reason for concentrating more on what could be described as the International

Concrete Poetry Movement – a loose group of poets, artists, critics, and publishers who were fascinated by the possibilities for poetry within an emerging global imaginary – rather than concrete poetry as *form*, which some critics, with varying levels of skill, apply to almost all poetry with a strong visual character, is to see what happens when we isolate poems within their moment. Which work comes to the fore? What gets left out? How can we understand such an impulse for inclusion or exclusion when it comes to thinking about literary history, or literature *in* history?

Kostelanetz astutely recognized the need for a new adjective to describe the work that was being produced in the wake of concrete poetry. Photography, in particular, as well as collage and happenings, were playing a much larger role in work poets and artists made in the late 1950s and early '60s. However, much of this work is better categorized as *poesia visiva*, a term that retains its Italian origin due to the history and popularity of similar work in Italy dating back to Filippo Marinetti and the Futurists' *Parole in libertà*. Despite the 1970s being seen as the decade of decline for concrete poetry, it was a time in which concrete poets developed highly personalized styles against the dominant idea of the negation of the subject present in the critical writings and manifestos of the international movement. Scobie points to the Scottish poet and artist Ian Hamilton Finlay and the Canadian bpNichol as two figures who adopted a distinctive style in the decade following the Stedelijk exhibition (*Earthquakes* 150–51), and I would add to these the Canadian bill bissett and the British Tom Phillips, whose poem project *A Humument* has been in continuous composition since the late 1960s.

While these poets were undoubtedly producing work in dialogue with concrete poetry, their work had departed qualitatively from that produced within what I argue is the International Concrete Poetry Movement, a distinction that is necessary to parse concrete poetry into historically situated contexts. Critics of concrete poetry encounter a poverty of terms in this regard, but a shift away from conflating subsequent or contemporary visual poetry as "concrete" would go a long way towards attaching history to poetic form. Poets and critics who refer to concrete poetry primarily as a form, who might consider a shaped poem from the seventeenth century beside a typewriter poem from the 1960s and a Flash-based digital poem from the twenty-first century, ask important questions about how language functions, how meaning operates, and what possibilities are open to poetry on the page. But there are questions that such an approach elides: how does language function differently in particular geographical, historical, political, and technological spaces? How does a concrete poem that might have been composed using Letraset or photo-offset printing in Brazil in the early 1960s *mean* differently than a poem that was produced in Photoshop, or HTML? These are the kinds of questions that drive my investigation, and are indicative of a method that owes perhaps as much to the discipline of art history as it does to literary criticism. Art historians, for example, might recognize in contemporary visual art techniques borrowed from the early twentieth century – readymades, nonsense, performance – but I imagine they would hesitate to categorize current practitioners as Dadaist or Surrealist artists, even if the work reminds them of those moments.

The boundary between concrete poetry and visual art becomes especially blurred by visual art's representation of language within movements like conceptual art and Fluxus, as well as in the work of the early twentieth century avant-gardes. Figures like Ian Hamilton Finlay or Tom Phillips, inasmuch as both are considered artists as well as poets, present a difficulty for disciplinary critics, a predictable difficulty when dealing with a genre that aims to fuse the linguistic and the visual. Poets such as the Romanian-Swiss Daniel Spoerri, or the German Ferdinand Kriwet, both of whom had contemporaneous careers in visual art alongside their concrete poetry activity, impede a clear delimitation of where their poetic work ends and their visual artwork begins, and challenge the very logic behind such a separation. Gomringer felt this anxiety around taxonomy, as well, and reacted in a rational, though perhaps conservative manner in his 1972/3 anthology of German language concrete poetry, *konkrete poesie: deutsprachige autoren*. In the text's introduction, he identifies a class of poets who function more as visual artists than poets, labelling them "also poets (auch-Dichter)," and defends his decision to exclude them from the anthology. Kriwet is notably absent (Gumpel 207). But there is a strong argument against treating language-based visual art and visual poetry as equivalent, as each practice functions within distinct yet overlapping discursive histories. They occupy different critical landscapes, and are focused on different horizons. They travel on different, though at times overlapping circuits of distribution. For instance, the emphasis on language in the conceptual art movement in the 1960s sought to utilize language as a transparent mode of communication, in opposition to what they considered the fetishized products of painting and sculpture. But a series of instructions by Lawrence Weiner, or a black and white Photostat print of a dictionary definition by Joseph Kosuth, should not be read as or considered concrete poetry. Concrete poetry, particularly in its Brazilian-Swiss context, was very much interested in making poems more like sculpture and painting, following the lead of Max Bill. While conceptual art utilized language to critique a system of referentiality within the institution of art, concrete poetry drew the reader's attention to the materiality of language, to its physicality, and its changing role within global communication. The dematerialization of the art object mirrored the rematerialization of the word: the canvas became a page and the page became a canvas.

I deal with the relationship between concrete poetry and visual art, and specifically conceptual art, in greater detail in chapter 4, but, by way of outlining what I have chosen to include and exclude in this study, further explanation of why I consider certain images poems and other images "not poems," and which poets to be "concrete" or "not concrete," for the purpose of this investigation, might be helpful. This kind of categorical boundary-building always comes with a certain amount of anxiety, but because there is already such a paucity of criticism that deals with concrete poetry as a movement, I feel that it is important to establish some provisional borders before advocating their dissolution. A figure like Ed Ruscha, for example, who was making word paintings in the mid-1960s, would likely not qualify as a concrete poet according to most criteria. This is hardly a controversial statement; I have never seen him referred to as a concrete poet or included in a history of visual poetry. He is an interesting case study, nonetheless, especially in the wake of the publication of *They Called Her Styrene* (2000), a collection of almost 600 word paintings Ruscha produced between the late 1950s and the late 1990s. The book's presentation of Ruscha's fascination with the visual representation of text, and of the materiality of language operating within the lexicon of advertising and design suggests possible affinities between visual art and concrete poetry. Indeed, a detailed analysis of his work alongside that of the concrete poets, addressing how painters and poets responded to new conditions of language in a consumerist mediascape, would likely produce interesting and illuminative results, especially if it included Ruscha's book projects and photographs. But I would still argue against categorizing his word paintings as concrete poetry for the following reasons: (1) he did not consider himself a concrete poet, nor did he speak of his work as related to poetic traditions, nor was he involved in any of the international anthologies, nor did he communicate with any concrete poet about his work; (2) his work was primarily on canvas, and painted, and the backgrounds on which the words were placed were as carefully produced as the words themselves; and (3) following from number two, his work was done by hand, whereas the concrete poets largely and significantly preferred work created by mechanical means, either by typewriter or letterpress.[4]

On the other hand, even though his poetic work was not anthologized until midway through the 1970s, Carl Andre, best known for his minimalist sculpture, was producing typewriter poems in the late '60s that fit formally within the critical discourse of concrete poetry.[5] The same is true for the aleatoric poetic composition of John Cage and Jackson Mac Low, each of whom is better known for work outside of concrete poetry, and closely linked to the multi-disciplinary Fluxus movement. Both Cage and Mac Low experimented with the rejection of the poetic subject in ways that complemented the ideas of the early concrete poets, which explains why they are more likely to appear in histories of both poetry and visual art of the time than those figures who are more specifically linked to visual art. Their presence in discussions of concrete poetry, although perhaps peripheral, makes much more sense because of their acute interest in the history of and potential for poetry.

Another figure who often becomes tangled with the history of concrete poetry is Isidore Isou, the founder and lead practitioner of the Lettriste movement. Because the Lettristes' project was framed as a stripping away, or rejection of meaning, because they sought to operate below the level of the word – at the letter – and because they make an explicit connection between the linguistic and the visual, critics and historians often pair it with concrete poetry's mid-century output, but there are significant differences between the respective programs. While concrete poetry operated in a loose, decentralized network of affiliations, the Lettristes were very much a French phenomenon. Isou, continuing in the tradition of Andre Breton as a high-priest of the avant-garde, staged scandals, decried the dead poetry of the day, and attempted to destroy film and poetry in order that they might be built up again. He had devised a theory that recognized two stages in the cycle of an art form: the Amplic (*amplique*), in which the art swells, and its function is integral to society; and the Chiseling (*ciselant*), in which a medium is reduced to its form alone, and is separated from daily life. Isou considered himself and his fellow Lettristes as occupying the terminal period of an Amplic phase, through which all poetry must pass before it can begin anew. He saw the salvation of poetry in the new alphabets and compositional techniques created by Lettristes. These techniques were largely expressive, and often improvisational, and would stretch into various media: painting, assemblage, performance, film, and sound. Lettristes avoided the personal pronoun *I*, believing it to be too romantic, but maintained a dependence on the idea of the artist or poet as a privileged, almost prophetic figure. In this they both parallel and depart from the concrete poets, who also rejected the compositional *I*, but who aimed for non-expression in many cases, following in the tradition of Max Bill and the concrete artists.

Isou and the Lettristes operated very much within the mode of the avant-garde developed by Surrealism, Dada, and Futurism in the early part of the century. Their work was oppositional, full of grand claims for its ability to transform culture and shepherd it into a glorious future in which all creative urges could be satisfied. Concrete poetry, on the other hand, functioned in the role of an *arrière-garde*, a category William Marx has applied to movements that compliment previous avant-gardes, which take up their concerns while acknowledging them as influences. The concrete poets might have had priests – Eugen Gomringer, Décio Pignatari, Augusto and Haroldo de Campos – but none of them were as high as Isou. And it would be incorrect to argue concrete poetry, in spite of its radical formal experiments, functioned as an avant-garde. It had none of the nihilism, activism, antagonism, or agonism Renato Poggioli argues are required in his *The Theory of the Avant-Garde* (1968), nor did it position itself against the institution of the bourgeois art market in the manner outlined by Peter Bürger in his *Theory of the Avant-Garde* (1974). It did, however, take up many of the issues that remained after avant-gardes had disappeared. In their "Pilot Plan for Concrete Poetry," the Noigandres group – whose very name is taken from Pound's *Cantos* – provides a litany of historically radical artistic figures, including Pound but also Guillaume Apollinaire, Sergei Eisenstein, Stéphane Mallarmé, James Joyce, Oswald de Andrade, João Cabral de Melo Neto, Anton Webern, Pierre Boulez, Karlheinz Stockhausen, Max Bill, Josef Albers, and Piet Mondrian (A. de Campos, H. de Campos, and Pignatari 71–2). As Marjorie Perloff explains:

> In military terms, the rearguard of the army is the part that protects and consolidates the troop movement in question; often the army's best generals are used for this purpose. When, in other words, an avant-garde movement is no longer a novelty, it is the role of the arrière-garde to complete its mission, to insure its success. The term *arrière-garde*, then, is synonymous neither with reaction nor with nostalgia for a lost and more desirable artistic era; it is, on the contrary, the hidden face of modernity. ("Writing as Re-Writing")

Keeping this definition in mind, connecting concrete poetry to Pound's engagement with Fenollosa's ideas of the ideogram – an engagement which some critics believe the concrete poets simply mimicked, or came to later (being from less developed countries than those which provided the bases for avant-gardes, those arguments imply) – does not contradict my position that concrete poetry is set apart from the poetic experiments of the early twentieth-century avant-gardes. Rather, it supports my argument that concrete poetry needs to be re-examined and re-formulated outside of the categories and critical methods that have for so long impeded its positioning as one of the major poetic movements of the twentieth century. Lamenting the pejorative tone applied to movements which look backwards, Marx argues that "there is a blind spot in our history of philosophy and art: the attention legitimately devoted to the avant-garde has made us forget the rest, and risks distorting our perception of history and unbalancing our point of view"[6] (5; my translation).

Placing concrete poetry in its literary, artistic, and historical lineage is, as a result of its dispersive and interdisciplinary tradition, an intimidating and difficult task. The problem of defining what, exactly, concrete poetry is, and what it is not, is represented in the general lack of criticism addressing it as a movement. In his preface to *Visual Literature*, which he edited in 1979, Kostelanetz claims that the book "is, as far as I can discern, the first symposium of *criticism* of visual literature in English" (9). It was twenty-seven years until another collection of English-language criticism was to appear, *Experimental – Visual – Concrete: Avant-Garde Poetry Since the 1960s*, which gathered material from a conference held at Yale University in 1994. Both these texts, however, as their titles suggest, did not concentrate on either the poetry or the international character of the movement. More recent criticism by Perloff, in *Unoriginal Genius*, by Olsson, in his examination of Swedish concrete poetry, by Antonio Sergio Bessa, in his study of Öyvindh Fahlström, and by Kenneth Goldsmith in his theorization of how contemporary "conceptual writing" functions in relation to concrete poetry, have served to energize the discourse surrounding the poetics of concrete, but there remains a need to address the poets within their technological and historical moment. Perloff recognizes as much when she claims that "we need [...] to ground concretism in its history, to understand, for example, its relation to the two world wars as well as to the varying cultures that produced it" (*Unoriginal* 52).[7]

Criticism to Date

There have been only three book-length studies of concrete poetry published to date in English: Liselotte Gumpel's *"Concrete" Poetry from East and West Germany: The Language of Exemplarism and Experimentalism* (1976), David Seaman's *Concrete Poetry in France* (1981), and Caroline Bayard's *The New Poetics in Canada and Quebec: From Concretism to Post-Modernism* (1989). While much of this work connects concrete poetry with historical poetic experimentation, it stops short of addressing the work in a wider context. The earliest attempts at analyzing concrete poetry often rely on identifying the *techniques* of the poem: a mirroring of the formalist strategy of locating literary devices like irony, rhyme, meter, genre, and mood. This was the tenor of readings by Mike Weaver, an early critical reader of the work who importantly took the work seriously as poetry. But such readings, though interesting and valid, and exciting for the departure they offer from readings of conventional poetry, do not go far enough in presenting concrete poetry as a critical movement in the history of experimental poetics. No criticism focuses on the movement's flight from national languages (or, in some cases, the alphabet), or the fact that this flight from language takes place predominantly within the Roman alphabet, completely eliding Cyrillic, Arabic, and most of the Asian ideogrammatic languages and thus making the work ideologically modern and inextricable from certain cultural, economic, and military infrastructures.

The critical reception of concrete poetry has been characterized largely by four approaches that have trouble addressing the work within its larger contexts. Studies that emphasize poetry within a specific nation or language have difficulty considering the relationship of the work to the shifts in nationhood and the emergence of a new understanding of the globe around mid-century. Approaches that position concrete poems against visual poetry from other epochs – such as Simian of Rhodes, Rabelais, or George Herbert – might tell us something about how poets have addressed the relationship between form and content in different ways, but they tell us very little about why concrete poetry emerged at the moment it did, or how its relationship to language grew out of innovations in communication technologies. Critics who address the work as a way of explaining structural or post-structural signifying practices tend to say more about the theories themselves than the poems or poets. And readings of the poems that treat them strictly within a literary context, that neglect to deal with the poetry's relationship to the other arts, and visual art in particular, are generally vitiated.

The national mode has persisted in concrete poetry criticism in spite of the fact that the movement had no geographical centre. Unlike earlier twentieth-century movements such as Dada, Surrealism, or Futurism (or, more recently, Lettrisme), which seemed to nest in major cosmopolitan centres such as New York, Paris, Berlin, Zurich, and Milan, concrete poetry grew out of Bern, Ulm, Darmstadt, São Paulo, Stonypath, Bloomington, and Stuttgart. Yet the national approach remains popular, against Gomringer's 1956 manifesto:

> International-supranational. It is a significant characteristic of the existential necessity of concrete poetry that creations such as those brought together in this volume began to appear almost simultaneously in Europe and South America and that the attitude which made the creation and defense of such structures possible manifested itself here as it did there. ("Concrete" 68)

Even Mary Ellen Solt, who published Gomringer's manifesto in her anthology, organizes the poetry in her text according to its national origin, circumventing the transnational style and ambitions of many of the poems: "We hope to show by this limited selection [of poems] that, *despite* its international outlook, concrete poetry displays both distinctively national characteristics and individuality, personal style" (*A World View* 14; my italics). Her lengthy introduction is divided into sections by nation,[8] giving three pages each to Switzerland and Brazil, the putative birthplaces of concrete poetry, four to Germany, four to France, and ten to the United States.[9] Her apparatus does not allow for the dual nationalities of the Bolivian-Swiss Gomringer, or the Romanian-Swiss Spoerri, or even the fact that Emmett Williams was a member of the *Materialgruppe* in Darmstadt in the '50s, and produced much of his work in close contact with Spoerri and the Swiss-German poet Dieter Roth, who were also members. This fact does not serve to negate Williams's American-ness but, rather, to problematize a characteristic that Solt and various other critics present as natural. In subsequent chapters I suggest this American emphasis on nationalism is significant at a time of the cold-war bifurcation of the world, and how much the idea of individuality contributes to that stance.

The national mode of criticism also prevents readers from discussions of how the very concept of nationhood was being challenged and transformed at mid-century, especially in relation to the redrawing of borders after World War II. In the context of Germany, Gumpel's 1976 study of concrete poetry

from East and West Germany argues less for an isolation of a national tradition than for an investigation of how meaning is created and maintained
under different economic and ideological systems. It is the habit of many
contemporary, post-unification thinkers to consider the differences between
West Germany (the Federal Republic of Germany) and East Germany (the
German Democratic Republic) as minor, but Gumpel's 1976 study begins
with the acknowledgement that the two regions were not only were politically different, but linguistically different as well. As both nations were only
created in 1949, Gumpel necessarily avoids the trap of many concrete poetry
critics whose instincts push them to link the work to earlier poetic eras and
to focus on how each contributed to the development of a national character.[10] The history of the nations in Gumpel's study coincides with the history
of concrete poetry, and she bases her study on the ways that the term *concrete
poetry* (konkrete poesie) grew within each nation.

The last joint edition of the German *Duden* (dictionary) appeared
in 1947, after which each nation started publishing its own, a fact which
supports Gumpel's claim for distinctive linguistic nationalisms within the
German language. In the seventeen years following there were one hundred
and eighty-two coinages in the GDR, as opposed to just twenty-two in the
FRG, evidence which points to the East Germans' concern over the power
of language to alter material consciousness. Making the point that language
changes with context, and vice versa, Gumpel notes that "every fortieth word
in the East *Duden* registered some morphological change, be this one of
the innumerable plurals or dual genitive forms (e)s/en. Some of the change
was no doubt caused by the shift in regional balance and a new stress on
the indigenous preferences of the 'Volk.'" Significantly, in the seventeen-
year period following the division of Germany, the East Duden recorded
182 new coinages, dwarfing the 22 new words included in the West Duden
(12). Gumpel's concern about national context affecting meaning spills over
into the East's use of *concrete*, which, based on an idea of socialist realism,
demanded that "informing about a fixed socio-political setting must
supersede the forming of esthetic objects" (16). In the West, the opposite
was true: "When the environment does enter into the picture, it is mainly
a question of concrete literary design emulating the commercial display of
advertisements that surround the poet in everyday life. Poem and poster thus
come to complement one another, regardless of their difference in essence"
(16). She demonstrates the techniques of western concrete by citing an
example from the critical writings of German concrete poet Max Bense, who
places a Gomringer poem against a text found on an advertisement for the

French apéritif Dubonnet to show how each utilizes permutation of syllables as linguistic material, although obviously with different intentions:

Dubo   americans and apricots
Dubon   american apricot
Dubonnet   apricot americans
                apricot and americans (16)

In citing this example Gumpel acknowledges two things: first, that concrete poetry is affected by the language and material conditions of everyday life of its time, and second, that it did not develop in isolation, but through engagement with the work done by poets and artists in other nations (even if the poet in this example does often work within the German language). Indeed, Gumpel recognizes the supranational character of Western concretism throughout her study, and significantly argues that, in contrast to the Eastern usage, it carries in its capitalist alignment an ideological residue. Such geo-political inflection offers an entrance into concrete poetry that has yet to be explored in depth, and one that flows into further investigations of how concrete poetry operated in its world.

In *Concrete Poetry in France*, David Seaman writes that "'Concrete poetry' is the name given to a movement which developed in the 1950s and '60s; the products of this school are full-fledged visual poems. Yet certain aspects of earlier poetry in the visual tradition can also be called 'concrete'" (2).[11] But this is a false syllogism. It presents as its rationale: if concrete poems are visual, then visual poems must be concrete. This is akin to placing Jean Dubuffet's *art brut* alongside the cave paintings of Lascaux and attempting to extract an aesthetic affinity. Such exercises only serve to undercut any useful critique of the work within its moment by exiling it to the rarefied sphere of pure form. This is what I refer to as the "ancient mode" of criticism, and it is one that has a particularly adverse effect on the historical positioning of the work. Dick Higgins, whose Something Else Press published Emmett Williams's *An Anthology of Concrete Poetry*, admits that he became curious about shaped poems around the same time that he discovered concrete poetry. He knew that many concrete poets were aware of the visual elements in the work of Stéphane Mallarmé, Guillaume Apollinaire, and F.T. Marinetti, but that very few were aware of the tradition of visual poetry and word imagery stretching back to ancient civilizations. His 1987 book, *Pattern Poetry: Guide to an Unknown Literature*, is the culmination of twenty years of research into pattern poetry stretching from the Greek to the Hebrew, Indian, and Asian cultures (iv). But even he, perhaps anticipating a conflict, refuses to include in his text any work by concrete poets, or even the Dadaists or Futurists. He sets 1900 as a cut-off date for his collection, and explicitly states in his introduction that the term "concrete poetry" "should really be reserved for works from the 1950s and 1960s which use the alphabet" (vii). It is a short and insufficient definition, but it supports the idea that concrete poetry is limited to a specific time period, one that adheres to the chronology of the 1955 meeting in Ulm and the 1970–71 Stedelijk Museum exhibition. More recently, in the exhibition catalogue accompanying an exhibition of text-based art responding to concrete poetry, curator Mark Sladen makes a distinction between concrete poetry as *genre* and concrete poetry as *movement*, and attempts to argue that the latter is historically specific while the former is ancient in its roots (4). But that strikes me as a convenient method for collapsing concrete poetry into a category that encompasses all visually distinct writing, whether it be in artistic, spiritual, literary, or commercial arenas. The effect of that approach is to create a set that becomes bloated with its contents, too unwieldy to be of any real critical value.

Certain concrete poets have also been complicit in perpetuating the "ancient mode." These poets often were producing work towards the end of the movement, and were more interested in the spiritual experience of visual word imagery than the constructivist tradition. Jean-François Bory was perhaps the first to collect ancient and mediæval visual poetry alongside the work of his own and that of his contemporaries in the anthology *Once Again: Concrete Poetry* (1968). Published by New Directions in the United States, the title is both a reference to the persistence of visual language throughout history as well as a recognition of the proliferation of concrete poetry anthologies. The collection chides the concrete poetry movement for taking its cues from posters and other para-literary linguistic phenomenon without recognizing what Bory sees as a tradition that has been maintained "from the code of Hammurabi through the manuscripts of the master calligraphers of the Middle Ages and on down to the 'Follies' of Nicolas Cirier" (5–7). But to contextualize concrete poetry in this way is to decontextualize it. Bory includes in his text a poem by Vladimir Burda that is simply a fingerprint with the German first person pronoun "ich" printed underneath it (see fig. 2.10; Burda 79). Bory holds this up as an example of real writing, primitive and connected to the impulses of the body: writing as marking. But what Bory's reading elides is far more pressing. First, the fingerprint is a relatively recent and sophisticated biometric, requiring tools of collection and magnification that are far from primitive. A handprint might carry the impression of

pair g
rl au pair
pair girl au
au pair girl
au pair girl a
rl au pair girl a
pair girl au pair gir
girl au pair girl au pair
pair girl au pair girl au pa
air girl au pair girl au pair
pair girl au pair girl au pa
u pair girl au pair girl a
irl au pair girl au pair
irl au pair girl

Figure 1.2
Ian Hamilton Finlay. "Au Pair Girl"

Homo sapiens, as distinguished from a paw or hoof, but a fingerprint made from ink is in a different category, especially after the nineteenth-century development of forensic techniques to tie a latent print to an individual. The finger print is no longer an anonymous, simple signal of being, or the trace of the body in some distant past, but now refers to a documented, regulated individual, and often one which comes under the suspicion of the law.

Further contributing to the historical reading of the poem is the fact that Burda was Czechoslovakian at the time of writing, which means he lived in a country that was first occupied by German and then Soviet-aligned forces, both of which suppressed cultural and political dissent. The poem, then, is less about physical, primitive writing than a reference to the idea of an occupied consciousness, one in which identification papers, perhaps marked with fingerprints, form a document which can stand in for a human being, and which can be used to both imprison and set free. The inclusion of the German "ich" for *I* is therefore also problematic, as it is unclear whether or not Burda is a native German speaker, or a Czech speaker who is concerned about the linguistic dominance of invading forces. That indeterminacy is localized, specific, and integral to the work, and is ignored by a reading that holds it up as a symbol of a universal humanism.

Another example of a text that is often presented as an inheritor of the long tradition of mimetic visual poetry is Ian Hamilton Finlay's "Au Pair Girl" (see fig. 1.2). But even this poem, which refers directly to those poems in which the subject determines the shape of the lines, and perhaps specifically to a poem published in France which presents a prose caricature of King Louis Philippe (who was known for his pear shape) should not be read solely for its form, but rather for its relationship to its time. Finlay famously wrote, in a letter to Pierre Garnier in 1963, that if he were asked why he liked concrete poetry, he could truthfully answer, "Because it is beautiful" (Finlay, "Letter" 84). But "Au Pair Girl" does not simply strive for a purity of form; it takes a term recently developed to describe a new shift in family economics and aestheticizes it, much in the same way that concrete poetry adapts the styles of advertising and shifts in linguistic practice to create a poetry which is appropriate and applicable to its moment. The figure of the au pair girl is historically specific; it began to appear just after World War II. Women who had become accustomed to working outside of the home maintained their economic independence by continuing to work, and the demand for childcare was filled by the au pair program, which matched young women with host families in participating nations, allowing for the proliferation of cross-cultural exchange. *Au pair* is French for "on par," indicating not only an equal economic exchange between the au pair and her hosts – work for room and board – but also the absence of traditional class structures associated with live-in servants. There is also a potential reading of the poem that implies looking through a keyhole at the au pair, which sexualizes it – "O, pear girl!" – and, in the process, humorously contrasts contemporary conditions of romance to a pastoral poetic tradition. The au pair program has historically included an erotic element, specifically the fantasy of the impressionable, adventurous young girl living in the same house as the father of a young child, a scenario which formed the context of many sex comedies in Europe in the 1960s and '70s. There was also a popular TV show set in Brighton in England in the '60s that operates as a more direct reference. All of this contributes to the complexity of Finlay's poem within an increasingly visual culture, and in doing so impedes the conventional critique of concrete poetry as overly mimetic or reductive. The poem is not, after all, shaped like an au pair girl.

Berjouhi Bowler's 1970 anthology *The Word as Image* is another text that falls into the trap of the "ancient mode," a point that Bowler makes explicit in the first sentence of her introduction, where she outlines a methodology that is deeply inflected by its historical position at the end of the 1960s:

> The researches into the material for this anthology were begun
> without a guiding thesis, without a single preconception. Odd doors
> were knocked on and chance inquiries made into the possibility
> of locating shaped writing in various cultures. As the material
> accumulated it became apparent that many of these early picture-
> texts were in some way connected with magic, ritual, religion or
> superstition, and that they had urgency evocative of the LOGOS
> itself – the incarnated word. (7)

Her text is broken down geographically, like Higgins', but she concludes with a chapter devoted to the "International Concrete Poetry Movement," citing Gomringer's call for a universal poetry, but misinterpreting it to mean across time as well as geography.[12] Her critical approach is reproduced in subsequent anthologies of visual language, specifically Massin's *Letter and Image* (1970), Klaus Peter Dencker's *Text-Bilder: Visuelle Poesie international* (1972) and Milton Klonsky's *Speaking Pictures: A Gallery of Pictorial Poetry from the Sixteenth Century to the Present* (1975); all of these texts place concrete poetry at the end of a long trajectory of word imagery, juxtaposing the ancient with the contemporary and in the process expelling history from the very place in which they sought to identify it.

Though I do not deny there were poets affiliated with the concrete movement who sought a spiritual experience via the merging of logos and imago, their work should not be read as exemplary within the movement. Describing his poetic "constellations," which would be the basis for his concrete work, Gomringer writes in 1954:

> our languages today are in a process of formal simplification. a reduced number of minimal forms are developing. the content of a sentence is often carried by a single word, while longer statements may be broken down to groups of letters. instead of many languages we are learning to work with a handful that is more or less universal. [...] headlines, advertisements & other groupings of sounds & letters that could serve as patterns for a new poetry, are only waiting to be discovered & meaningfully applied. (*The Book of Hours* n. pag.; lower case in the original)

This articulation of the condition of language at mid-century in no way forecasts or lays the foundation for the alchemical work which would come later in the movement, or explains why the creators of such work would regularly point to Gomringer as their priestly father. The only argument offered within the critical body of concrete poetry for linking the contemporary work to the shaped and visual poetry of past epochs is one based on history, not form, and is proposed by Geoffrey Cook in his idiosyncratic short essay "Visual Poetry as a Molting" (1979). He identifies visual poetry in three epochs preceding the mid-twentieth century: the Alexandrine period, the Carolingian renaissance, and the Baroque period. He suggests all three possess a character of decadence, noting that visual poetry in each emerged at the death of one cultural epoch and the beginning of another, functioning as a "visual statement that nothing more meaningful can be said till we can restructure the basic vision that is an historical culture" (141). This critique supports those critics who have positioned concrete poetry in the space between modernism and postmodernism, as a hinge, but requires a study that moves beyond the simply formal toward the historical.

It is inevitable that critical methodologies – including mine – sacrifice specific terrain in order to emphasize others, but the historical placement of concrete poetry within its global context seems to have been sacrificed too often. In a telling passage from the introductory chapter to *The New Poetics in Canada and Quebec: From Concretism to Post-Modernism*, Caroline Bayard writes:

> It did not escape my attention that the texts I was dealing with took place and developed within a specific historical context and that their language was irretrievably part of that history. I realized that it would be a misguided fallacy to suggest that avant-garde and post-modern texts [...] appeared strictly within the precincts of a literary canon and were unrelated to the large fabric of a general interdiscursivity. [...] I realize the necessity to situate texts within a linguistic as well as civilization context. But, because I was looking at language constructs and because these experiments were situated within the precincts of language, I determined that my first and primary responsibility was to the prosodic and linguistic components of the texts in question. (6–7)

This passage comes shortly after Bayard's litany of theoretical influences and a placement of her theoretical subjectivity, a passage that solidly roots her work in the context of late 1980s literary scholarship. Shortly after, Bayard notes she feels regret for the limits of her study, but decides to put off the other questions for the future in favour of an examination of concrete poetry in relation to a debate about language that flows from Plato's account of Socrates's dialogue with Kratylus about the ties between words and their referents, through the writings of Jean-François Lyotard and Jacques Derrida. This is what I refer to as the "theoretical mode," a critical approach to concrete poetry that, just as much as the "ancient mode," considers the work in a rarefied sphere, in this instance that of theory, reading backwards onto the poetry the linguistic theory that played such a strong role in the scholarly literary criticism of the 1970s and 1980s.[13] The privileging of theory over historical function is evident in Bayard's critique of a poem by Augusto de Campos, whom she does not bother to name, for its apparent failure to adequately fuse form and content (25; see fig. 1.3). Her reading of "sem um numero" focuses on the form of the central "o" in the poem and its link to the concept of zero without ever connecting the poem to its eminently *modern* subject: the difficult practice of enumerating the peasant population of northern Brazil in the national census of 1962. The poem is explicitly about the conflict between the rapid modernization of Brazil and its traditional character, a fact that can be gathered from even the most rudimentary research into the concrete poetry tradition, and one which leads into a wider investigation of how statistics and

```
sem um numero
     um numero
        numero
           zero
            um
             o
              nu
               mero
                numero
                 um numero
                  um sem numero
```

Figure 1.3
Augusto de Campos. "sem um numero"

Figure 1.4
bpNichol. "Blues"

data production link up to models of mass production in twentieth-century modernism.[14]

Bayard's reading of bpNichol's "Blues" falls prey to a similar impulse. The poem, which plays with the word "love" and its backwards form, "evol," serves as a prompt for Bayard to discuss the relationship between love and evolution, which she then links to "a wide spectrum of interpretive references (from Plato to Christian theology, if one wishes to limit oneself to Western master codes, and from the Gnostics to other Middle Eastern spiritual traditions if one refuses to operate within Graeco-Judeo-Christian perimeters)" (146; see fig. 1.4). Her reading overlooks the title of the poem – "Blues" – which alludes to a tradition of lyrics within the music genre, one that ties love to pain and the eventual downfall of the singer. And bpNichol, who is known for both his playful poetics and his emphasis on the sound of texts, was most certainly aware of the irony that "love" read backwards sounds like "evil." In this way, the poem works to reference both song and poem, both written word and vocality, and the tension that comes with the visual score of a linguistic performance. Meter and rhyme operate differently, visually as well as acoustically. Like many concrete poems, "Blues" exists in flux; readers cannot be certain of where the poem begins, or where or if it ends, a confusion which only adds to the tension between the visual and the acoustic. Bayard's evolution reading is not to be discarded, but by no means is it exclusive, or even primary, and it is telling that her default critical impulse is to place concrete poems within a decontextualized, pan-historic frame of philosophical writings on language.

Other critics' attempts to place concrete poetry within a language-based theoretical frame have also contributed to its peripheral position in the history of twentieth-century poetics. Loris Essary, in her essay "On Language and Visual Language," attempts to match the ideas of Ferdinand de Saussure with those of Maurice Merleau-Ponty to describe how humans experience language, but she assumes that all humans experience language in the same way across time and geography. Also operating within the structuralist/post-structuralist arena, Stephen Scobie, in *Earthquakes and Explorations*, begins his chapter on concrete poetry with an epigraph from Jacques Derrida, and then refers to Roman Jakobson and Claude Levi-Strauss in order to situate concrete poetry within the history of structuralist examinations of language. I do not wish to discourage or devalue investigations of the theoretical structures of language and the discourses inherent in poetic or literary production: the shift from formalist literary analysis to theoretical engagement within the textual turn has been an immensely productive and integral one for literary and cultural criticism. But concrete poetry did not benefit from such an approach as completely as other sites of investigation. For example, neither Essary nor Scobie makes any real attempt to engage with the information theory that informed the concrete poets, perhaps an effect of its link to the structures that post-structuralism aims to destabilize. But, significantly, the concrete poet Max Bense was a professor of Information Sciences in Stuttgart, as was Pignatari in Brazil, and Bense engaged often with the information theory of Claude Shannon. Eugen Gomringer begins one of his collections with an epigraph from communication theorist Colin Cherry, but no attempt has been made to follow that line of investigation. Stephen Bann mentions the Gomringer epigraph in the introduction to his anthology but does not provide it; Johanna Drucker mentions Gomringer's affinity for machine languages that were popular at mid-century, but adds in a footnote, "Precisely what Gomringer was reading is unclear – Frege, early Wittgenstein, or Claude Shannon are possibilities" (*Figuring* 135). This resistance to examinations of concrete poetry that go beyond the dominant post-structural theories of language that developed within literary criticism since the 1970s is a widespread problem in the critical reception of the movement, and what I refer to as the "disciplinary mode." This mode, which seems to disproportionately affect English language criticism, is likely a side-effect of the pressures of knowledge organization within scholarship, pressures which only intensify as readers recognize the various cultural, geographical, and linguistic conditions that surround the works' production: across nations, across disciplines, across languages, across modes of distribution, across spaces of reception. Critical readings of the poems require an interdisciplinary and cultural compartivism that ventures out of conventional disciplinary terrain.

The visual character and various modes of display of concrete poetry have generally impeded its popularity amongst literary critics, and its linguistic and often ephemeral character have largely kept art historians from examining it in depth, exiling it to its current position as the "other of post war writing," a putatively formal eccentricity whose historical poetic/ artistic impact never matched up to its scandalous avant-garde cousins: Dada, Futurism, and Surrealism (Drucker, *Visible* 227). The strongest analyses of the work to date is by those who acknowledge the literary and visual art traditions that meet in concrete poetry. The critic Mike Weaver early on identified an expressionistic character in poems whose shapes mimic natural phenomena. Later critics counterposed the category of *constructivist*, which applied to poems that implemented geometric or mechanical compositional

```
        lackblockblackb
        lockblackblockb
        lackblockblackb
        lockblackblockb
        lackblockblackb
        lockblackblockb
        lackblockblackb
        lockblackblockb

lackblockblackb  lackblockblackb  lackblockblackb
lockblackblockb  lockblackblockb  lockblackblockb
lackblockblackb  lackblockblackb  lackblockblackb
lockblackblockb  lockblackblockb  lockblackblockb
lackblockblackb  lackblockblackb  lackblockblackb
lockblackblockb  lockblackblockb  lockblackblockb
lackblockblackb  lackblockblackb  lackblockblackb
lockblackblockb  lockblackblockb  lockblackblockb

        lackblockblackb
        lockblackblockb
        lackblockblackb
        lockblackblockb
        lackblockblackb
        lockblackblockb
        lackblockblackb
        lockblackblockb
```

Figure 1.5

Ian Hamilton Finlay. "Homage to Malevich"

strategies. This is not necessarily a difficult connection to make, as there are many works by concrete poets that refer directly to the history of visual art, such as Jiří Kolář's poems that mimic sculptures by Constantin Brancusi and Jean Tinguely, and Ian Hamilton Finlay's "Homage to Malevich," a grid of the words "black" and "block" which evokes the Suprematist paintings of Kazimir Malevich (see fig. 1.5). Weaver offers a close reading of Finlay's poem, going so far as to diagram its lexical permutations, but leaves out its historical and cross-disciplinary character. As a result, the reading is counter-productive in its ostentatious comprehension of the supposedly incomprehensible: poetry that is not meant to be read. No explanation is offered for a Scottish poet's reference in the 1960s to a Russian artist from the time of the revolution, or how such a poem fits into the larger domain of visual poetry.

Although they are in the minority, there are examples of historical, material readings made by critics of concrete poetry. Gumpel's work is valuable for the links it draws between concrete poetry and the geo-political ramifications of a divided Germany. Her discussion of the histories of form does not stop at a disciplinary limit; she discusses Kurt Schwitters's Merz project as being inextricable from *kommerz*, the German word for "commerce," and expands this into an idea of an "environmental constructionism" that she then applies to the concrete techniques practiced by both the East and West German poets (51). In *Radical Artifice*, Marjorie Perloff writes about how American poetry follows the shift in advertising from the text-heavy to the iconographic and illustrates her point via references to work by Gomringer and the Noigandres group, although she neglects to expand her perspective beyond the territory of the United States, against the evidence of an emerging global culture. In her study of the experimental typography of the early twentieth century and its influence on modern art, Drucker also does well to draw a connecting line between journals printed for the advertising trade and the appearance of Dadaist and Futurist texts, but she does not apply a similar method in her analyses of concrete poetry. Claus Clüver, a colleague of Mary Ellen Solt's at the University of Indiana, Bloomington, has been writing about concrete poetry for close to forty years, theorizing its "intermedial" character and its relationship to concrete art. His work has, unfortunately, suffered a dislocation similar to that of the poetry. He writes about the poetry's relationship to art and media, challenging disciplinary boundaries, much in the same way the poetry often blurred the line between literature and visual art. But he also writes criticism in English, German, and Portuguese, operating in a polylingual space that the structure of academic publishing, at least in North America, is not designed to facilitate.

Despite these examples, however, the bulk of writing about concrete poetry is locked within disciplinary boundaries, removing it from its historical motivations and promoting a critical disjuncture between culture and history, a separation that impedes understanding of how cultural production influences and shapes our everyday lives, and how shifts in our everyday lives, conversely, influence our cultural production. While such a critical approach has already been put to valuable use in a wide selection of literary and artistic re-readings, concrete poetry, specifically within English-language criticism, has remained largely overlooked by it.

Globalizing Concrete

What is required in order to move beyond the national, ancient, theoretical, and disciplinary modes is the type of critical approach that refuses the dogma of conventional critical positions. Concrete covers too grand a space to be encapsulated by a particular method, and therefore requires readers to occupy the poetry with an openness and curiosity that will be rewarded by a proliferation of critical vectors. This is exactly the opposite of what would result from that which previous commenters have considered the reductively mimetic or decorative character of the work. Combining this kind of critical encounter with a recognition of the *situatedness* of the work in its international context provides an entrance into concrete poetry that previous criticism has opted to circumvent.

The study of ways in which concrete poetry in the middle part of the twentieth century permeated both physical and linguistic borders seems especially salient in today's political environment, when issues around security have led to a hardening of borders, either through surveillance, documentation policies, or physical walls and fences, while global capital moves with fewer restrictions than ever before. What is at stake, therefore, is an understanding of the ways that culture moved within and imagined global spaces at a time that predated, but in some ways initiated, the trends we now see more fully developed in current theories of globalization. Critical developments within globalization studies offer a methodological reasoning for avoiding the nation as the dominant mode of cultural organization. Arjun Appadurai, in his essay "Grassroots Globalization and the Research Imagination," makes a valuable distinction between the knowledge of globalization and the globalization of knowledge, identifying in the latter a neo-colonial project of cultural and intellectual dominion (4). He points out that the geographies which area studies have traditionally depended on are unstable and heuristically problematical (7). Geographies based on processes, rather than traits such as location, language, and social customs, appear to be more productive. Writing out of anthropology, James Clifford describes "a modern 'ethnography' of conjunctures, constantly moving between cultures, [which] does not [...] aspire to the full range of human diversity or development. It is perpetually displaced, both regionally focused and broadly comparative, a form both of dwelling and of travel in a world where the two experiences are less and less distinct" (9). This investigative shift from the national to the global is what geographer Cindi Katz advocates, as well, in her formulation of topographical social critique: "Topography is associated not just with description of place but also with measurements of elevation, distance, and other structural attributes that enable the examination of relationships across spaces and between places" (1229). Using what she calls "contour lines," which connect disparate elevations across geographies, she provides a convincing rationale for making connections where disciplinary, national, and economic boundaries have long been in the habit of claiming there are none. These approaches form a productive basis for the study of concrete poetry proposed here, one that consciously moves against formalist approaches that too often emphasize technique without any reference to technology or larger shifts in culture. More categories of concrete poetry are not useful, as is shown by the relative obscurity to which the previous criticism has assigned the international movement since its demise in the 1970s.

There are anxieties that come with delineating a movement, and those anxieties can often metastasize as disciplinary and chronological borders that close down as many questions as they spur. This book means to both set boundaries and encourage the transgression of them, so that subsequent discussions of concrete poetry and its various cousins might have a new space in which to meet and share perspectives. Chapter 2 reads poems against two mid-century shifts in the ways we are able to imagine the world. Early computer technology, which was driving a mathematical understanding of communication and language, changed the way poets thought about methods of composition, and possibilities for expression. Grids, lists, and lexical permutations point to a reconsideration of poetic subjectivity. The second mid-century technology that changed what poetry could be was the development, military use, and regular testing of nuclear weapons. Within current globalization discourse, the economic distribution of goods and people around the world occupies a privileged position. While economic and migratory factors are most certainly the engine driving globalization at this moment, I want to think about how "the bomb" worked affectively in the postwar period to create a new understanding of global citizenry, quickly and terrifyingly produced as a category by the possibility of total annihilation.

Chapter 3 moves away from the apocalyptic and towards the utopian, though in this chapter, as well, the poems are read against rockets. This rocket, however, has a more benign, though no less effective globalizing technology attached to it: a camera. In the same way that the fear of nuclear fallout gathered the world population under the same umbrella, making it impossible to ignore each other, the first forays into outer space and the photographic representation of the earth from *somewhere else* made the imaginary borders between nations even more imaginary, and spurred a collective pride in the possibilities for humans to discover new things. I place this view from *way* above against the similarly optimistic project of the International Style of architecture, particularly the construction of Brasília, a planned city whose buildings are only possible thanks to the technology of reinforced concrete.

The relationship between concrete poetry and visual art is, combined with concrete poetry's insistent internationalism, one of the primary reasons the work has so long suffered from critical neglect. It falls into a space between disciplines, where art historians feel nervous addressing the work's poetic lineage, and literary critics feel hesitant to deal with its material form and the poets' double-role as poet *and* artist. The few texts that take up the challenge of concrete poetry's connection to visual art tend to concentrate on the connection to concrete art. When discussing the Brazilian poets, it is difficult to avoid mentioning the *1 Exposição Nacional de Arte Concreta* (First National Exhibition of Concrete Art), the 1956/57 exhibition that had such great influence on the nation's poetic culture. Similarly, any discussion of Eugen Gomringer's connection to visual art leans toward his position as secretary to Max Bill, whose exhibitions and presence in São Paulo in the early '50s were integral to the development of Brazilian concretism. My approach in Chapter 4 diverts from this tradition in that it focuses on the contentious relationship between concrete poetry and conceptual art, a primarily Anglo-American movement that was also interested in the possibilities of language functioning as art. In spite of their obvious affinities, conceptual artists largely disavowed concrete poetry, and concrete poets were often less than impressed by the linguistic experiments of conceptual art. The reasons for this go beyond aesthetic preferences, and include commercial, disciplinary, and philosophical differences that highlight conditions for visual art and poetry that in many ways still exist.

Coming at the end of the book and dealing primarily with the end of the movement, chapter 5 deals with the surge of international anthologies that Scobie argues marked the culmination of a moment, and poses the question: how does the form of the anthology, or the exhibition catalogue, contribute to the meaning of the work? Here the form of distribution engages with the form of the poetry, the anthology and catalogue each taking advantage of technologies of colour printing and global trade networks to access new and expanded audiences. This chapter also introduces the idea of a post-concrete poetry, one that takes a different approach to mechanical understandings of language and communication, and that questions the role of the human in an increasingly electronic, enthusiastically networked society.

What all concrete poets between 1955 and 1970 have in common is that they were producing concrete poetry between 1955 and 1970. Beyond the redundancy of this statement, it is possible to assert that even those poets who were not explicitly engaged in technological innovation, those who wanted to create a national poetry, and those who saw themselves outside of poetry or inside of a spiritual tradition investigating the link between logos and imago, were all participating in a discourse that was defined in large part by networks of communication and artistic exchange that were impossible before World War II. There will necessarily be ellipses and gaps in this study, but there is a value in the acceptance of those gaps that also seems rooted in the lessons of concrete. My method is meant not to encompass concrete poetry, or to pen its history, but to adopt and personify a heuristic cultural pose. No doubt those scholars immersed in the poetry and biographies of specific poets will bristle at the speed with which I move between poems and locations, but this text is meant to challenge the structures built by particular critical approaches. How can we talk about a poet who never produces a collection of poems? How do we talk about a poet who travels, who slips between nations, and between languages? How do we talk about a poet who is also – even *primarily* – a graphic designer, or who is an information theorist? All these impediments are not frivolous. Deep knowledge and situated reading are tools of impeccable criticism, but there remain gaps formed through our mass-produced methods, gaps in which entire movements can become mired. While the disciplines of comparative literature and area studies, more broadly, have been the conventional gatekeepers of concrete poetry criticism, I want to offer a different mode of comparitivism, a new area of study customized to the poetry itself. This practice cannot aim for completion, but proceeds with the ambition that a method might develop by which any concrete poem might be productively approached. I entered this investigation optimistically, proceeded immanently, and analyzed openly, spurred by a constantly renewed bewilderment. These are the conditions concrete poetry demands.

Why concrete poetry? Why then?

2/

A POETICS OF THE GLOBAL

Global Poetics

In the period immediately following World War II, the world experienced dramatic changes in the way people consumed and shared ideas. Shifts in the kinds of media that were not only available but increasingly dominant in everyday life were at the base of many of those changes. For example, even in Britain in the late 1930s, for every person who purchased a daily newspaper, two people bought tickets to see a film; the transistor, invented in 1947, allowed radio to reach even the most remote locations; and television, the long playing record, and magnetic recording tape irreversibly transformed the mediascape (Hobsbawm 193; 264; 265). The concrete poets emerged out of and wrote in response to these shifts that allowed for greater connectivity across a reformatted globe, but that also prompted philosophical questions about how information is processed and received.

In 1957, Augusto de Campos published an article in the *Jornal do Brasil* daily newspaper that began with a sentence fragment paragraph – more like a software command than an opening to a literary essay – that captures the position concrete poetry operated in: "Instigating question: What does a concrete poem communicate?" The line's purposeful ungrammaticality goes unremarked by de Campos, though, in subsequent paragraphs he does draw the reader's attention to something else he feels might be odd: the idea that a poem might *communicate* rather than *express*. He offers this idea in counterposition to the American philosopher Susanne Langer who, particularly in her book *Problems of Art*, resists speaking of poetry in terms of "communication," reserving the term for what happens in everyday discourse, "language in its literal use" (Langer 71). In another formally idiosyncratic critical gesture, de Campos provides a list of seven passages from Langer's text that illustrate what he considers her romantic, conservative definition of poetry and art as something that operates in a region beyond the discursive, everyday language, in a rarified and inspired space where "what is created is a composed and shaped apparition of a new human experience" (148). Concrete poetry rejects this division, de Campos argues, and embraces the possibilities of communication as a way of intervening in the discursive spaces of the everyday.

In addition to his stripped down critical style, de Campos communicates something else in his article, specifically in relation to the work he chooses to engage. Langer is not a literary critic, but a philosopher of language, and operates in de Campos's text as evidence of the breadth of Brazilian concrete poetry's intellectual engagement. De Campos, his brother Haroldo, and their collaborator Décio Pignatari were not just interested in responding to a literary tradition in Brazil, the United States, and Europe, nor simply to a history of avant-garde art and music they were also familiar with, but were attempting to attach poetry to an idea of language and culture that was consistently agitated by technologies of communication. The electronic exchange of messages produced a pervasive sense of acceleration, and by choosing that specific text of Langer's – a text that was published also in 1957 – de Campos, a Brazilian poet in São Paulo, was showing how quickly the spaces that were generally considered remote and peripheral had become connected to those considered the centres. I can only conclude that de Campos received an advance review copy from the publisher; the publication date of his article was 9 January 1957 (de Campos 167).

A year before de Campos's article, Eugen Gomringer, in an introduction to a planned – though never published – international anthology of concrete poetry, articulated a similar fascination with the new, technologically-produced global spaces. He strikes a confident tone throughout his text, celebrating the poetry's connection to the "contemporary scientific-technical view of the world" and its contribution to the "synthetic-rationalistic world of tomorrow." His meeting with Décio Pignatari in 1955 maintains a central influence in his thinking:

> International-supranational. It is a significant characteristic of
> the existential necessity of concrete poetry that creations such
> as those brought together in this volume began to appear almost
> simultaneously in Europe and South America and that the attitude
> which made the creation and defense of such structures possible
> manifested itself here as it did there. (Gomringer, "Concrete" 68)

Two concepts loom large in Gomringer and de Campos's texts, and form the central questions for this chapter. The first is the relationship between concrete poetry and the technological developments of the period. How did poets embrace and/or resist the media transformations of their moment? Which shifts in everyday living brought about by advances in communication technology were they responding to? The second concept is the emerging feeling of the global – to be distinguished, in later chapters, from the "international" – that comes out in the poets' postures towards the limits of national languages. How did this feeling of the global come about? Who were its champions? Who were its opponents? What was to be embraced, and what to be feared?

Four years after his orphaned introduction, Gomringer's penned his manifesto "The Poem as a Functional Object," where he reiterates the concrete poets' aim to compose poetry on a global scale. His text matches its title's modernist, industrial character by outlining a rational approach to poetic production, claiming that the purpose of concrete poetry is not the "reduction of language itself but that of greater flexibility and freedom of communication." Linking the poetry to the everyday experience of travel and circulation, he argues that poems should strive to be "as easily understood as signs in an airport or traffic signs" (70). He rejects readings that function within a national scale, exemplifying a position within concrete poetry that parallels contemporary debates over how to read and consider literature in its global cultural context. The juxtaposition of the radical formal experiments of the concrete poets against the development of technologies that altered the scale of the globe for its citizens grounds concrete poetry within its historical context, but also opens up questions about which methodologies are most effective for negotiating world literature.

Poems by Décio Pignatari and the Czech collaborative pair Josef Hiršal and Bohumila Grögerová serve as the ground for an initial investigation. Pignatari's "Beba Coca Cola" (1957), as published in Mary Ellen Solt's anthology, provides a critical record of the emerging global imaginary that concrete poetry sought to engage. Printed in Coca-Cola red and white, the Portuguese slogan "beba coca cola" permutes into "babe cola," "beba coca," "babe cola caco," "caco," "cola," and finally, simply "cloaca" (108; see fig. 2.1).[1] The English translation, by Solt and Maria José Quieroz, using the reverse colour scheme – red ink on a white background – appears at the bottom of the page, and although it expresses the basic anti-advertisement status of the poem, it is problematic for what it leaves out. It cannot, for example, express the linguistic shifts and overlaps between Spanish and Portuguese that occur in the poem. And it neglects, in its attempt to faithfully reproduce the form of the poem, to include the multiple meanings of some of the words. "Cola" doesn't just mean *glue*, but can mean *tail*; "caco" can mean *thief*; and "cloaca" can mean *sewer pipe*, but can also refer to a digestive tract. Solt and Quieroz consequently diminish, in their emphasis on the physical (drink, drool, glass, shard), the anti-imperialist stance of the poem. It is not a poem against advertising, but a poem against the advertisement of a specific economic and ideological position, one that might have been better expressed by the translation of "caco" as *thief*, or "cola" as a perhaps more explicit term for *tail*.

Coca-Cola was, after all, a powerful cultural image of the United States' aggressive economic colonization, or "coca-colonization" as it has come to be known in contemporary globalization discourse.[2] Describing the political force the soft drink possessed in the reconstruction of France under the Marshall Plan, the historian Irwin M. Wall writes that "Coca-Cola was 'the most American thing in America,' a product marketed by mass advertising, symbolic of high consumption, and tributary to the success of free enterprise; for its president, James Farley, a politically powerful anti-Communist, it contained the 'essence of capitalism' in every bottle" (65). Possessing such a full symbolic value on an international scale, Coca-Cola iconography could function as an immediate signifier of the American cultural and political project in the postwar period. A *Time* magazine article from March 1950 reports the French resistance to what they also referred to as the "coca-colonization" of French culture, and significantly emphasizes the effect of Coca-Cola's advertising on the French language as a concern. The article cites a letter from a M. Dreyfus to the *Paris Herald*: "I like Coca-Cola, [...] but [Coca-Cola's advertising] has ripped deep into what the French treasure most – their language. One now sees posters and trucks bearing the inscription

drink coca cola
drool glue
drink coca(ine)
drool glue shard
shard
glue

cesspool

Figure 2.1
Décio Pignatari. "Beba Coca Cola"

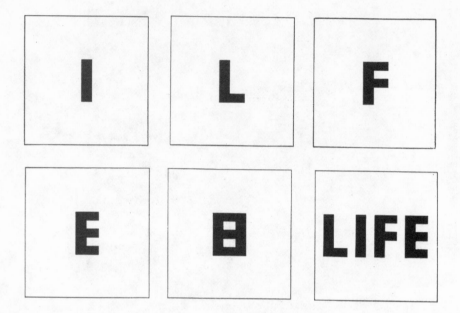

Figure 2.2
Décio Pignatari. "LIFE"

'Buvez Coca-Cola.' You can say 'Buvez du Coca-Cola' or 'Buvez le Coca-Cola' but you cannot say 'Buvez Coca-Cola' because this is pidgin French" ("Pause" 33). The example highlights the effect advertising had on culture through the very techniques that Gomringer identifies in his manifesto: the reduction of language, the standardization of communication, and the insertion of poetry into expanded spaces of circulation. While different poets adopted different postures towards the commodification of language, with some, like the Brazilians, positioning themselves against it, and others taking advantage of its possibilities for a greater audience, the strategy of international-supranational poetry was central to the formation of the international movement.

Also emphasizing an emergent global condition, Pignatari's "LIFE," as published in *Noigandres* 4 (1958), is a kinetic poem, with one large letter on the first four pages, forcing the reader to experience the sans-serif letters *I*, *L*, *F*, and *E*, as an accumulation of intersecting lines (see fig. 2.2). The vertical line that comprises the *I* has a slightly thinner line attached to its base to create the *L*, then another line, identical to that attached to the foot in *L*, is added to the centre of the thicker, vertical line, and the whole letter is rotated 180 degrees on its horizontal axis to create an *F*. A third line in the dimensions of the previous two horizontal lines is added to make the *E*, to which is then added another line the size and thickness of the original *I*, enclosing the figure in what appears to be a digital-clock's eight, but that is also a representation of the ancient Chinese calligraphic symbol for the sun. The poem's final panel has the four letters arranged into the word "LIFE," at first glance suggesting a natural relationship between the Chinese and English representations of a common terrestrial phenomenon: the life-giving capabilities of the sun.

This poem would be relatively uninteresting if it were limited to the formal coherence that allows such a reading, however. What sets it up as an important cultural index for a new global identity is not the fact that it is a poem written by a Brazilian in English, nor that it refers to an ideographic language that previous critics of concrete and visual poetry have been only too eager to embrace as metaphor, following the path of Ezra Pound and Ernest Fenollosa. The significance of the poem comes in large part from its font and its final panel, where "LIFE" is printed as it would appear on the cover of *LIFE* magazine, an international, glossy mechanism for the dissemination of American ideas and desires, paralleling it with the ancient concept of the sun, the cosmic entity that provides light, warmth, and the possibility of life. The reader would flip through the poem the way s/he would flip through a popular magazine; neither the solid, geometric letters nor their position on manifest

1 2 3 4 5 6 7 8 9 ; : !
q w e r t z u i o p ü
a s d f g h j k l ö ä
y x c v b n m , . - ?

Figure 2.3
Bohumila Grögerová and Josef Hiršal. "Manifest"

the page invite close attention. Solt, despite recognizing the anti-advertising quality of "Beba Coca-Cola," and despite recognizing Pignatari's reference to the font of *LIFE* magazine, mistakes the political for the principally poetic when she writes that the poem "affirms life in a visual succession based upon the architectural structure of the letters of the word LIFE (out of usual order) culminating by the kind of happy accident possible in concrete poetry in the Chinese ideogram for the sun out of which the word LIFE radiates" (Solt, *Concrete* 15). There is much more to the work that a largely apolitical American anthologist might overlook. The contemporaneous global implications of Chinese and American iconography placed within their respective ideological conditions – America under Dwight Eisenhower, China under Mao Zedong – and the position of a Brazilian poet with a socialist, anti-imperialist perspective provides the terrain for understanding concrete poetry's position in the production of a new global cultural imaginary. The modularity of the poem, as well, in both its page/panel construction and in its accretive use of the constituent lines or marks of the letters, links to contemporaneous experiments in modernist architecture, where standardization of form sought to homogenize urban spaces around the world, and in the process create a rational collective human society.

A poem by the collaborative pair of Czechoslovakian poets Bohumila Grögerová and Josef Hiršal, printed as part of Hansjörg Mayer's *Futura* pamphlet series in 1966, displays a similar posture towards the internationalization of language (see fig. 2.3). The fact that Hiršal and Grögerova are a collaborative pair is in itself deserving of notice, and might perhaps be significant for understanding the pose towards authorship that concrete poetry allowed for through its veritable excision of the lyrical "I" and its embrace of the collective experience of language. In the case of "Manifest," the reader apprehends the letters as they would appear on a keyboard, but if the reader is North American or British, or Spanish or French, s/he feels a disruption as s/he reads the letters from left to right. Instead of QWERTY, the top layer of letters reads "QWERTZ." The *Y* many typists are accustomed to seeing between the *T* and the *U* is missing, and it takes a little while to find it exiled to the lower left-hand corner, where the *Z* usually is. Further examination of the arrangement of letters uncovers three additional letters, all with umlauts, on the right hand side: ü, ä, and ö. This would seem natural to a German speaker, for it is, in fact, a German QWERTZ keyboard, where the *Y* and the *Z* are positioned based on the probability of their use, as they would be in English. For touch-typists used to the QWERTY layout, the poem's defamiliarization of a specific kind of alphabetic arrangement is one they feel in their hands. It prompts a bodily response, one of estrangement. The memory of a keyboard layout is not a visual memory. Ask typists to recall the layout of a keyboard and they will likely close their eyes, or look at their fingers, which they will move as they recite each letter: muscle memory. A German speaker encountering the poem will not have the same, bodily defamiliarization with the letters, and it is that schism between readers that makes the poem's function complex when positioned within an international sphere.

Adding to the poem's power is the fact that the poets are Czech, and face the same linguistically occupied and varied consciousness I discussed in relation to Vladimir Burda's fingerprint poem in chapter 1. In this context, the poem becomes even more entangled with histories of industry and violence, as Czechoslovakia had only been a nation separate from the Austro-Hungarian empire for twenty years before it was invaded by the Nazis near the beginning of World War II, an occupation that brought both language and German technology back into a space that had only recently begun to experience a national independence. And while it is important to recognize that Czech-language typewriters also use a QWERTZ layout, the presence of the ü, ä, and ö is specifically German. None of those letters appear in the Czech alphabet. Letters that do commonly appear, and that are left out by the poets – and the typewriter manufacturers in many cases – are Á, Č, Ď, É, Ě, Ch, Í, Ň, Ó, Ř, Š, Ť, Ú, Ů, Ý, and Ž.

By presenting the letters as they are popularly experienced, the poets situate their work within the mechanical, materially-determined arena for language that is a consequence of the mass-production and consumption of typewriters. The title they give to the piece, or the word that appears on the top of the page, "manifest," adds a further ambiguity to the poem. Does it refer to the tradition of the manifesto in poetry and art of the twentieth century? Does it hold up the typewriter as a tool of political and cultural defense, offering it as both a symbol of writing as well as a standard technology of increased circulation and production of ideas? Or, perhaps most interestingly, does it refer to the list of a transport ship's cargo, to be checked by customs officers who guard national ports of entry? Writing in the eastern bloc nation of Czechoslovakia, Grögerová and Hiršal likely meant it in all three ways.

The attention paid by the above poems to the contemporaneous conditions of language and to constituent elements beyond what the human eye or ear is accustomed to also played a central role in the mechanical approach to language and information that characterized early experiments in computation, experiments that connect to the larger modernist project in very specific ways: the development of a new global understanding, the flattening of culture, the dream of a universal, scientific language, and so on. Although the idea of the *global* is by no means specific to the middle of the twentieth century or limited to modernism, it seems clear that concrete poetry, in its compositional techniques and attention to distribution across various, disparate geographies, provides a record of a *qualitative* shift in the understanding of what comprised globality in the wake of World War II.

Bombs and Bombes

There are a number of historical forces that position Pignatari's "Beba Coca Cola" and "LIFE" within a politically charged context. The first is the Hydrogen bomb, whose globalizing power is easy to understand. Nuclear fallout does not recognize national borders, and although the Cold War is popularly recognized as hardening those borders, its constant threat of terrestrial annihilation forced nations to recognize structures beyond themselves. The vehicle by which that threat was delivered was often the large-format pages of *LIFE* magazine, which chronicled the American nuclear tests from Operation Crossroads in 1946 through the 1960s. That the Americans developed and used the most devastating technology of destruction, and then continued to develop and test even more destructive technology, is not a trauma limited to the United States and Japan alone. In the 1950s and '60s, tests of nuclear weapons were being held by France, the Soviet Union, Britain, and China, and the proliferation of weapons had reached a point where the Earth could be destroyed several times over.[3] The continued presence of trace quantities of Strontium-90 – a bone-seeking radioactive isotope released into the stratosphere by fallout from nuclear testing – in humans around the globe allows us to conceptualize a disturbing but eminently modern global community. It is difficult to imagine from a twenty-first-century perspective just how transformative an *invention* nuclear technology was. In many ways, it invented a cohesive world by threatening to end it.

The wider cultural output of the time speaks to the centrality of nuclear weapons in the global consciousness. Stanley Kubrick's *Dr Strangelove or: How I Learned to Stop Worrying and Love the Bomb* (1964) persists as one of the most effective records of the anxiety of the period, as it satirically unravels the argument used by nuclear nations that the weapons were designed for peace, not war. The plot of the film centers on a doomsday mechanism designed to ensure that if a war were initiated by the United

States, the Soviet Union would automatically launch its entire nuclear arsenal in retaliation, resulting in the complete annihilation of the planet. When a rogue American brigadier general – Jack D. Ripper, played by Sterling Hayden – suffering from paranoid fantasies of communist infiltration of the water supply, initiates an attack on the Soviet Union, it is a series of breakdowns in the chain of command and a communication malfunction that lead to a mechanically unavoidable mutually assured destruction. The sequence that opens the film depicts two planes refuelling in midair, set to music that suggests the aircraft are performing a sort of mechanical copulation. After the credits, the first scene takes place at an airforce base, where large rotating satellite dishes emphasize the central role of communication in modern military culture. The first character to appear does so in a room lined with large computers, emerging from behind a large paper printout. This is Group Captain Lionel Mandrake, played by Peter Sellers, the rational character foil to Hayden's Ripper. Ripper orders the confiscation of all radios and shuts down communication into and out of the base in oder to ensure his plan goes undiscovered, but Mandrake comes across a portable radio and turns it on to discover it is playing soothing jazz music rather than an emergency broadcast about a Soviet nuclear attack. At this point, communications technologies emerge as a sort of character within the film, part fool, part malicious spirit. Much of the rising action of the film stems from a phone conversation between the president of the United States and the prime minister of the Soviet Union in which the audience hears only the president's side. In combination with the damaged radio in the B52 bomber en route to attack the Soviet Union, the phone call between superpowers signifies a strong critique of the faith in communication and weapon technology to safeguard the lives of humans, and represents the expanded reach of particular nations and their conflicts into the realm of global catastrophe.

Recent large-scale museum exhibitions have also exposed how influential the threat of nuclear war was on the painting and visual art of the period, and it is difficult for even our contemporary, terror-stricken global population to understand the weight and power nuclear war presented.[4] Reconsidering concrete poetry with this in mind charges the work with an urgency and significance that has to this point been neglected by critics in large part – and ironically – because of its expansive, consciously global circulation. The global is a space that has only relatively recently become fathomable in a consciousness that for so long fooled itself into identifying as *post*war, and hence beyond the bomb. The threat of a final and permanent violence within a putatively peaceful world is an anxiety we can only recognize now, having become accustomed to it. What is more difficult to imagine is a world without it, contained and indefinite.

There is another "bomb" that is similarly absent from examinations of concrete poetry, one which both highlights the globality of the work and has implications for the formal qualities of the poems. It is Alan Turing's Bombe, the rudimentary computer designed by the British mathematician and his group – though modelled in large part after a machine designed by the Polish cryptanalyst Marian Rejewski – to crack the Nazi's Enigma code by mechanically sifting through millions of potential word combinations obtained from intercepted Nazi radio transmissions.[5] The Enigma machine encrypted messages by a mechanism that used three to four rotors in a fixed position, which meant that if one did not have the key for that particular message, there were seventeen thousand, five hundred and seventy-five settings that would result in completely unintelligible language, and just one which might make sense as a military command. The number of combinations swelled to close to half a million potential messages when the Nazis switched to the five rotor model later in the campaign. Turing's Bombe was able to mechanically read all the potential messages and would stop on any that mathematically adhered to German phrases, at which point a translator would check to see if it was significant. While the activities of Turing and his code-breaking colleagues at Bletchley Park remained classified until the mid-1970s, the technical knowledge produced during the war by Rejewski, Turing, et al., would seep out into the development of early commercial computer technology.

This mathematical approach to language comprehension and *deciphering* would, just over a decade later, find an aesthetic parallel in the work of the German concrete poet Max Bense, as well as in the aspirations for a universally recognizable poetry expressed by Gomringer. The effect of the mechanical or statistical treatment of language appears in many concrete poems whose composition adopts a permutational strategy, linking process to form in a manner that recognizes the diminished communication involved in commercialized or propagandistic discourse. For example, in Haroldo de Campos's "ALEA I – VARIAÇÕES SEMÂNTICAS (Uma Epicomédia de Bôlso)" (1962–3), a list of positive words are presented above a nearly identical list of negative words, the only difference between the two being the substitution of one or two letters per word (see fig. 2.4).[6] "O ADMIRÁVEL" in the first list, which Scottish concrete poet Edwin Morgan translates as "THE UNSURPASSABLE," becomes "O ADMERDÁVEL," or "THE UNSHITPASTABLE," in the second. This poem displays the anxiety of communication in an age of mechanization, where transmissions in which a single letter might be misunderstood could have serious ramifications for peace. Language had moved onto a sharper ledge with the expanded scale of communication.

The bottom section of the poem begins with two nonsense words, "NERUM / DIVOL," which shift and combine with each other until the end of the poem, when they re-order into "MUNDO / LIVRE," or "FREEWORLD." On their way they also morph into words that seem potentially meaningful, yet foreign; many of them appear to be Latin roots, which de Campos was hyperaware of, being a translator and speaker of several languages. Morgan translates a note by de Campos printed on the same page as the poem as "*program* do it yourself / the reader (operator) / may go on at pleasure / doing new semantic variations / within the given parameter," but because he chooses to translate "MUNDO LIVRE" as a single word, "FREEWORLD," he leaves out the rest of the note, that translates as "The possible permutations of the different letters of two five letter words add up to 3 628 800" (105–6), and that solidifies the mathematical approach to the scale of language in certain permutational poems.[7] The slight differences between antonymous words and between nonsense and sense words relates directly to the mechanical approach to language provided by early computational experiments that relied on programs to recognize logical constructions: if x then y; if y then z, etc. The terminal lines of the poem, "MUNDO LIVRE" / "FREEWORLD," therefore points directly to the emancipatory promise of technology, a promise of which de Campos, like Pignatari, was sceptical.

The compositional strategies made possible by the contemporaneous computer technologies received a heavy emphasis by the curator Jasia Reichardt, whose 1968 exhibition at the Institute for Contemporary Art in London, *Cybernetic Serendipity*, included work by engineers, artists, scientists, and poets in a manner that refused to identify which work belonged to which field. In her introduction to her edited collection *Cybernetics, Art, and Ideas*, where she reflects on the lessons of the exhibition, she brings into focus both the influence of mechanical modes of communication on concrete poetry and the new, international spaces these modes had created: "One thing that foreigners, computers and poets have in common is that they make unexpected linguistic associations" ("Cybernetics" 11). In another essay in the collection, the German poet Max Bense, one of the most prolific theorists of the concrete poetry movement in the 1960s and a professor of the philosophy of technology, scientific theory, and mathematical logic at the Technical University of Stuttgart, points out:

Today we have not only mathematical logic and a mathematical linguistics, but also a gradually evolving mathematical aesthetics. It distinguishes between the "material carrier" of a work of art and the "aesthetic state" achieved by means of the carrier. The process is devoid of subjective interpretation and deals objectively with specific elements of the "aesthetic state" or as one might say the specific elements of the "aesthetic reality." ("Projects" 57)

This idea of a diminished or absent subject position recurs in several of the poets' writings, but Bense's is perhaps the most extreme, celebrating the new, disinterested aesthetic of calculation, probability, and algorithms. The Noigandres group address a similar antisubjective pose in their "Pilot Plan": "Concrete poetry: total responsibility before language. Thorough realism. Against a poetry of expression, subjective and hedonistic. To create precise problems and to solve them in terms of sensible language" (A. de Campos, H. de Campos, and Pignatari 72). The poets were interested in subjectivities beyond those created by national language, and machines and their maths seemed to be nationless. The subject the poets required, and that is implicit in their refutation of the traditional poetic subject, was an emergent collective consciousness, created by a common emphasis on the experience of language in an internationalized social sphere. The barriers of nuanced semantic meaning crumble under a reduced, and therefore more accessible, sign system that aimed for a basic understanding across geographies: a kind of poetic Esperanto based on the rational functions of mathematics and the primary geometry of letters. That this collective understanding was created in large part by structures of capital, within the rapid expansion of communication technologies, advertising, and the circulation of goods and products within a mid-century period of affluence, is largely unaddressed by both the poets and critics.

In Henri Chopin's "Poem to Be Read Aloud," which dates from the mid-1960s, the concept of both the H-Bomb and Turing's machine meet in a permutational poem that is simply a column repeating the pattern "bombA / bombB / bombC / [...]." The poem announces its typewritten character, with some of the letters overinked and the terminal uppercase letters floating just out of alignment with the lowercase "bombs," a fact that distinguishes the work from the cleaner, fine printing aesthetic of Gomringer or the Noigandres poets. There is no variation on the pattern until "bombX," which Chopin repeats before moving on to "bombY / bombZ" (79; see fig. 2.5). The experience of looking at the poem is deceiving, as the eye assumes it recognizes the

ALEA I — VARIAÇÕES SEMÂNTICAS
(uma epicomédia de bôlso)

Haroldo de Campos
1962/63

O ADMIRÁVEL o louvável o notável o adorável
o grandioso o fabuloso o fenomenal o colossal
o formidável o assombroso o miraculoso o maravilhoso
o generoso o excelso o portentoso o espaventoso
o espetacular o suntuário o feerífico o feérico
o meritíssimo o venerando o sacratíssimo o sereníssimo
o impoluto o incorrupto o intemerato o intimorato

O ADMERDÁVEL o loucrável o nojável o adourável
o ganglioso o flatuloso o fedormenal o culossádico
o fornicaldo o ascumbroso o iragulosso o matravisgoso
o degeneroso o incéstuo o pusdentoso o espasmventroso
o espertacular o supurário o feezífero o pestifério
o merdentíssimo o venalando o cacratíssimo o sifelíssimo
o empaluto o encornupto o entumurado o intumorato

N E R U M
D I V O L
I V R E M
L U N D O
U N D O L
M I V R E
V O L U M
N E R I D
M E R U N
V I L O D
D O M U N
V R E L I
L U D O N
R I M E V
M O D U L
V E R I N
L O D U M
V R E N I
I D O L V
R U E N M
R E V I N
D O L U M
M I N D O
L U V R E
M U N D O
L I V R E

programa o leitor-operador é
convidado a extrair outras
variantes combinatórias
dentro do parâmetro semântico
dado
as possibilidades de permutação
entre dez letras diferentes
duas palavras de cinco letras cada
ascendem a 3.628.800

Figure 2.4
Haroldo de Campos. "ALEA I – VARIAÇÕES SEMÂNTICAS"

ALEA I — SEMANTIC VARIATIONS
(a mock-pocket-epic)

Haroldo de Campos

translated into English by Edwin Morgan

THE UNSURPASSABLE the laudable the notable the adorable
the grandiose the fabulous the phenomenal the colossal
the formidable the astonishing the miraculous the marvellous
the generous the excelse the portentous the stunning
the spectacular the sumptuous the faerifying the faery
the supereminent the venerable the supersacred the supercelestial
the unpolluted the uncorrupted the inviolate the intrepid

THE UNSHITPASTABLE the lowbabble the nauseable the malodorable
the ganglious the flatulous the fetoranimal the cutarsadical
the fornicable the astinking the iratulous the matrocitous
the degenerous the insext the pustiferous the stomafuching
the tentacular the suppurous the faecifying the fevery
the supermuckent the veneravid the suprasacral the supersyphilable
the pollust the upcorpsed the violoose the tumorped

FEWERDOLR
FOWLREDER
DREERFLOW
LOWFEEDRR
FROWLEERD
REERFOWLD
FLEDWEROR
FREDERLOW
WEEDFLORR
FERROWELD   *program* do it yourself
REDFLOWER   the reader (operator)
FLEERWORD   may go on at pleasure
FREEWORLD   doing new semantic variations
                        within the given parameter

pattern of the alphabet in this list of bombs – or bomb targets if "bomb" is read as an imperative verb – and only really catches the stutter at "bombX" when reading it aloud, following the instruction of the title. It is at this point that the reader sees and feels the poem differently, via a disruption Chopin often sought to locate in the relationship between language and the body. The poem operates as a warning against the fetishization of patterns, and of the too enthusiastic embrace of language as data to be fed into a programmed reader or machine. Is it a mechanical failure – a glitch? – on the part of the poet that has produced this error, or does the double X represent death, in the way that cartoons or comics place Xs over the eyes of corpses? Or does it reflect an anxiety over the increased mechanization of communication, like Kubrick's *Dr Strangelove*? There is a critique of both bomb(e)s in this poem through the violence of the proliferation of the bomb as weapon as well as the disrupted pattern of a mechanical presentation. Other questions arise as well, especially in relation to how quotidian bombs had become in the post-war period, a period which was only postwar to some, as new, anticolonial wars in North Africa often strayed into France in the 1950s and '60s, and as the Cold War's nuclear testing dominated political discourse and kept the world on edge.[8] What happens at "BombE," where the English word "bomb" becomes the French, *bombe*? And how significant is the acoustic similarity between "bomb" and "poem" / *bombe* and *poème* for a poet who believes in the disruptive power of spoken language?

Language Machines

The idea of mechanical language or communication that Chopin was working both in and through grew out of the rise in communication studies during the postwar period. An explanation of exactly how information was understood at the time will provide a context for how the permutational compositional strategies and reduced language of concrete poetry operated within the promise of advancements in communication networks and the contemporaneous theory. In this approach I am following Friedrich Kittler's lead in identifying a media-influenced discourse network, and the psychophysics – the effects that technologies have on the way humans at various times store and process information – involved in the production and reception of concrete poetry. Kittler distinguishes his method from what he disparages as the sociology of literature, critical readings that remain at a thematic level. He argues that literature does not simply provide

```
bombA
bombB
bombC
bombD
bombE
bombF
bombG
bombH
bombI
bombJ
bombK
bombL
bombM
bombN
bomb0
bombP
bombQ
bombR
bombS
bombT
bombU
bombV
bombW
bombX
bombX
bombY
bombZ
```

Figure 2.5
Henri Chopin. "Poem to Be Read Aloud"

metaphorical access to historical shifts in production, where its characters might speak the anxieties of an age that have not been recorded in dominant histories. In his view, literature is much richer than that: "literature [...] processes, stores, and transmits data, and [...] such operations in the age-old medium of the alphabet have the same technical positivity as they do in computers" (*Discourse Networks* 370). The wider field of media archeology similarly aims to comprehend how media affected populations throughout history, taking into account their relationship to previous media as well as the cultural ramifications of their adoption, recorded through material other than sale records and infrastructure development. As Erkki Huhtamo and Jussi Parikka point out, media archaeology owes a great debt to Kittler's investigations, and offers a counter-position to the study of new media, which often neglects the historical in favour of a celebration or panic over the possibilities of a new technologized future. My approach to the technological moment of the concrete poets is to show how recent shifts in media – both communicative and militaristic – offered new possibilities for thinking "language," or thinking "the globe."

The evidence that the poets were thinking about language *through* communication technologies is abundant. Haroldo de Campos writes about it explicitly in his critical essays; both Décio Pignatari and Max Bense taught information studies at post-secondary institutions; and poets themselves implemented mechanical modes of composition, both electronic and manual, in the production of their work. Eugen Gomringer, in a recent interview with Annette Gilbert, talks about how significant the concepts of cybernetics were to the Swiss-German poetic discourse, referring to an influential visit by the American cybernetician Norbert Wiener arranged by Bense. He also notes that in 1972, some time after his initial fascination with mechanical approaches to language, he was able to enter the title of one of his permutational poems "'kein fehler im system' [no error in the system] into one of the world's first computers, which was in [his] publisher's office filling a whole room. The permutation of the eighteen letters produced a two-sided output of several meters in length" (Gomringer, "Interview" n. pag.). The excitement Gomringer feels about language proliferating on its own, beyond a composing, feeling subject, is a major part of many concrete poets' engagement with the conditions of language at the time. An examination of what those conditions were, and how they provided both opportunities and challenges for a movement eager to cross borders and interrogate boundaries, both disciplinary and geographical, will help fill in some of the gaps in the critical treatment of concrete poetry to date.

Claude Shannon and Warren Weaver's *The Mathematical Theory of Communication* – first published in 1949 in *Scientific American*, as a condensed explanation of a 1948 study commissioned by the Bell Telephone Laboratories – and Norbert Wiener's work on cybernetics were both central to the development of new attitudes towards communication networks and the role of technology in everyday life. Weaver carefully defines *communication* early in his explanation of Shannon's more technical text as less an exchange of language than a description of "all the procedures by which one mind may affect another." This very broad definition, which implies a shift from human language to machine language and all its infrastructural components, is made even broader shortly after, through a significant and eerie expansion to the "procedures by means of which one mechanism (say automatic equipment to track an airplane and to compute its probable future positions) affects another mechanism (say a guided missile chasing this airplane)" (Shannon and Weaver 3).

Shannon and Weaver's scientific approach was a search for the quantifiable in a field where only the qualitative had previously been measured. They concerned themselves with measuring how much information could be communicated in a place and how well messages could be understood. Information was therefore separated from meaning: "Two messages, one of which is heavily loaded with meaning and the other which is pure nonsense, can be exactly equivalent, from the present viewpoint, as regards information […]. To be sure, this word information in communication theory relates not so much to what you *do* say, as to what you *could* say" (8). The semantic and material aspects become irrelevant; what is of primary concern is how accurately, or cleanly, a signal is received from a transmitter.

The move away from human communication toward a more general, mechanical communication replaced the Saussurean diagram of two faces whose minds are connected via mouths and ears with a series of boxes and arrows representing on one side the information source and transmitter, and on the other the receiver and destination. In the middle is a noise source, which is responsible for any degradation of the message in the process of transmission. The shift in diagrams (see figs. 2.6 and 2.7), on a very basic level, moves from the figurative to the geometric, a vector that can also be identified in concrete poetry's eradication of the lyrical poetic subject in favour of a detached coordinator of linguistic material. The Saussurean image even makes a point of distinguishing one of the heads from the other through slightly different facial features, perhaps in order to discourage the reader from confusing the diagram for one

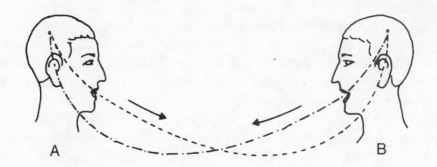

Figure 2.6
Ferdinand de Saussure. Diagram of communication model

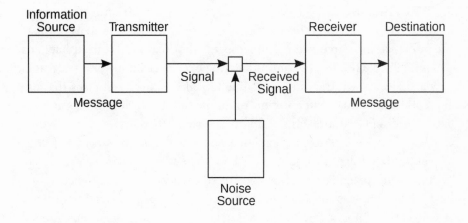

Figure 2.7

Claude Shannon and Warren Weaver. Diagram of communication model

of an inner monologue, or a mirror relationship, or twins. The Shannon and Weaver diagram displays no such anxiety, and celebrates the geometrical exactness of its diagram as a representation of standardized, mechanical communication, sourced in humans or otherwise. Added to the pattern are the transmitter and the receiver, two stages which structural linguistic analysis had no reason to identify, being satisfied with one human brain as the information source and the other as the destination. But what happens when those two brains are communicating over a telephone or a telegraph, or via radio waves? The brains become joined by exterior devices that are susceptible to noise or interruption, or, in the case of mechanical communication, are replaced altogether. This is a system of communication which does not require face-to-face explanation or dialogue; messages are consequently pared down to be quickly comprehended, a technique concrete poets would implement in order to expand their potential audience across barriers of time – as simultaneously present on the page instead of ordered in conventional poetic lines – and language – in a reduced and easily glossed vocabulary. Close proximity was no longer a requirement. The space of communication had exploded.

The mathematical character of Shannon's work comes in the statistical analysis of information. As Weaver points out, "That there are probabilities which exert a certain degree of control over the English language [...] becomes obvious if one thinks, for example, of the fact that in our language the dictionary contains no words whatsoever in which the initial letter j is followed by b, c, d, f, g, j, k, l, q, r, t, v, w, x, or z; so that the probability is actually zero that an initial j be followed by any of these letters" (11). The measure of uncertainty which exists within a system of communication comprises for Weaver the concept of entropy: "a measure of the degree of randomness, or of 'shuffledness' if you will, in the situation; and the tendency of physical systems to become less and less organized, to become more and more perfectly shuffled" (12). Information, then, in any system, increases as the ability to predict a message decreases; entropy and information are in this way positively linked.

The concept of noise in a communication channel – the measure of degradation, disruption, or error in any transmission – can only result in increased uncertainty of a message, that according to the logic of Shannon and Weaver's "entropy = increased information" formula, means that increased noise results in an increase in information. Weaver is aware of the contradiction:

This is a situation which beautifully illustrates the semantic
trap into which one can fall if he [sic] does not remember that
"information" is used here with a special meaning that measures
freedom of choice and hence uncertainty as to what choice has been
made. [...] Uncertainty which arises by virtue of freedom of choice
on the part of the sender is desirable uncertainty. Uncertainty
which arises because of errors or because of the influence of noise is
undesirable uncertainty. (19)

This idea of a desirable uncertainty, as it relates to the concept of entropy, is a
curious one throughout Weaver's text, as if the discovery of entropy within a
theory of communication, as opposed to a theory of heat or energy transfer,
has unlocked the scientific possibilities of linguistic analysis and opened a
frontier of mechanical thought.

This was the frontier Haroldo de Campos saw concrete poetry discovering, and how deeply he was influenced by notions of exactitude and quantification stemming from contemporary technologies comes through in his
1960 essay "The Informational Temperature of the Text":

Information theory provides us with precise tools, free of visceral
emotional appeals. In this way we can attempt to identify
straightforwardly the linguistic and aesthetic characteristics
which gave rise to the aforementioned censure and proceed to
locate them and the poetic object which they distinguish in
a wider process of formal evolution, as well as in the cultural
context from which they derive their necessity and their
justification. (223)

The essay is a riposte against those critics who condemn concrete poetry
for impoverishing language. De Campos counters that the poets are simply writing within the constraints of their moment, in the same way meter or form might have influenced poets in earlier moments. He cites the
work of Max Bense in making his argument for an aesthetic emerging out
of the mechanical. Displaying the depth of his engagement with the subject,
de Campos moves through the ideas of mathematician Benoit Mandelbrot,
the linguists George Zipf, G.A. Miller, and Charles Ogden, whose concept
of Basic English would seem attractive to a poet who sought an expanded,
international audience through a reduced language and a maximization of

communicative efficiency. This concept of increased meaning though a re-duced lexicon comes through in a passage de Campos cites from Miller's writing: "An increase in the size of the vocabulary is balanced by [a] decrease in the size of audience. A decrease in vocabulary is balanced by an increased audience. There seems to be no simple way to have a large vocabulary and a large audience at the same time" (quoted in de Campos 225). De Campos fuses this rational, logical approach to poetic production with the language of modernization, describing his and his fellow concrete poets as involved in an "industrial process," one which is historically distinct from the craftsman-ship that literature had to that point conjured, and which de Campos had earlier challenged in his response to Susanne Langer's philosophy. Concrete poems are "prototypes," emphasizing structure over "swarms of inarticulate feelings": "In this way [concrete poetry] coincides with the sense of a pro-gressively technical civilization within which it is postulated" (226).

The language de Campos uses in not only this essay, but in his earlier writing on concrete poetry as well, is rooted in a cultural shift towards the comfort of the mechanical that James Beniger locates within the innovations in manufacturing and travel in the nineteenth century. In his 1986 book, *The Control Revolution*, Beniger describes this shift as taking place within an understanding of "control," which he defines in a way that sounds very much like Shannon and Weaver's presentation of information: "the purpose-ful influence of behaviour, *however slight*" (8). He points to technological and structural changes that affected society in the eighteenth and nineteenth centuries – using the examples of rail travel, telegraphy, mass printing tech-nology, postal systems, and synchronized time zones, amongst others – as socially transforming our understanding of how information is distributed and received, and thus how, as social beings, we interact with each other. He offers the concept of rationalization, which he claims "might be defined as the destruction or ignoring of information in order to facilitate its pro-cessing," and as linked to the rise of the bureaucracy. He uses the example of "paperwork," specifically the limited spaces for input on standardized forms, as something that actually reduces the variability of data while also accumulating huge amounts of it (14–15). Like the Wittgensteinian maxim that the limits of our language are the limits of our world – because we exist in language we cannot imagine a space outside of it – this standardization of information controls our social being. From a poetic standpoint, this kind of control has historically been attractive for those who adhere to a revolution-ary political model, and would ideally be designed to include as many people as possible. When attempting to influence the behaviours of people who speak other languages, it is necessary to have a common ground on which to meet them, however rudimentary that ground might be.

Central to this metaphor of control is the concept of information processing, and how humans could be understood as information-processing machines. Norbert Wiener spent a considerable amount of time theorizing the human being as a programmable organism that functions within a feedback loop between its sensory organs, which send information to the brain for processing, and its external environment. Part of the reason why this perspective became so widely embraced by thinkers in various fields was the introduction of statistical analysis into the field of physics, which offered a new approach to an area of research that could match the growth of scientific discovery. The crystalline laws of Newton that governed much of the advancement in physics in the eighteenth and nineteenth centuries were, in the twentieth century, beginning to crack. The application of statistical analysis of particle movement, for example, resulted in a recognition of the impossibility of complete accuracy. This turn, according to Wiener, had the effect that "physics now no longer claims to deal with what will always happen, but rather with what will happen with an overwhelming probability" (10). An effect of this embrace of *probability* was an optimistic sense of *possibility*.

N. Katherine Hayles identifies in Wiener's thinking, and in the discourse around cybernetics more generally, the beginnings of a post-structuralist understanding of language and human subjectivity: "[Wiener] questioned whether humans, animals, and machines have any 'essential' qualities that exist in themselves, apart from the web of relations that constituted them in discursive and communicative fields" (91). And indeed, the understanding of energy and information that grew out of the discipline of cybernetics had a lasting effect on how information continues to be conceptualized. In the Macy Conferences on Cybernetics, which were held annually from 1946–53, mathematicians, engineers, social scientists, and psychologists gathered to discuss the implications of the mechanization or rationalization of information, and the role of the human subject in processing that information. The purely quantifiable mode of information, the kind favoured by engineers and early computer scientists, was divorced from context in order to function with greater stability of meaning. This stability is paramount for formulae to function, and for theories of information to work across disciplines, but it exists only in abstraction. This position has a particularly modernist flavour to it, as it imagines a universal calculating subject, who apprehends the world as varying sources of information, all of which operate within a theoretical logic of quantification.

The attendees of the Macy Conferences who challenged this mechanistic perspective were the social scientists, particularly the social anthropologists Margaret Mead and Gregory Bateson, and their daughter, Catherine Bateson. Catherine Bateson, in particular, disputed the idea that information can ever function in a closed system, for the energy of the observer necessarily influences the information gathered. Hayles writes through the Batesons' and Mead's anxieties around cybernetics to argue that such approaches to information assume a separation of mind and body, continuing a Western tradition antithetical to the body. This tradition – and the debate initiated by cybernetics – continues to be relevant today, where economic data and bio-data, both operating on a scale that would have been unimaginable to the participants in the Macy Conferences, carry a global significance for governmentality and geopolitical structures of power.

"The Ethics Residing in the Audacity of Change"

The theorization of how advances in communication and information technologies impacted social organization and human subjectivity was developed much more comprehensively in the work of Marshall McLuhan, a literature professor and contemporary of Wiener. Since the publication of his first book, *The Mechanical Bride* (1951), which treated popular advertisements as high-culture to be carefully parsed and decoded, McLuhan had become fascinated by how media influences the ways that we deal with the world and each other. He manifested his theories in various modes, relatively quickly abandoning the academic treatise with its conventional lines of type and the mode of thinking those lines – these lines – encourage and taking up a more explorational method of criticism, using images, typography, film and sound to materially situate his argument that our media shape our consciousness. Following *Understanding Media: The Extensions of Man* (1964), in which he coined the phrase "the medium is the message," McLuhan collaborated with graphic designer Quentin Fiore[9] to produce *The Medium is the Massage: An Inventory of Effects* (1967), a text which, like concrete poetry, tries to match its form to its epoch by pairing words with images, and questioning the linear conventions of book technology. The text is laden with photographs, some captioned and some left on their own, with short texts interspersed. The authors explain their strategy:

> The medium, or process of our time – electronic technology – is reshaping and restructuring patterns of social life. It is forcing us to reconsider and re-evaluate practically every thought, every action, and every institution formerly taken for granted. Everything is changing – you, your family, your neighborhood, your education, your job, your government, your relation to "the others." And they're changing dramatically. [...] It is impossible to understand social and cultural changes without a knowledge of the workings of media. (8)

This passage serves to contextualize the newness concrete poetry was writing through as a movement that emerged during a period of dramatic shifts in media. The traditional book, with its pages of unbroken text, had become insufficient in a time of electronic communication. The concrete poets felt the same way about the line, and the idea of the poetic subject: it was outdated, impotent.

What the advances in technology allowed for, intellectually, socially, and globally, and how these changes affected the strategies and concerns of the concrete poets remain significant questions, ones that challenge the very status of the book. McLuhan and Fiore embrace a return to pre-Gutenberg subjectivity, although with a language that should now strike readers as naïve and Eurocentric: "Ours is a brand-new world of allatonceness. 'Time' has ceased, 'space' has vanished. We now live in a global village ... a simultaneous happening. We are back in acoustic space. We have begun again to structure the primordial feeling, the tribal emotions from which a few centuries of literacy divorced us" (63).[10] The concrete poet Pierre Garnier welcomes a similar shift in a text that shares the embrace of new structures of meaning with his compatriot Chopin, who is quoted above:

> These kinds of poetry in their diversity as well as in their shared tendencies are driving forces, they are man come back, liberated from a pre-established language imposed from childhood on with its burden of ideas and moralities, at the root of the forces and working there aided by the most modern techniques and consciousness, like the cosmonaut in space – the ethics residing in the audacity of change. Joy in the absence of narrow certainties,

joy in the world open as it is, joy of creation in creation infinitely spacious, these kinds of poetry are not "fixed," they are constantly becoming. ("Position I of the International" 80)[11]

Both the concrete poets and McLuhan and Fiore implement similar techniques to evoke these recent perceptual shifts. The concrete poets emphasized the materiality of language: "Today 'Concrete Poetry' is the general term which inlcudes [sic] a large number of poetic-linguistic experiments characterized [...] by conscious study of the material and its structure [...]: material means the sum of all the signs with which we make poems" (Gomringer, "The Poem" 69).

Illustrating this point, Dieter Roth's "Some Variations on 4⁴" (1957) is simply an arrangement of *b*'s, *d*'s, *p*'s, and *q*'s in ways that emphasize their shapes over their sound referents, so that they become purely visual information (n. pag.; see fig 2.8). The poem illustrates the significance of orientation or perspective, even on the level of the letter. As readers – or should I say viewers? – we recognize some of the arrangements as letters: *dd* over *bb*, or *db* over *bd*, but others we recognize simply as shapes, as circles with lines attached. But we only have to rotate the page ninety degrees to see those shapes as letters again, proving that it is our habits that determine our readings, and our inflexibility that impedes recognition. Alternatively, a machine, which has no habits, could read the poem without any trouble if it were programmed to interpret specific shapes in various orientations or combinations. The machine is unimpeded by culture, and by the habits of a language community. It is the variations of the orientation, and of the relationship between the discrete groups of letters/shapes that give the piece its poetic charge, fulfilling the disruptive requirement of poetry. Roth inserts variability into an alphabet to make it opaque, to collapse signifier and signified, in order to expose the barriers we take as natural in our apprehension of language. The poem is a challenge to our habits and our stubbornness, and expresses a faith in the reader's ability to move outside of conventional reading strategies, encouraging us to reconsider the modes of thinking and communication that have brought us to this point in history.

This same challenge to habits, and to the knowledge those habits produce, is what drives McLuhan and Fiore. But *The Medium is the Massage* is less interested in foregrounding the materiality of language than the materiality of the book. Across two pages there is simply a photograph of two thumbs holding open a page as if they were the reader's, with "the book" printed at the top (34–5; see fig. 2.9). Significantly, the thumbs belong to different bodies, perhaps, like Saussure's diagram, emphasizing the interrelational, necessarily collective condition of language.[12] Text is printed backwards on two subsequent pages, forcing readers to hold the book in front of a mirror to read it, and as a consequence to encounter an image of themselves in the corporeal act of reading; they are confronted with their own mirrored bodies looking at something other than their bodies, something that moves differently in the image than it feels in their hands. On the next two pages the text is printed upside down, again disrupting readers' expectations of how information gets communicated through the book form (54–7). These corporeal investigations of the act of reading, though in this case visual, share the strategy of disruption Chopin uses in his "Poem to Be Read Aloud," where it is the process of vocalization that makes the reader see the unseen, that breaks the trance of the printed word. And just as Roth reorients letters to disrupt the space of the poem, McLuhan and Fiore break the plane of the book, forcing readers to experience the tactility of media.

McLuhan and Fiore, as well as the concrete poets, emphasize the materiality of language and its implications for the body in an increasingly mediated sensory environment, and use similar techniques to argue their position.[13] Both use the fingerprint as metaphor for embodied information: an example of how the body is written, as well as how, by even the most basic interaction with a mark and surface, it writes, and is physically interpellated into an order of signification. An enlarged fingerprint on one page of *The Medium is the Massage* is repeated in mirrored form and reduced on the following page, beside the paragraph heading "You" (10–11). As discussed in chapter 1, Jean-François Bory matches their style in his anthology *Once Again* (1968), where the Czechoslovakian poet Vladimir Burda's (presumably) fingerprint is printed as a poem, accompanied by the German word for *I*, "ich," as well as Fluxus artist Alison Knowles's "Poem," which is a fingerprint repeated until the ink no longer registers. The eye of the Western reader, trained to experience a page from left to right, top to bottom, follows the illegibly white record of bodily information to an illegibly black record of bodily information, which is the opposite direction the poem was produced in (Burda 79; Knowles 96; see fig. 2.10 and 2.11). The traditional poetic, thinking subject is replaced by a material record of the bodily, feeling subject, as the signifying order is disrupted and readers and viewers are required to abandon their techniques of comprehension and to open up to new structures of communication, be they visual or tactile.

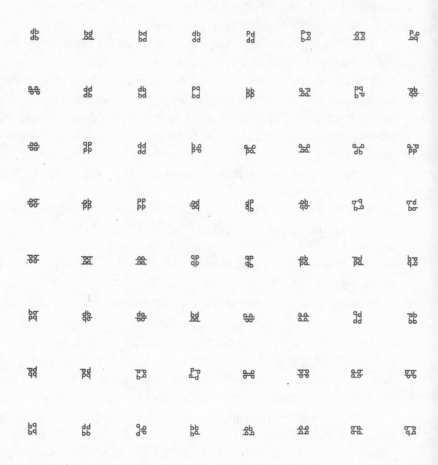

Figure 2.8
Dieter Roth. "Some Variations on 4⁴"

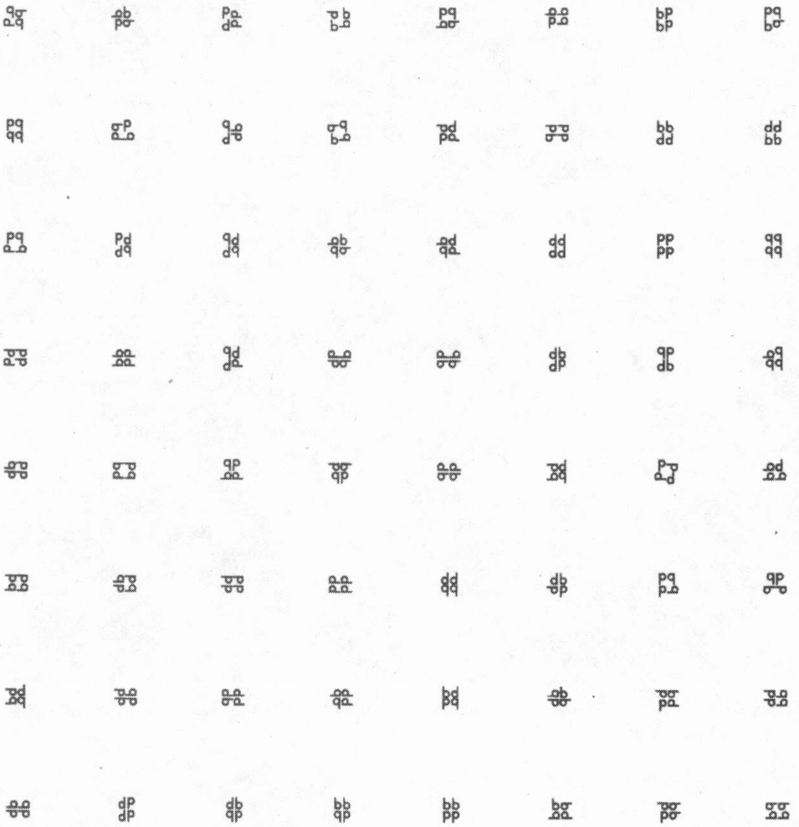

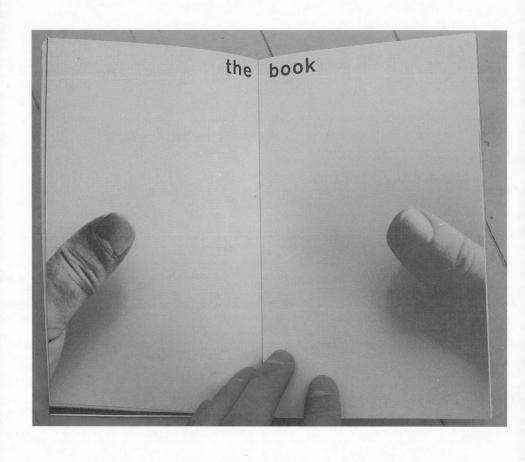

Figure 2.9

Marshall McLuhan and Quentin Fiore. Excerpt from *The Medium is the Massage*

ich

Figure 2.10
Vladimir Burda. "Ich"

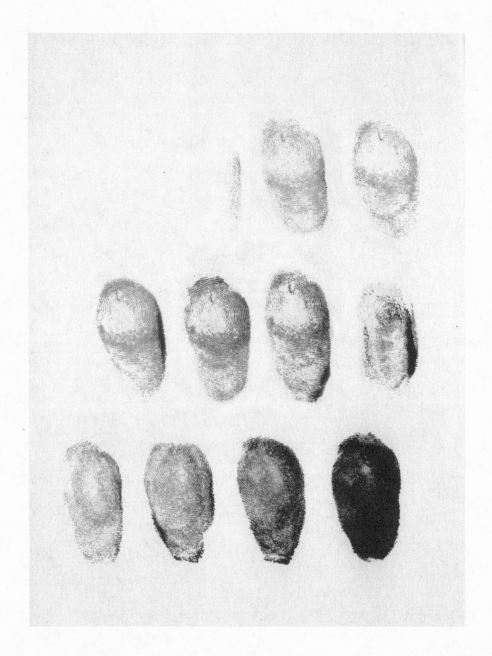

Figure 2.11
Alison Knowles. "Poem"

Mapping the Transnational

The increased role electronic media played in everyday life across various geographies had tremendous historical ramifications for cultural production and social organization. It is difficult to overestimate the effects that shifts in technology, rapid postwar economic development, and new understandings of how nations operate in relation to each other had on the world around the middle of the twentieth century. Where Wiener and McLuhan might feel that speculation about the social effects of world communication is sufficient, the historian Eric Hobsbawm places the shifts in everyday life and global understanding within their socio-political context. In his immodestly titled book *The Age of Extremes: A History of the World, 1914–1991*, Hobsbawm negotiates a space between argument and statistics. Like his contemporary, the media theorist Friedrich Kittler, who links communication technologies and war,[14] Hobsbawm parallels the development of major social trends with the practices of the wars that marked the first half of the twentieth century. He points out that "twentieth century wars were mass wars in the sense that they used, and destroyed, hitherto inconceivable quantities of products in the course of fighting. Hence the German phrase *meterialschlacht* to describe the western battles of 1914–18 – battles of materials" (Hobsbawm 45). The infrastructure for war production was then integrated into a global market that produced and consumed increasing amounts of goods in a modernization project unprecedented in world history in its scale and rapidity.

Mass war demanded mass production, which, after the war, demanded mass labour and mass consumption: "World output of manufactures quad-rupled between the early 1950s and the early 1970s and, what is even more impressive, world trade in manufactured products grew tenfold" (Hobsbawm 261). Hobsbawm links this drastic increase in production to rapid urbaniza-tion across the globe – "For 80 per cent of humanity the Middle Ages ended suddenly in the 1950s; or perhaps better still, they were *felt* to end in the 1960s" – but also to a triumphant phase of capitalism. Posed against the stagnating economies of communist nations, which were lagging behind in technology, the visible wealth of the middle classes and the generous welfare states cre-ated by the influence of Keynesian economic policies in developed nations were the most effective strategy for the containment of communism. It is out of this period, Hobsbawm argues, that the transnational economy emerged. He makes a clear distinction between the transnational and the international economies, however, noting that the latter was not a new development – nations had been exchanging goods for as long as there were nations to trade with – although it was increasing rapidly, as a result of expanding markets and wealth. The transnational, though, began to appear in the 1960s and then developed more fully in the 1970s, and can be defined as "a system of economic activities for which state territories and state frontiers are not the basic framework, but merely complicating factors" (277). David Harvey provides some nuance to this process, locating it, in part, in the breakdown of the Bretton Woods System, which regulated international trade and currency exchange, beginning in 1968. What changed, Harvey argues, was not that national economies disappeared, but that the influence of one national economy in particular – the United States' – diminished. A global system in which the United States wielded a great deal of power gave way to a different global system "that was more decentralized, coordinated through the market, and [that] made the financial conditions of capitalism far more volatile" (Harvey, *Spaces* 61). The rhetoric that accompanied this shift emphasized its flexibility, consequently shifting the spatial understanding of the centralized *nation* to the more dispersed concept of the *globe*.

This supranational level of activity, for Immanuel Wallerstein, centres on the concept of a world-system, which he developed in the early 1970s as a way to contest the increasing compartmentalization of knowledge. He explains his critical approach to the transformed geography of the period as

> first of all the substitution of a unit of analysis called the "world system" for the standard unit of analysis, which was the national state. On the whole, historians had been analyzing national histories, economists national economies, political scientists national political structures, [literary critics national literatures,] and sociologists national societies. World-systems analysis raised a skeptical eyebrow, questioning whether any of these objects of study really existed, and in any case whether they were the most useful loci of analysis. (16)

The world-system is not necessarily a globe-system; world-system analysis can be and often is applied to regions such as Europe, Asia, and Africa, without discussing their connection to other regions. But importantly even these regional approaches strive to operate on a supranational level. When dealing with cultural production, for example, it is not necessary to connect all output from one region to that of another, but where connections can be made that might elucidate the relationships between social and artistic contexts, the lack of a cohesive national or linguistic background should not impede investigations that increase the understanding of how culture moves between global spaces. As such, world system analysis proves an extremely valuable source for theorizing a method of reading concrete poetry beyond national, linguistic and disciplinary borders.

While there might have been in the past attempts to theorize the relationship between German and Brazilian concrete poetry, or British and North American, or Portuguese and Brazilian, the challenge of the movement is to account for the activity of poets who compose in languages and spaces not often studied in university departments, or at least not in conjunction. After reading the Japanese concrete poets, how can we read the Swedish, or the Danish? After reading the Mexican poets, how can we talk about the Czechoslovakian? There needs to be a critical method of approaching the work that allows for those unexpected and often counterintuitive routes, for it is those very routes the poets were imagining in their comprehension of the global. While discussions around how to integrate cultural production from a range of spaces, at a range of scales, have energized recent debates within globalization studies and cosmopolitanism generally, and comparative literature more intensively, there is yet to be accord on how to responsibly approach the rapidly expanding terrain of a global culture. An investigation of the challenges in conceptualizing an expanded space of cultural production when we are so accustomed to the nation, or other critical circuits etched by repetition in various disciplinary approaches – particularly globalization studies, cosmopolitanism, and comparative literature – will help readers navigate the stubbornly dispersed texts of concrete poetry.

The world-system Wallerstein theorizes rose out of the emergence of capitalism in the long sixteenth century, which was solidified by the 1648 Peace of Westphalia, an agreement that granted a level of sovereignty to specific nations in Europe; was developed further by the 1789 French Revolution, a bourgeois revolution that marked the beginning of radical, antisystemic movements; and reached its current stage only with the "world revolution of 1968" (Wallerstein x). Like Hobsbawm, Wallerstein places strong emphasis on the sharp rise in production and wealth that took place in the postwar years in most Western European and North American countries, but he accentuates the increasingly central role of the United States in that process. The Marshall Plan in Europe and the aggressive economic policies of containment during the Cold War had tremendous influence on global culture.

The writings of both Fredric Jameson and Arjun Appadurai have been integral in identifying how cultural production is rooted in Marshall Plan economic restructuring, as well as how global identities have emerged from circuits of mass media. In this way, globalization theorists have provided an update to Benedict Anderson's influential 1983 text, *Imagined Communities*, that linked the development of nations to the rise of print capitalism. Appadurai argues that electronic media, which can function outside the skills of reading and writing central to Anderson's argument, are the current instigators of what will become a global, postnational imaginary (*Modernity* 22). In this he falls in step with the project of the concrete poets who placed similar emphasis on the potential for the global reach of culture to create new communities, and who would use technological advancements to reach beyond the spatial limitations of the nation or national language. Gomringer's writing, in particular, expresses a parallel desire for transformation through connectivity.

The idea of a cosmopolitan subjectivity, also nascent in Gomringer's writing, travelling the networks of media and finance in the age of globalization, is one that grew alongside globalization theory at the end of the twentieth century and the beginning of the twenty-first. Bruce Robbins and Pheng Cheah theorize cosmopolitanism as a way of imagining a global citizen, or at least the difficulties of deciding what that citizenship would entail. They make the important distinction between globalization, which approaches the material conditions that arise from the interaction of global and local forces, and cosmopolitanism, which is a reaction to certain kinds of globalization processes, and is concerned with developing a cross-national political solidarity to counter the exploitation that arises from the new, accelerated shifts in social organization. Both Robbins and Cheah refer to the loosening of the hyphen between nation and state, a nice way of understanding the cosmopolitical processes that resonate with Wallerstein's concept of the world-system, while reinforcing Anderson's thesis that citizens' feelings of belonging are produced linguistically and culturally, not by the space defined by the borders of the nation-state.

But there are also voices that rise against the quick embrace of a world-subject as one who is characterized by *opportunity*, or the kind of negative freedom brought by circuits of capital. Timothy Brennan critiques the optimistic mode of the global imaginary, one which Appadurai – in *Modernity at Large* more than his later work – shares with the at times technologically determinist concrete poets.[15] He focuses on the discourse around cosmopolitanism, and its cousin *cosmopolitics*, both of which often conceptualize a universal subjectivity and relation to global modes of production. This is the cosmopolitanism Karl Marx and Friedrich Engels put to polemical use in *The Communist Manifesto*, in their attempt to articulate a universal position for the worker *vis a vis* the expanding realm of bourgeois production in the mid-nineteenth century (Marx and Engels 10–11). Whether used by communists or neoliberals, cosmopolitanism often falls into the trap of participating in a kind of reverse orientalism, one that imagines subjects in foreign spaces who desire an emancipation from their material conditions, whether it be via revolution or an entrance into a market economy. As David Harvey argues in an essay that calls for greater attention to be paid to the spaces out of which ideas emerge, all cosmopolitanism has within it an "embedded geopolitical allegory" ("Cosmopolitanism" 557). Brennan moves around cosmopolitanism by advocating a return to internationalism, though a renewed and fairer version of it:

> The cosmopolitan ideal envisages less a federation or coalition
> of states than an all-encompassing representative structure in
> which delegates can deliberate on a global scale. By contrast,
> internationalism seeks to establish global relations of respect and
> cooperation, based on acceptance of differences juridically, before
> material conditions exist for doing so equitably. *Inter*nationalism
> does not quarrel with the principle of *national* sovereignty, for there
> is no other way under modern conditions to secure respect for
> weaker societies or people. (77)

It would be unfair to read onto the project of the concrete poets the biases of recent globalization theory, just as it would be unfair to condemn them for a naïve embrace of the technology of computation. They functioned within a historical and geographical context – a world – that had different promises, and different potentials. What is more pressing, and more challenging, is to consider how the poetry operated during its moments: which fantasies it engaged, which ideas it sprung from. It remains clear from their critical writing that the poets, by trying to escape national language by reducing it to a visual, easily comprehendible format, conscientiously attempted to produce a global (cosmopolitan) subject though an international poetic style. The fact that the major theorists come from Brazil supports this position, as their national language keeps them and their compatriots slightly outside of their immediate South American cultural milieu, but also keeps them from identifying with one particular European or North American modernist tradition over another: the English, French, German, Soviet, Italian, and to a much lesser extent, Spanish modernisms are all similarly distant both culturally and geographically, a condition that does not apply to European or

North American poets, and which affects their understanding of the spaces of the *global*.[16]

A New World Literature

Addressing the problem of how to deal with a world literature that, after the work done by theorists of globalization and cosmopolitanism, can no longer pretend that culture develops in nations without influence from other regions (and can no longer even pretend that was *ever* the case), a series of articles by Franco Moretti attempts to provide a new model for literary critics to confront the scale of their field. His "Conjectures on World Literature" begins with Goethe's oft-quoted passage from 1827 which proves the concept of a literature of the global is not a recent development: "Nowadays, national literature doesn't mean much: the age of world literature is beginning, and everybody should contribute to hasten its advent."[17] Trained as a comparativist, Moretti admonishes his field as failing to sufficiently engage with world literature, instead mapping what often becomes an even more entrenched Western European tradition.

> The sheer enormity of the task [of reading world literature] makes it clear that world literature cannot be literature, bigger; what we are already doing, just more of it. It has to be different. The *categories* have to be different. "It is not the 'actual' interconnection of 'things,'" Max Weber wrote, "but the *conceptual* interconnection of *problems* which define the scope of the various sciences. A new 'science' emerges where a new problem is pursued by a new method." That's the point: world literature is not an object, it's a *problem*, and a problem that asks for a new critical method: and no one has ever found a method by just reading more texts. That's not how theories come into being; they need a leap, a wager – a hypothesis, to get started. ("Conjectures" 55)

The sheer enormity he speaks of echoes the exponential increase in information that is the impulse behind much of the writings of the cyberneticians, and which Turing's Bombe had the potential to address. The concrete poets, in their permutational works as well as in their efforts to function within a simplified or reduced language – remember Gomringer's claim that poems should strive to be "as easily understood as signs in an airport[,] or traffic signs," – were dealing with a similar anxiety – a similar *problem* with *world literature* – albeit forty years previous to Moretti's argument. Their response to the increased scale of knowledge and culture comes out in their permutational and geometrical methods. Closer to our present moment, Gayatri Spivak argues in *Death of a Discipline* that the development of Area Studies within universities created a false understanding of culture and language as contained within specific geographies.[18] She extends this critique to the tendency of a certain manifestation of Comparative Literature, "whose hallmark remains a care for language and idom," to reinforce a Eurocentric and discrete understanding of cultural production (5). Willard Bohn, who has produced masterful and virtuosic readings of visual poems in several languages within modernist and avant-garde literature, admits that in his study of visual poetry from 1914–28, "the absence of the Slavic poets, like the Dutch, was necessitated by a lack of linguistic competence. Given the complex interplay between verbal and visual elements, working with translations is inherently unsatisfactory" (7). But perhaps against the conventional emphasis on language competency we might find a way to productively engage that dissatisfaction, to use it as a side entrance into an adjusted comparativism that asks questions of texts without already knowing the answers. Again, the idea of scale becomes a barrier. How many languages can one know? How many geographies can one concentrate on without losing site of the global?

Moretti's project works both for and against Spivak's argument. He defends his methodological approach against advocates of close reading by outlining his desire for an overarching *system* of literary analysis. For Moretti, the problem with insisting on close reading, including methods promoted by New Criticism as well as deconstruction, is that "it necessarily depends on an extremely small canon" ("Conjectures" 57). What he advocates in its place is an idea of "distant reading":

> At bottom, [close reading]'s a theological exercise – very solemn treatment of very few texts taken very seriously – whereas what we really need is a little pact with the devil: we know how to read texts, now let's learn how *not* to read them. Distant reading: where distance, let me repeat it, *is a condition of knowledge*: it allows you to focus on units that are much smaller or much larger than the text: devices, themes, tropes – or genres and systems. ("Conjectures" 57)

The very mention of "distant reading" is enough to make any literary critic suspicious; it is a shocking and counterintuitive proposition. But the distance

Moretti advocates is unavoidable when approaching a contemporary understanding of world literature, one that operates in many languages across
many geographies, and one in which for too long the dominant languages or
regions have held primary positions.

> Sociological formalism has always been my interpretive method,
> and I think that it's particularly appropriate for world literature
> [...]. But, unfortunately, at this point I must stop, because my
> competence stops. Once it became clear that the key variable of
> the experiment was the narrator's voice, well, a genuine formal
> analysis was off limits for me, because it required a linguistic
> competence that I couldn't even dream of (French, English, Spanish,
> Russian, Japanese, Chinese, and Portuguese, just for the core of the
> argument). ("Conjectures" 66)

Concrete poetry allows for this incompetence in its readers. Indeed, it takes
it as a starting point, and revels in it. Removing the poetic subject and performing a global, glossed style circumvents the national critics who, although
valuable, are often cloistering and girding in their methods. In the previous
critical treatments of concrete poetry there has been no apparatus for reading it that gets away from modernist concerns (Mallarmé, Pound, the early
twentieth-century avant-gardes) and national histories in order to emphasize its fluid geographies and internationalist concerns. Ideas of space within
theories of globalization, Wallerstein's world-system, and Moretti's concept
of distant reading all offer potential – though inevitably partial – remedies.

Moretti's subsequent essays attempt to develop an abstract model for
world literature based on a statistical model of cultural and economic influence, and it is here where critiques of his method point to an apparent planet-
ary hierarchy. His primary genre, at the expense of all the others, is the novel,
from which he designs a theory of movement and adaptation from the core
to the periphery.[19] Efraín Kristal objects to this approach, and argues that by
following economic development, and the model of a core and periphery
development as it seeps into cultural output, Moretti perpetuates a Western
bias that sees the bulk of culture from outside of the "core" as a negotiation,
or compromise of Western forms and local conditions.

Kristal also challenges Moretti to account for the development of poetry:

> I am arguing [...] in favour of a view of world literature in which
> the novel is not necessarily the privileged genre for understanding

literary developments of social importance in the periphery; in
which the West does not have a monopoly over the creation of
forms that count; in which themes and forms can move in several
directions – from the centre to the periphery, from the periphery
to the centre, from one periphery to another while some original
forms of consequence may not move much at all; and in which
strategies of transfer in any direction may involve rejections,
swerves, as well as transformations of various kinds, even from one
genre to another. (73–4)

Moretti responds: "Yes, forms *can* move in several directions. But *do* they?
This is the point, and a theory of literary history should reflect the constraints
on their movements, and the reasons behind them" ("More Conjectures" 75).
When it comes to concrete poetry, forms certainly move from the periphery
to the core, if we remain within the thankfully now-dated terminology of
Moretti and Kristal. The Brazilians were, along with the Bolivian-Swiss
Gomringer, the major developers of the poetic form, and the most articulate
and prolific theorists of the movement. Daniel Spoerri, a Romanian living in
Germany, and Dieter Roth, a Swiss-German who moved to Iceland in 1957,
were also major figures in the form's development.

Using the example of architecture, and one that is relevant to subsequent chapters, Valerie Fraser notes that the French architect and theorist
Le Corbusier did not start working with curvilinear forms until after he had
visited South America and seen Rio de Jineiro from an airplane. But it is not
simply the forms that move from the periphery to the core; it is the periphery and the core that move, and which co-exist in poets who occupy various
spaces and overlapping national identities. Even Germany in the mid-1950s
would occupy a disputed position as a member of the developed core, experiencing a recent division into the GDR and the FRG, and learning to live in an
occupied and reconstructing space. These poets were all members of what
Stephen Bann describes as the first generation of concrete poetry (7). It is
only in the second wave that figures like the Scottish Ian Hamilton Finlay,
or the American Mary Ellen Solt, or the French Pierre Garnier begin to start
producing work and theory. So in this example, forms do move in directions that do not necessarily follow economic development, and other factors
need to be accounted for to trace their historical determinants. Moretti's idea
about the development of the novel coming out of a negotiation of local narratives and spaces with a Western form is countered by the concrete poets,
who, though the Brazilians and the Germans were certainly responding to

their locales (the Brazilians in their leftist politics and the Germans in their response to their East/West split), were attempting in many cases to create a literature without locale that could be adopted and understood in any region without a hierarchy of influence through the photographic/electronic/visual basis of their experimentation. Pignatari's "LIFE" is a prime example of this, as is, to a slightly lesser extent, because of its lexical markings, Hiršal and Grögerova's "Manifest." This does not negate Moretti's idea that a theory of literary history should deal with the constraints on the circulation of form, or "the reasons behind them," but it does challenge the idea that a unifying theory of world literature is necessary, or even possible when dealing with different genres or forms. There need not be a global key, but rather an awareness of contingencies, and a critical attitude that is open to the possibility of entering a field of investigation without a determined outcome set in the critic's mind.

Christopher Prendergast addresses Moretti's theories in his review of Pascale Casanova's *La République mondiale des letters*, a book that also deals with the ways in which world literature is framed. Prendergast applauds Casanova for refusing "to traffic in the term 'globalization' and its tacky Third Way *idées reçues*," which, having been written in 2001, provides evidence for how quickly academic trends rise and fall in contemporary discourse (100). Prendergast here substitutes a personal prejudice for a critical stance, though; the term *globalization* need not refer solely to the economic verve with which corporations and neo-liberal economists embrace the cost benefits of outsourcing production, which is how it is often used by the legions of protestors against such policies. *Globalization* primarily refers to an increased connectivity and common imaginaries, and in doing so does not limit itself to the age of transnationalism that developed during the latter half of the twentieth century. As a term, *globalization* carries with it the residues of all those meanings, which is part of what makes it so valuable and, at times, frustratingly vague.

Prendergast perceives the field of world literature – a term that has, post-Gutenberg, referred almost exclusively to printed literature – as contaminated and hierarchical. The national literatures that quickly adopted writing became dominant:

> The European Enlightenment established a link between "reason,"
> "civilization," and writing, thus confining oral culture to a position
> of inferiority, often attaching the pejorative valuation "barbaric" or
> "savage." The argument that a culture attains to civilization only

when it is capable of "inscribing" itself not only devalues the oral
tradition in the name of a specious fable of "development," but also
overlooks the very real ambiguity of the acquisition of writing;
at once an immense cultural gain, but also helping to institute
structures of power and domination, within which those who have
the skills of writing and reading enjoy advantages over those who
do not. (102)

Relating this to concrete poetry raises the question as to whether the poets
were attempting to move away from these structures of dominance by
embracing the photographic, or by critically mimicking the aesthetic of media
in an increasingly visual and electronic mediascape. In order to create a more
evenly distributed system of reference, were the concrete poets attempting
to combine geographies instead of separating them? Max Bense seems to
think so: "Concrete poetry does not separate languages; it unites them; it
combines them" ("Concrete Poetry" 73). Was the incompetence of the reader
a poetic strategy? Incompetence should not here be considered pejorative,
in the same way that illiteracy would in the system Prendergast identifies
above, but as a necessary condition in an expanding, poly-linguistic global
environment. Such incompetence might have been a material condition for
a form that would aim to make poetry as globally accessible as the traffic
signals and signs in airports that Gomringer points to in 1960. This poetic
strategy is perhaps most strikingly present in the sound experiments of
Henri Chopin and Paul de Vree, who used the expressive potential of the
human voice to move outside of visual signage, but who also used electronic
means, such as the tape recorder and tape-splicing techniques, to distinguish
their experimentation from previous sound poets like Hugo Ball and Kurt
Schwitters.

But the strategy is there in visual concrete poetry, as well. Augusto de
Campos's "Olho Por Olho," (1964) which he refers to as "popcrete," is simply
symbols cut out from magazines, mostly eyes and mouths, and arranged tri-
angularly (98; see fig. 2.12). The fragmentation of the body parts, especially
the sexualized eyes and mouths of magazine models, at the top of which are
traffic signs whose explicit function is to direct the movements of traffic –
no left turn, right turn only, etc. – triggers questions of behaviour, desire,
and representation in media culture. Pignatari's "Semiotic Poem," from the
same year, is similarly not made of words at all, but of shapes, a lexical key
for which is provided on the lower left side of the page (85; see fig. 2.13).
The poem deals with the fascination of Brazil with the football star Pelé, a

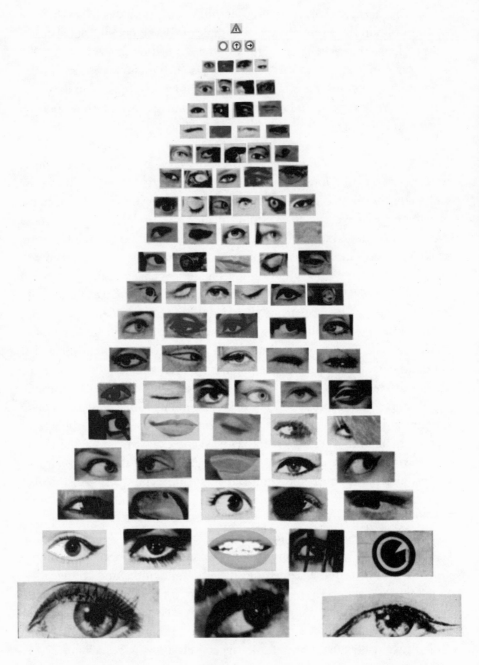

Figure 2.12

Augusto de Campos. "Olho por Olho"

chave léxica
lexical key

            pelé

            a pátria é a família
                (com televisão) amplificada
                the country is the amplified
                family (with television set)

            no fim dá certo
                at the end all ends well

Figure 2.13
Décio Pignatari. "Semiotic Poem"

fascination made all the more intense by his constant television presence and the fact that Brazil had won the FIFA (Fédération Internationale de Football Association) World Cup in 1958 as well as 1962. Brazil had through these victories become in some global networks almost synonymous with football, and for the first time football was an event mediated in large part by television, instead of radio, photography, and written news accounts. In this way the poem relates to the tension of Brazil's cultural and political moment – a military junta assumed power the same year the poems were published – in a complex manner, perhaps surprisingly to readers who would dismiss it for being overly simplified. The lexical key becomes part of the poem's composition. Translation is not here the subordinated capitulation to the conditions of an inter-linguistic audience, but an integral part of the work. The fact that the key – itself a kind of inter-sign translation – is translated into English from the original Portuguese troubles the prejudice against translation as being necessarily a degradation of the original, situated work. The form is accessible to any reader provided with only the most basic definition for the three symbols Pignatari makes use of.

Pelé, represented by a black circle in the poem, exists in a spatial relation to the nation of Brazil, "the amplified family (with television set)," and in affective relationship to the idea that "at the end all ends well." At the top of the poem, Pelé exists in multiple, outside of the amplified family, but within the feeling that things end well. The subsequent arrangements can be understood in various ways, with some of the lexical shapes intersecting or fragmenting in meaningful arrangements. The challenge for the reader or decoder is to keep the concepts associated with the shapes in mind while apprehending the arrangements. It is quite simple in the case of Pelé; the black circle stands in for a single person, easily comprehensible. But the more complex definitions associated with the rectangle and the rhombus are more difficult to manage in one's mind, and much more difficult to imagine in their various modulations. How exactly does a feeling split in half? Or rotate forty-five degrees?

The issue of translation is also central to concrete poems which function within language, not just to those that use only symbols, alphabetic or otherwise. Eugen Gomringer's work engages with the issue of cross-linguistic understanding, and occupies a critical ground for the imagination of a new space, beyond the language-based nation theorized by Benedict Anderson. Having spent the first eleven years of his life in Bolivia before moving to Switzerland, he wrote his first constellations in Spanish before attempting compositions in German and English. His early correspondence with Décio

Pignatari was in French. Gomringer's poem "Wind," on first viewing, seems to be a rather banal, mimetic poem about wind, as the letters *w*, *i*, *n*, and *d*, are scattered about the page as if wind had dispersed the language material (37; see fig. 2.14). But readers only fully grasp the poem's meaning when they realize that "wind" refers to the same phenomenon in English as well as German, meaning that there is not only a difficulty in reading the letters, as they are not arranged on conventional lines, but even the sounds of the words and letters are indeterminate. The English "wind" becomes the German *vind*; the English *w* (dʌb(ə)ljuː), *i* (aɪ), *n* (ɛn), and *d* (diː), become the German *w* (vɛ), *i* (ɪ), *n* (ɛn), and *d* (de). The poem is then not about a relationship between signifier and signified, but about one between linguistic communities and about a common visual experience of language. The collapse of the signifier into the signified opens up spaces to communities that might have been excluded by levels or certain modes of literacy. The embrace of a new global literacy, though one that was and still is perhaps problematically created by the sphere of commerce, was a strategy of cultural expansion for the concrete poets. In the case of Gomringer's poem, the letters' potential to *mean* in various arrangements is as much the force of the poem as the specific word choice, and although the primary relationship in the poem is between English and German languages, it is also meaningful to speakers of languages that use the Roman alphabet, in their ability to vocalize the text, and to those speakers of languages that use other alphabets, in their apprehension of the letters as shapes arranged in an odd pattern on the page.

Gomringer was enthusiastic about concrete poetry's ability to travel. He pointed to the poetry's intentional polyglotism as a way to "bring some living languages into contact with each other as at a party, for instance, or on a flight [where] people from different backgrounds, abilities, and languages as well as outward appearances can be observed" ("Concrete" 68). The Brazilians, especially, operated within various linguistic communities, and were skilled translators, especially of American modernism. Elizabeth Walther-Bense recalls of Haroldo de Campos: "Besides Latin and Greek, he learned German, French, English, Italian, Spanish, Russian, Japanese, and Hebrew. Maybe some other languages, too. His goal was never to master foreign languages completely, but to be able to read literary texts and to translate them" (358). And for Eugene Wildman, the editor of the Chicago Review's *Anthology of Concretism*, the activity of concrete poetry across language plays a central role in his understanding of the significance of the movement. Writing in 1969, two years after his anthology was published, he identifies a folk aspect in concrete poetry, as it is written in a language meant to provide access to those with a basic understanding of language, whether they are foreign or native speakers. Wildman uses the example of a calendar image in the Chicago Review's office, unchanged since July 1967, whose caption, "A new bridge over the Biferno (Molise)," is printed in five different languages: Italian, French, English, German, and then Spanish, with the last two words identical in each. Wildman asks: "But is this not a concrete poem?" (164–5). He considers it a found poem that acknowledges the indeterminacy of the commodity in an environment of global trade while recognizing the value of disparate spaces of consumption; the calendar could be bought by an Italian, French, Spanish, German, or English consumer, each of whom would be confronted by an artefact that would remind them that there are other language communities in the world which demand recognition. This emphasis on reminding, on foregrounding the structures that impede communication and the strategies for circumventing – or circumscribing – those impediments, appears throughout the program of the concrete poetry movement.

Wildman's emphasis on the importance of translation comes out in his inclusion of an English translation of Hiršal and Grögerová's poem "The Old / New (*from the book of JOB:BOJ*)," which is a prose passage that has certain verbs, nouns, and adjectives paired with their opposites, so that the beginning of the text reads "The aesthetic of the old / new work of art is primarily determined by the subject/material [...]" (34). As readers continue, they are confronted with potential readings that double with every choice between two words, adding up to four million one hundred and ninety-four thousand three hundred and four possible readings.[20] Is this the aesthetics of entropy, "the tendency of physical systems to become less and less organized, to become more and more perfectly shuffled" (Shannon and Weaver 12)? The immensity of the work is only compounded when the reader is confronted with Hiršal and Grögerová's poem again ninety pages later, but in a different English translation. While there is indeterminacy and proliferation of relationships in all poetry – and certainly in the conventional poetic techniques of rhyme, alliteration, enjambment, disjunction, allusion, and so on – the foregrounding of disorder, and especially the mathematically formulated disorder in Hiršal and Grögerová's poem, is of a particular character that relates to the contemporaneous conditions of language on an international, often mechanized scale. A poem is never an ordered space, nor is language, as post-structuralism taught us. There will always be slippage and traces. But what is significant in Hiršal and Grögerová's work is the purposeful engineering of ambiguity, the literary switches that form a logical, mathematical character within the poem. What is being expressed is not a feeling of the poet but an idea of stability/instability in language. It is there in all poetry, but here it is insisted upon, made concrete and present, and offered as a site of pleasure for the reader.

Two poems also included in Hiršal and Grögerova's collection *JOB:BOJ*, gathered under the title "Vývoj I" (Developer; 1960–62), perform a synthesis of the mathematical/mechanical, the global, and the visual turn. The title is a reference to the photographic chemical product used to make visible the light captured by photographic paper during the development process, a product which needs to be in contact with the paper for a very specific period of time or risk over- or underexposure of the image. The poem uses a permutational method reliant on word-length in which a word is gradually morphed into a word from a different language while creating diagonal patterns of repeated letters. The five letters in the German word for *love*, "LIEBE," turn gradually, through nineteen letter combinations, into the Czech word for *love*, "LÁSKA," in one example, while the seven letter Czech word for freedom, "SVOBODA," travels through thirty-four combinations of gibberish before settling into the English "FREEDOM," engaging both the mathematical structure of information technology developed by the rudimentary computer technology as well as the social significance of cross-linguistic communities (146; see fig. 2.15). Post-World War II Czechoslovakia was attempting to shift identities from one occupied consciousness, the German, to another, the Soviet, making the inclusion of the English word "freedom" an especially loaded political statement at the height of cold war relations. Does "freedom" translate? How does it translate at the end of a gun? What does this particular linguistic morphology represent at the beginning of the 1960s in Eastern Europe? It should here be noted that although Liselotte Gumpel's *Concrete Poetry in East and West Germany* does identify concrete visual poets operating in East Germany, particularly Carlfriedrich Claus, for the most part concrete visual poetry is identified with the West, and deals with a specific media and capitalist infrastructure (advertising, consumerism, advanced communication technologies) popularly identified with the United States and its allies in the cold war.[21]

In the catalogue accompanying the exhibition *Between Poetry and Painting*, which she curated in at the Institute for Contemporary Art in London in 1965, Jasia Reichardt describes concrete poetry as the "first international poetry movement," emphasizing the fact that beyond imagism or Dada or Surrealist poetry, concrete poetry was the first to engage with disparate linguistic communities and internationalism as a defining problematic (9). In order to understand the reasons behind the movement's development,

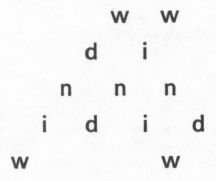

Figure 2.14
Eugen Gomringer. "Wind"

```
                                        S V O B O D A
                                        V O B O D A S
                                        O B O D A S V
                                        B O D A S V O
                                        O D A S V O B
                                        D A S V O B O
                                        A S V O B O D
                                        F V O B O D A
                                        V O B O D A F
L I E B E                               O B O D A F V
I E B E L                               B O D A F V O
E B E L I                               O D A F V O B
B E L I E                               D A F V O B O
E L I E B                               A F V O B O D
L Á E B E                               F R O B O D A
Á E B E L                               R O B O D A F
E B E L Á                               O B O D A F R
B E L Á E                               B O D A F R O
E L Á E B                               O D A F R O B
L Á S B E                               D A F R O B O
Á S B E L                               A F R O B O D
S B E L Á                               F R E B O D A
B E L Á S                               R E B O D A F
E L Á S B                               E B O D A F R
L Á S K B                               B O D A F R E
Á S K B L                               O D A F R E B
S K B L Á                               D A F R E B O
K B L Á S                               A F R E B O D
B L Á S K                               F R E E O D A
L Á S K A                               R E E O D A F
                                        E E O D A F R
                                        E O D A F R E
                                        O D A F R E E
                                        D A F R E E O
                                        A F R E E D O
                                        F R E E D O M
```

Figure 2.15

Josef Hiršal and Bohumila Grögerová. "Developer (Vývoj I)"

it is necessary to consider what exactly was the condition of nations or the experience of language, visual or otherwise, at the time of writing. The global imaginary is an old idea, but one that underwent dramatic change as a result of the conditions brought about by the technologies of World War II. Both the H-Bomb and the computer technology rooted in Turing's Bombe radically shifted our understanding of nationhood and communication. The link between language and mathematics is also not a new phenomenon, as any basic history of ciphers demonstrates; the same is true of the combination of the visual and the linguistic, as any examination of early writing, or of early twentieth-century avant-gardes, shows. But there were shifts around the mid-twentieth century that were forceful enough to prompt a new strategy of poetic composition, one that took the recognition of an altered mediascape as a challenge to create work that could speak to a new global reader whose consciousness was becoming unbound by linguistic borders.

3 /
FIFTY YEARS' PROGRESS IN FIVE

Juscelino Kubitschek was elected president of Brazil in 1956 after running on a populist platform that included the promise to build a new capital city in the undeveloped central plateau of the country, and in the process move the locus of power away from the major metropolises of São Paulo and Rio de Janeiro. The relocation was meant to promote greater equality and balance as the nation moved forward on a program of rapid modernization. Though it was central to Kubitschek's political platform, the idea of Brasília was born much earlier, in the religious milieu of the nineteenth century. In his journal entry for August 30, 1883, the Italian João Bosco, who would become the patron saint of Brasília, writes about his dream of travelling by train across the Central Plateau:

> I saw the bowels of the mountains and the depths of the plains.
> I had before my eyes the incomparable riches [...] which would one
> day be discovered. I saw numerous mines of precious metals and
> fossil coals, and deposits of oil of such abundance as had never
> before been seen in other places. But that was not all. Between
> the fifteenth and the twentieth degrees of latitude, there was a
> long and wide stretch of land which arose at a point where a lake

was forming. Then a voice said repeatedly: when people come to excavate the mines hidden in the middle of these mountains there will appear in this place the Promised Land, flowing with milk and honey. It will be of inconceivable richness. (quoted in Holston 16)

This is an oddly industrialized spiritual vision, one that must have spoken loudly to a nation with such fraught ties to the Catholic church and to the projects of modernity. The Promised Land does not come through devotion or obedience, but through industry – specifically *mining* – the products of which can then either be sold for profit or absorbed into the infrastructure of the nation. Brazil was not blessed with wealth, but blessed with the natural resources that could – if managed properly – lead to prosperity. Later in his journals, Bosco specified that the city would be built three generations on from his vision, which, assuming generations last twenty-five years (which Kubitschek's government conveniently did), puts the date for its construction in the late 1950s.

"Fifty years' progress in five" was the popular slogan of Kubitschek's government, and the ground on which that concept would be constructed was Brasília. The new capital was the synthesis of what Kubitschek called his Target Program for national development, an economic plan closely following the contemporaneous theory of developmentalism that was alternatively imposed upon and embraced by several South American nations in attempt to "catch up" to the industrially developed states in Europe and North America. Developmentalism stressed state-directed industrialization as a means for rapid economic growth that would then allow South American nations to participate in an expanding global trade structure. Despite its emphasis on short-term national economies, developmentalism was marketed conceptually as an entrance into an increasingly connected global market.

The poetry produced within Brazil at the time would deal with this tension between the national and the global in various ways. Augusto de Campos's "sem um numero," a poem dealing with the problems surrounding the census of 1962 in providing an accurate count of the inhabitants of the Amazon region in Northern Brazil, has already been discussed in a previous chapter, as has Décio Pignatari's "Beba Coca Cola," which expresses the poet's anxieties about where exactly the development of Brazil would lead to in a global market. Ronaldo Azeredo's "Velocidade" (1957) is another work that requires examination in this context. At first glance the influence of the Futurists seems to come through in the depiction of speed, the repeated *V*s of the initial line becoming shorter and shorter as the word emerges from its grid, which along with the regular and even permutation places it solidly within the concrete method. Visually, the repeated *V*s perform as a field of directional cues, pointing downward and gradually to the left, to the beginning of the final line, "VELOCIDADE." When read aloud, the poem sounds as if it is a car shifting gears, finally reaching the highest gear in the annunciation of the Portuguese word for *speed*, "VELOCIDADE." But is the poet inside the car or stationary on the side of a highway? In the latter case, the diminishing repeated *V*s might still function as engine sounds, but of cars going faster and faster past the listener/viewer. As the automobile industry in Brazil played a large role in its industrial growth, it would be difficult to read into Azeredo's work the same kind of enthusiasm for industry and technology that Marinetti and his group possessed in Italy at the beginning of the twentieth century (Azeredo 171; see fig. 3.1). Considering the poetic milieu in which Azeredo was writing, it is likely he would share the concerns of Pignatari and the de Campos brothers over exactly what development meant to Brazilian society, and who benefited the most.

José Lino Grünewald's "Preto" is another example of poetry tied to the economics of national development and global trade. Haroldo de Campos describes it as a placard poem in the tradition of Mayakovsky's "agit-plakat techniques," and it certainly has an aura of protest to it (Grünewald n. pag.). A vertical repetition of "preto," the Portuguese word for *black*, is interrupted every two lines by the addition of four nouns: "um jato" (a jet), "um óleo" (an oil), "um fato" (a fact), and "petróleo" (petroleum). The poem shifts on the last line of the first section into another vertical column of the repeated "nosso" (our), and terminates in the emphatic "nosso petróleo" (Grünewald n. pag.; see fig. 3.2). This poem is less interesting for its visual dimension and structural integrity than it is for its emotional thrust, a rare trait for a concrete poem. Beyond the similarities of the words (*jato* and *fato*, *oleo* and *petróleo*, *preto* and *petróleo*), the poem represents the graphic score of a crowd's chant. The upper section functions as a visual representation of a call and response; the lower section, which is transitioned into with the subject of the protest, "petróleo," is dominated by the word "nosso," meaning *our*, and emphasizes a collective resistance through repetition. This protest has an obvious political dimension, aimed as it is at the exploitation of Brazil's vast oil holdings by foreign investment, and is rooted in the tradition of Pignatari and de Campos where the fusion of the political and the visually poetic functions on both a local (national) and global scale.

This is where concrete poetry's ambition to create an expansive and new audience can be read alongside the emphasis on the collective voice and will

VVVVVVVVVV
VVVVVVVVVE
VVVVVVVVEL
VVVVVVVELO
VVVVVVELOC
VVVVVELOCI
VVVVELOCID
VVVELOCIDA
VVELOCIDAD
VELOCIDADE

Figure 3.1

Ronaldo Azeredo. "Velocidade"

```
preto
preto    um jato
preto
preto    um óleo
preto
preto    um fato
preto
preto    petróleo    nosso
                      nosso
                      nosso
                      nosso
                      nosso
                      nosso
                      nosso
                      nosso    petróleo
```

Figure 3.2
José Lino Grünewald. "Preto"

of the people, as expressed enthusiastically by political protestors and the anticolonial agitations of nations in South America, Africa, and Asia. This was the moment of Dien Bien Phu and the Cuban revolution, which Augusto de Campos marked with the publication of a poster poem, *cubagramma* (1960–62; in Cid Campos 43). The text links the revolution with the process of writing via the word "gramma," which contains the Latin root for *writing*, "gram," and at the same time refers to the ship *Granma* that carried Fidel and Raul Castro, Che Guevara, Camilo Cienfuegos, and close to eighty other members of the 26th of July Movement from Mexico to Cuba in 1956, marking the beginning of the three-year guerrilla war to overthrow Fulgencio Batista. The Brazilian concrete poets' desire to increase literacy – not just through social critique, but through formally reduced compositions, as well – and to distribute poetry to the masses in a visual style and grammar they could comprehend was a political gesture, and the post-Noigrandres Invenção group, which was made up of Pignatari, Haroldo and Augusto de Campos, Cassiano Ricardo, and Edward Braga, amongst others, made the best of their opportunities to access the masses, managing to publish a weekly insert in the newspaper *O Correio Paulistano* in São Paulo from 1960 to 1961.

The concrete poets, especially in Brazil but also internationally, have a very complex relationship to the spaces and forces of modernism. The aim of this chapter is to think through the poetry as it operates within various spatial shifts, and to think about the poets' fascination with linguistic material at a moment when the world was also enthralled by new opportunities for travel, and new possibilities for building. When considering Azeredo's "Velocidade," one could make the common and largely acceptable critical maneuver to concentrate on the poem's relationship to the automobile as machine, or the factory as a place of accelerated production, as in Charlie Chaplin's *Modern Times* (1936). But what is more pressing in this case is the surface that allows for such increases in speed, the concrete streets and highways that form an urban architecture no less important than the skyscraper and, I would argue, no less grand. By looking at how concrete, as a material, provided not just the physical but also the aesthetic foundation for modernist architecture, readers can better understand the geography of concrete poetry. While there might be some doubt about what vantage point the poetic subject operates from in Azeredo's poem, that doubt dissipates in later poems as modernism picks up speed, moving from city streets to superhighways and from the human scale of the airplane to the extra-planetary scale of space exploration. While the period of concrete poetry appears to be quite compressed, the technological, social, and spatial transformations of that moment are more dramatic than at any other point in history. In a fifteen-year span, humans developed the technology to both destroy the earth as well as to leave it. The ramifications of such a rapid reformulation of what is possible were wide and varied, alternating between hope and anxiety, cooperation and violent exclusion.

One of the landscapes that carries both the hopes and anxieties of modernism most intensely is the city of Brasilia. Although the Brazilian concrete poets had no real connection to the planning of the city, the jury that would eventually decide on the city's design shared their emphasis on the primacy of form, and the process of selecting a plan offers some striking parallels with the aims of concrete poetry. In 1956 the Brazilian government held a competition to decide the shape the new city would take, and in 1957 proclaimed the design of architect Lucio Costa the winner. Costa

> submitted his proposal on five medium-sized cards containing fifteen freehand sketches and a brief statement of twenty-three articles. His presentation featured not a line of mechanical drawings, no model, land-use studies, population charts or schemes for either economic development or administrative organization – in short, nothing more than the idea of a capital city. (Holston 63)

The design competition had stressed that it was searching for design ideas, not a construction plan, which is likely part of the reason they chose Costa's proposal over that of the firm of M. M. M. Roberto, which included "scores of blueprints, voluminous statistical projections of population and economic growth, and detailed plans for regional development and administration" (64). The jury was looking for a project for the future, not a map of the present. Costa's proposal offered just that promise, a plan as undeveloped as the land Brasília was to be built on, and as full of prophecy as that of Bosco's vision. The text he submitted alongside his drawings begins, "It was not my intention to enter the competition – nor indeed, am I really so doing. I am merely liberating my mind from a possible solution which sprang to it as a complete picture, but one which I had not sought" (quoted in Holston 64). At least one jury member was moved by Costa's quasi-mystical posture. The British architect and town planner William Holford wrote of his experience of Costa's proposal:

> At the first reading of the report, one realized that here was a thinker, an urbanist, of the first order. On second reading one realized that there was not a single unnecessary word in the report,

and not a single unnecessary line in the sketch plan or diagrams: yet everything essential was said ... Even to me, who am no Portuguese scholar, the original version was immediately lyrical and striking. (Holford 398)

Although the conventional colonial romanticization of the Other might play a role in Holford's description, his language is interesting for the connection it draws between the efficiency of Costa's drawings and that of the poetic output of Brazil at the time. Both emphasized a stripped-down aesthetic in order to maximize the efficiency of expression, as well as to highlight the tension of the constituent elements. The concrete poets moved away from the poetic line to the space of the page; Costa moved away from blueprints and development studies to the index card sketch, replacing a stolid, rigid way of thinking with an invitation to imagination. Holford's admission that he is "no Portuguese" scholar – indeed, we can assume his Portuguese was quite rudimentary, and that he depended quite heavily on translation – contributes to the rationale for concrete poetry to communicate across national languages, and for its emphasis on visual forms. As the Noigandres group puts it in their Plano-Piloto Para Poesia Concreta, published in 1958, a year after Costa's Plano-Piloto de Brasília[1]: "With the concrete poem occurs the phenomenon of meta-communication: coincidence and simultaneity of verbal and non-verbal communication; only – it must be noted – it deals with a communication of forms, of a structure-content, not with the usual message communications" (A. de Campos, H. de Campos, and Pignatari 72). The combination of efficient language, efficient diagrams, and ease of translation in Holford's account legitimizes concrete poetry's claim to be a poetry of the time, one in which global communication and circulation of culture has real effects on the everyday lives of people around the world, including the development of an entire city from a single idea judged adequate by a panel of diverse national perspectives.

Doorway to Brasilia, a 1957 collaborative book by the Brazilian artist and graphic designer Aloisio Magalhães and American artist, designer, and printer Eugene Feldman contains many of the same postures towards technology, planning, and internationalism that Costa's approach shared with the contemporaneous shifts in poetry. At the back of the book, the authors draw a parallel between their decision to use photo-offset lithography "as an artform" and the promise of Brasília:

It is the belief of the designers that this medium has a potential
limited only by the boundaries of the imagination and creative
talents of the artists who choose to use and develop it. Brasilia [sic],
the new capital city in Brazil was chosen as subject matter because
of the mood it suggests – a frontier city with strong graphic shapes
and a vitality that is both timely and timeless. (Magalhães and
Feldman n. pag.)

The introduction, written in English by the American modernist writer John
Dos Passos and then, like the rest of the text, translated into Portuguese and
French to match the languages of the Brasília jury, continues the genuflection
to the planned character of the city. Describing the physical scene as
"hundreds of miles from nowhere" and describing the glorious sounds of
industry and construction echoing through the jungles of the central plains
as he stands with a young engineer, Dos Passos writes:

The sun sets in purple behind distant ranges. The engineer shades
his eyes to point out, in the thickening dusk, the white oblong of the
palace and the tourist hotel and blocks of new buildings shapeless
under scaffolding. "Soon you'll see rising behind them the Congress
buildings and the downtown district. You can imagine them
already," he says catching his breath. "Soon the neon lights will go
on. You'll see them reflected in the lake." (n. pag.)

The admiration of the poet for the engineer and the link between their
complementary cultural projects becomes explicit. The engineer is the
modernist hero, the visionary who will conquer nature and bring industrial
harmony to the spaces that have resisted it, the secular version of Bosco, the
prospecting Jesuit. The moonlight that had been for millennia a sign of the
poet's hypnotic wonder for nature, has been replaced by neon.

The city of Brasília was built in less than five years, from 1956 to 1961, a
period that closely parallels the orthodox period in Brazilian concrete poetry.
But the link between Brasília and concrete poetry, though never operating
on the level of official culture, comes out most clearly in a comparison of the
methods of construction for each. Justin Read argues that the "concrete"
in concrete poetry is a "direct reference to Brazilian architecture and its
predilection for reinforced concrete" (255). His point is strengthened by
a poem written by Augusto de Campos in 1956, called "concreto," which

begins with the word "concentro" (focus; concentration) and moves through similar words: "certo" (certain), "concerto" (concert), "corte" (cut; hack), "contra" (against), "conceito" (concept), and "centro" (centre) before finishing with "concreto" (concrete; 145). The word "certo" appears in bold as its letters appear diagonally in the five words following "concentro," functioning as a verbo-visual reinforcement of the poem, its meaning augmented by its position. The poem is a solid, confident structure that links the possibilities of concrete as a cultural movement to the potential of actual reinforced concrete to transform cities and spaces of living (see fig. 3.3). This poem dates from the moment that the Noigandres group and Eugen Gomringer in Switzerland had just agreed upon *concrete poetry* to describe their work, but it would be simplistic to read the poem as a strict celebration of that term. If this poem were by Gomringer, there would be an urge to read it as homage to the European concrete artists, dating from van Doesburg to Max Bill. While the Brazilians enjoyed a close and productive relationship with the Brazilian concrete artists, particularly the Ruptura group, also based in São Paulo and comprised of figures such as Waldemar Cordeiro, Luiz Sacilotto, and Hermelindo Fiaminghi, who designed the cover of *Noigrandres* 4, they were more engaged with a literary tradition.[2] More than Gomringer or the European poets, they express their artistic debt to modernist and early twentieth-century avant-garde poets, from Guillaume Apollinaire to James Joyce, from Gertrude Stein to Ezra Pound, from João Cabral de Melo Neto to e.e. cummings.

While it is true that there are concrete poems which prompt readers to dismiss them as simply mimetic, in the tradition of the shaped poems from the Axe of Simius to George Herbert's "Easter Wings" – one thinks immediately of the playful but over-anthologized "Apfel" by Reinhard Döhl – the Brazilian concrete poems tend to deal with structure within words instead of concepts.[3] In de Campos's poem, the suggestion of cutting or hacking against concept in order to get to a centre, which is "concrete," is only possible because the words share so many letter-shapes. The same is true of Pignatari's "Beba Coca Cola": the poem can only end in "cloaca" (cesspool) because the letters are already present in "Coca Cola"; the poetry is immanent, contained within the structure of the words. Thus the emphasis on the visual character of language is not expressive but formally constrained: what we see is what we get, but the concrete poets' position is that there is more to language than what we are accustomed to seeing. There is a materiality in the language of concrete poetry that is overlooked by conventional approaches to literature. The emphasis on what is hidden, or contained within words that

Figure 3.3
Augusto de Campos. "Concreto"

seem innocuous has a political character that is not present in the work of the Swiss poets. In a later interview, after the 1964 coup that deposed Kubitschek and installed a military dictatorship, Augusto de Campos cites this as the primary difference between the Brazilian and the Swiss-German concrete poets, that the Brazilians "thought about their work politically, under conditions that required them to" ("Entretien" 377).

Reinforcing "Concrete"

The emphasis on structural integrity and the reduction of expression to a material base is what connects concrete poetry to concrete art, but it also connects it to the sphere of modernist architecture. The modernist tradition did not arrive in Brazil in 1956 with the initiation of Brasília. Both Lucio Costa and Oscar Niemeyer, who would design the majority of the monumental structures in Brasília, were admirers of Le Corbusier, and both had worked with him on the design of the Ministry of Education and Culture in Rio de Janeiro, which was built between 1936 and 1943. Niemeyer worked with Le Corbusier again in the 1940s on the initial plans for the headquarters of the United Nations in New York, and Costa was to be the first Brazilian representative in the Congrès Internationale de l'Architecture Moderne (CIAM). Le Corbusier's lectures in Brazil in 1929 and 1936 were well received, and both the architectural community and the artists and poets of the time had a firm idea of what role concrete, and specifically reinforced concrete, played in the worldwide movement of modernist architecture.

When historicizing *concrete* as a term in relation to concrete poetry, therefore, it is necessary to historicize concrete as a material, as well. It is not enough to try to understand concrete art and poetry in relation to what we think of when we hear the term *concrete* – a near ubiquitous material holding up the buildings around us, making up the streets and sidewalks on which most of us travel daily – but to consider what *concrete* meant to both the poets and artists who used the term to describe their work. For although concrete is an ancient material, dating back to the Romans, it was not widely used in building until the eighteenth century, and then only in a rudimentary form that had more in common with adobe than modern concrete. In the eighteenth and nineteenth century concrete was still made with ordinary lime mortar, a poor binding agent; it is for this reason that the structural walls of the buildings from that time were made of stone. It was only through the innovations of the nineteenth century that concrete became popular in general construction, and became linked to the industrial revolution as a quick and solid *technology* of construction.

Building on the discovery of France's François Coignet, who in the mid-nineteenth century solved the issues of strength and solubility that had prevented concrete from being used structurally, the Briton Joseph Tall was the first contractor to realize that great expense could be saved by minimizing the work in the shaping of concrete by building forms: "By concentrating on standardization, he had the distinction of exploiting for the first time one of the most beneficial characteristics of concrete construction which, if perceived at all by his contemporaries, would have been condemned by them as contrary to Ruskinian principles of genuine craftsmanship and the dignity of human labour" (Collins 40). It was, however, by no means a smooth transition into concrete construction. At first, structural concrete walls were accepted by architects only if they were to be covered up by brick work, stucco, or other ornament, a requirement made less quaint by the fact that concrete at that time was not the clean, smooth, sterile mid-grey of modernism, but the rough sepia of Victorian England. The first private buildings to be made of concrete in England were either industrial or railway buildings. These structures were not bound by the same codes as residential buildings, which were still not permitted to be made of concrete even as late as 1908.[4] The reticence could perhaps be forgiven if one takes the United States as an example, where in 1906 part of the Eastman Kodak plant in Rochester, New York collapsed, followed the next year by more building collapses in Long Beach, Philadelphia, New York, and San Francisco.

Reinforced concrete, as a term, only came into use at the end of the nineteenth century (1898), and it was not until 1927 that interest in the possibilities of concrete really began to develop in architectural circles. Despite being embraced by Art Nouveau for its organic shaping abilities, concrete became the subject of serious articles only in the 1930s.[5] This repositions Theo van Doesburg's first and only issue of *Art Concret* in 1929 as a journal very much determined by the contemporary shifts in the technology and aesthetics of concrete as a cutting edge building material. As Peter Collins points out, this was a "period in Europe when concrete was being energetically welcomed by the modernists because of its capacity to produce new forms and denounced equally vigorously by the traditionalists for the same reason" (Collins 146). Thus concrete as it functioned in the first half of the twentieth century was not the equivalent of stone, as we would consider it today, but carried within it the potential for new forms and possibilities, especially in the discourse surrounding modern architecture. The Russian Futurist poet Vasily

THE CUNARDER "AQUITANIA," WHICH CARRIES 3,600 PERSONS,
COMPARED WITH VARIOUS BUILDINGS

Figure 3.4

Le Corbusier. Diagram of architectural scale

Kamensky made this connection explicit in designating some of his poems as "ferroconcrete" in 1914. Published in an edition titled *Tango with Cows*, that also included illustrations by David and Vladimir Burliak, Kamensky's fragmented poems were meant to evoke a poetic wandering through a modern city, one which put the recent technology of reinforced – ferro – concrete to use in the pursuit of the rapid technological development Futurism embraced (Harte 546). While some might argue that reinforced concrete is a material generally not associated with speed and movement, for witnesses to the velocity of modernity at the beginning of the twentieth century, the jump from stone masonry to poured forms in the construction of buildings was a giant leap forward for the possibilities of urban design and, through that design, a new way of living.

Nine years after Kamensky's text was published, Le Corbusier's *Vers Un Architecture* embraced the potential for reinforced concrete to transform the way people lived through architectural functionalism and mass-produced housing. Explaining how these houses would be built, he writes: "The concrete was poured from above as you would fill a bottle. A house can be completed in three days. It comes out from the shuttering like a casting. But this shocks our contemporary architects, who cannot believe in a house that is made in three days; we must take a year to build it, and we must have pointed roofs, dormers and mansards" (*Towards a New Architecture* 230–1). This passage is indicative of the overall tone of *Vers Un Architecture*. Reading like an aphoristic manifesto, the text is valuable for understanding the awe that materials like reinforced concrete and steel instilled in the architects of the time. It is in this book that Le Corbusier formulates his support for the engineer's aesthetic, which he illustrates visually by juxtaposing an ocean liner with various monuments of French architecture: the Notre-Dame cathedral, the Arc de Triomphe, etc. (see fig. 3.4). The ocean liner dwarfs the structures, and in doing so mocks the imagination of previous generations, pitying them for their primitive technologies (92).

The engineer's aesthetic is not one that is imposed upon materials, as Art Nouveau would impose shapes on concrete, but comes as a result of the material. Thus the concrete house finished in three days, though it looks like a box as a condition of the form, becomes a celebrated aesthetic object for the potential the process of its construction carries within it. It functions, in the same way as previous buildings did, and in the same way as literature for Kittler, more complexly as an index of its technological moment. If early concrete construction – the buildings that used stucco or stone to cover up the concrete skeleton, or the work in the style of Art Nouveau – went against the grain by removing signs of labour, and thus offending the popular Ruskinian idea of the dignity involved in human labour, concrete construction in Le Corbusier's time was desired specifically for that reason: for the displacement of labour onto technology, and through that displacement a promise of a life free of toil, characterized by abundance.

A negation of the human in the modernist architecture that lauded straight lines and geometric order found a parallel in concrete poetry, where technology was privileged over subjectivity, invention over labour, structure over lyric. Primarily, concrete poetry is characterized by an appearance of *ease*, by the absence of the traditional traits of poetry: a lyrical subject struggling against the constraints of language, a conventional spatial syntax of left to right, top to bottom, and so on.[6] Heinz Gappmayr's "Zeichen" (1965), discussed at the opening of this book, can be read as containing both the frustration and the promise that Le Corbusier ascribes to the shudder of architects discovering the poured concrete form method of building a dwelling (Gappmayr 39; see fig. 1.1). The poem is simply – like a concrete house is "simple" – a large black square of ink. There are remnants of letters peeking out from three of the sides, but it is impossible to tell what they are, or what words, if any, they belong to. Some of the shapes bleeding through might not even be letters; they might be ink stains or smudges, a result of an excess of material that is neglected in conventional poetry, or maybe a gesture towards the imperfections in the modernist aesthetic of order and cleanliness. As a poet who was employed in a printing house, Gappmayr made work that implemented printing methods in ways that referred directly to the production of books and images – ink on paper – at mid-century (Mon, "Letter Sounds" 199). In this poem, the technology of print is taken for granted; its production is made invisible. "Zeichen" refuses to be complicit in that desire for print language as a transparent mode of communication, and forces the reader to confront both the material process through which poetry is produced as well as the impediments readers face when experiencing national languages that they, as speakers of a different language, have limited or no access to.

In its confrontation with national language, printing technology, the possibilities for utterance, Gappmayr echoes the work of the turn-of-the-century German poet Christian Morgenstern, whose work is central to Friedrich Kittler's analysis in *Discourse Networks 1800/1900*. Morgenstern's poem "The Great Lalulā," from 1905, also insisted on the incomprehensible, using nonsensical language that would be echoed in the Dadaist and sound poems of Hugo Ball and and Kurt Schwitters, as well as the concrete sound poems of

Ernst Jandl and Bob Cobbing. But Morgenstern also included the stubbornly unpronounceable in his poem, signs that frustrated enunciation in ways similar to the half-letters peeking out from Gappmayr's square. Morgenstern, in the final stanza, includes a semi-colon surrounded by parentheses and, two lines later, a single space surrounded by brackets. Kittler argues that these notations are an example of how to "write writing" (212) and associates it with how the standardization of information production tools and techniques – the discourse network grounded in the dominance of the typewriter, in this case – changes readers' relationship to language. Speaking of the typewriter and the possibilities for mechanically producing arrangements of language that might operate poetically, Kittler writes

> in principle it is possible to inscribe and describe more and different things than any voice has ever spoken. Of course, such notations have no purpose beyond notation itself; they need not and cannot be dematerialized and consumed by a hermeneutics; their indelible and indigestible existence on the page is all that the page conveys. (212)

This understanding of "writing writing" offers a way to consider Gappmayr's poem, and concrete poetry more generally, as operating within and responding to a technological and cultural milieu – a discourse network – that included a new reader, as well. The psychophysics of this reader were as new and transformative as the building techniques advocated and celebrated by Le Corbusier.

In 1955, Augusto de Campos wrote that "in synch with terminology adopted by the visual arts, and to a degree, by avant-garde music (concretism, concrete music), I would say there is a *concrete poetry*." That poetry is based upon an "irreversible and functional idea-generating sound-optical structuring [that] creates an entirely dynamic 'verbivocovisual' entity [...] of ductile words capable of being molded and amalgamated in to the shape of the poem" (quoted in Perrone 29). What this explanation makes clear is less what concrete poetry is than the conditions from which it emerged. The language he uses here is programmatic, and borrows from both literary and architectural modernisms. Words like "ductile," "molded," and "amalgamated" link up with the "verbivocovisual dynamic" to strengthen the concrete metaphor: "ductile," which refers to a physical weakness of concrete before technologies were developed to reinforce it; "molded," which refers to the processing of pouring concrete into built forms, and then letting it set in shapes that perform both structural and aesthetic – architectural? – functions; and "amalgamated," which points to the chemical properties of concrete as they advanced in the twentieth century, becoming a much more reliable, predictable, and consequently *useful* material for building.

In Brazil, the engineer's aesthetic was transformed into the engineer's poetics. This was true out of necessity in the case of Niemeyer's Brasília, where many of the monuments and buildings he designed in concrete would not have been feasible in Europe or the United States.

> Because Niemeyer operated in a semi-industrialized context, he could not be confined to the rigidity of regular pre-fabricated components. On the contrary, the most cost-effective building materials at his disposal were those that could be assembled on-site – concrete poured over steel frames, precisely the technique which allows maximum flexibility for experimentation with curvature. The architect's use of unconventional forms in Brasília thus stands as a direct index to the nation's level of industrialization at mid-century. Since many parts and components could not be pre-fabricated, Niemeyer was forced to improvise, which in turn promoted an architecture of improvisation. (Read 266)

With labour being cheaper than materials, Niemeyer was able to allot more time to the construction of complex forms that would be just as strong as simpler, rectangular forms, while in the process using less concrete and distinguishing the architecture of Brasília from the modernist buildings being constructed in more developed nations in Europe and North America.[7]

The International Typographical Style

According to Augusto de Campos, during the first period of Brazilian concrete poetry, which he refers to as a period of orthodoxy, and delimits between 1953 and 1960, the poets sought a rational, disciplined space that would use rational, geometric type in order to create a collective, anonymous style for concrete poetry. They accomplished this in part by making Futura their standard font. As de Campos explains in an interview from 2001:

> Donc la relation avec le design, la publicité et, de façon plus particulière, la typographie, était dès les débuts fermement

établie. Le Bauhaus et le concept de la « bonne forme » ont eu une influence décisive, et le type « sans serif, » ou caractère bâton, fut choisi, plus spécialement le futura, pour sa clarté et sa précision, la microgéométrie de ses lettres favorisant la création de la macrostructure géométrisante du poème concret de la première phase.[8] (Buschinger 151)

Many of the early Swiss and German concrete poems are set in Futura font as well, which is perhaps less surprising when one considers their proximity to the Bauhaus, the birthplace of rational typography. Hansjörg Mayer would produce a series of concrete poetry pamphlets called *Futura* in the mid-1960s, and used the font himself in the majority of his compositions. Futura's design emphasizes its geometrical character, with the letters based on the primary shapes of circles, squares, and triangles, continuing the epoch's embrace of the rational. In his discussion of type designer Jan Tschichold, Simon Loxley explains the expressive function of typefaces in terms that closely echo Le Corbusier:

"The essence of the New Typography is clarity." Tschichold argued that with the increasing amount of print and information battling for the reader's attention, greater economy of expression was needed. Old typefaces were concerned with beauty, but this was achieved by superfluous ornamentation, which now had to be stripped away in the search for purer, clearer forms. (148)

The standardization of type would find its zenith in a Swiss typeface created in 1957 and named after the Latin word for Switzerland, *Helvezia*. The Helvetica typeface is a refined version of Futura: it does not adhere as strictly to the geometric impulse of orthodox modernism. But it carries within it a similar international impulse, one that the designer Rick Pyner associates with the postwar idealism that arose out of reconstruction efforts in Europe (*Helvetica*). If Futura is the font of the Bauhaus, Helvetica is the font of the Marshall Plan. In the 1960s it began to be adopted on a grand scale. As a font it performed the role projected by the concrete poets: it was ubiquitous, transnational and designed for legibility. Rather than the internationalism – and international style – that the Brazilian concrete poets and their modernist heroes envisioned, however, Helvetica quickly became the standard font for transnational corporations around the world. Helvetica's ubiquity remains today. The American designer Paula Scher claims her antipathy towards the font developed out of its position as a de facto font of the Vietnam War, as many of the corporations that profited from the war used Helvetica in their advertisements and logos. When asked in an interview, "If Helvetica was the font of the Vietnam war, what is the font of this [the Iraq] war?" she answers "Helvetica" (*Helvetica*).

The desire for a standard, global type expressed by fonts like Futura and Helvetica is integral to concrete poetry. From the beginning Gomringer's manifestos speak of supranational poetry, universally understood, functioning in the same way as signs in an airport. Those concrete poets who used Futura font did so in hopes that the ideology of the Bauhaus and its the faith in design might allow poetry to exist in a sphere as rational as geometry. Those poets who avoided typesetting in favour of the typewriter, and who used the typewriter's standardized letters and spaces as a design tool were following a similar, if more mechanical impulse. But this impulse needs to be read both as a holdover from the modernist experiment as well as an anticipation of the creep of global capital and transnational organization that would take hold in the 1970s, and that we can still recognize today in discussions of globalization. A closer examination of Brasília within the intellectual context of the International Style will point to the conditions that contributed to the emergence of a globalization style, and the social ramifications of how people negotiated, and in many ways contributed to, the redesign of urban spaces.

Cidade / City / Cité

In the first manifesto of the Congrès Internationale d'Architecture Moderne in 1928, the group called on the League of Nations to legislate a single technical language to be taught to architects on an international scale, using standardized systems of measurement for domestic equipment and appliances. This would facilitate the construction of utopian cities by removing the impediments facing CIAM members who wished to design buildings and cities around the world, and would allow materials to be produced en masse and shipped to construction sites globally, or factories to be built in nations that could both fuel their national architectural revolutions and supply their neighbours with needed products, knowing they all needed the same materials, in the same dimensions. In *Building the New World*, Valerie Fraser ties that desire for homogeneity to the larger project of modernism:

The CIAM argued that architecture – or rather *building* – was unavoidably linked to political and economic factors; that in order to replace the slums that resulted from uncontrolled urban expansion with decent housing, architecture had to transform itself from a craft-based practice into a building industry by rationalization and standardization of component parts; and that there would have to be a move away from individual towards more collective living arrangement. (6)

The flattening of difference in this collective imagining of global cities ties closely to the supranational ambitions of concrete poetry, as expressed by Gomringer, the Noigandres group, and Max Bense, who all emphasized, though in slightly different ways, the contemporaneous encounters with information. It also relates directly to the mode of knowledge production coming out of the wider project of managed living, from scientific management in factory production to the development of census practices and the gathering and processing of statistics (see discussion of Augusto de Campos's "sem um numero" in chapter 1).

The designers of Brasília, Costa and Niemeyer, closely followed the program of CIAM and its leading theorist, Le Corbusier, and attempted in their designs to impose standardized living upon the future residents of the city. A government report from 1963 on the living conditions in Brasília was unwavering in its support for the project that would eventually bankrupt the Kubitschek government and precipitate the military junta's seizure of power the following year:

The apartment blocks of a *superquadra* are all equal: same facade, same height, same facilities, all constructed on *pilotis* [columns], all provided with garages and constructed of the same material – which prevents the hateful differentiation of social classes; that is, all the families share the same life together, the upper-echelon public functionary, the middle, and the lower. (Holston 20)

Unfortunately, the problem with Brasília became the same hateful persistence of social class stratification it was designed to remedy. The architecture did not prevent the wealthy from moving out of the *superquadras* and across the lake, where they built homes that looked like the homes of other wealthy Brazilians, or from organizing exclusive private clubs to counter the open social clubs included in the plans for the apartment buildings. In Dos Passos's introduction to *Doorway to Brasilia*, at the same time that he his presenting the engineer as saviour, he introduces a worker into the scene, who he describes as "thoroughly grimed with charcoal" and as having "sinewy dark carcass [that] shows through his scanty rags." He is a woodcutter from Motto Grosso that lives in the valley that will be flooded to create Brasília's lake, but Dos Passos sees only delight on the worker's face when the engineer asks him about losing his home. The engineer, on the other hand, who returned to Brazil from his studies at the University of Miami, and who expresses disbelief that there are people in Rio "who don't believe in Brasilia [sic]," has "already bought himself a lot [...] in the residential suburb across the lake from the city" (n. pag.).

What the design of Brasília did end up preventing, however, was social interaction, replacing the idea of a city square with a monumental square, removing it from living spaces by a network of grand freeways meant to separate the sectors of work from those of leisure. This is the engineer's aesthetic applied directly to the social organization of city space. As Holston describes it:

> Architecture as the conductor and condenser of a new way of life – this is a metaphor drawn from the model of the machine. These social condensers would transform human nature as electrical condensers transform the nature of current, turning the bourgeois individualist and the denatured laborer of capitalist society into fully developed members of the socialist collective. (52)

This architecture of the machine follows, chronologically, the popular metaphor of the body and its pathologies to describe the nineteenth-century city: town planners were imagined as surgeons, cutting into the city in order to open up veins for circulation, providing space for the city to breathe again, and so on. The concrete poets, adopting the updated roles of poetic engineers, emphasized structure and mechanical strategies of composition in order to perform a similar rejection of the conventional order. Not only architecture, but poetry could be a modifier of behavior. The concrete poets aimed to mass produce readers, to capture them on sidewalks and in newspapers, in airports and galleries. The lyric subject was replaced by the computing subject; poetry was no longer meant for personal edification in a moment of meditation, but as another experience in a mechanized scheme for living: image poems that can be quickly comprehended and appreciated conveniently, contributing efficiently to the overall maximization of modern life. It was poetry subsumed into design; it was *planned* poetry.

The modernist city is the horizon for the dream of a standardized subjectivity, its International Style attempting to produce a global citizenry following the post-revolutionary French model for a national citizenry. James Scott connects the history of standardized measurement in Europe to the expansion of trade networks and national unity and points out that in France in the eighteenth century, the metric system would be to industry and commerce what mathematics was to science: "A rational unit of measurement would promote a rational citizenry" (32). A standard meter is tied directly to the French Revolution, and served to limit corruption and abuse by merchants, making agents of commerce equal under law and in the same way imagining a homogenous community of consumers. What CIAM attempted to do with architectural internationalism was a similar pursuit of a new citizenry, but on a much grander scale. In 1963, it seems as if Augusto de Campos was still a supporter of the ideal, as his poem "Cidade / city / cité" suggests. The work is a long series of letters that appear to be gibberish until one comes to the end of the line, where "cidade," "city," and "cité" are printed in a vertical column (see fig. 3.5). Only then does it become clear that the string of letters are all Latin roots that, when combined with the three words at the end, form words in Portuguese, English, and French. The word roots are organized alphabetically: the first five letters, "atroc," become "atrocidade," "atrocity," and "atrocité." The second cluster is "caduc" making "caducidade," "caducity," and "caducité," and so on. That de Campos wanted to create a poem that could function simultaneously in diverse languages is significant but not surprising, given the past statements by concrete poets about how the visual character of the work allows it to be read across different languages. Although the visual character in this poem is less pronounced than those works produced in the moment that de Campos describes as Brazilian concrete poetry's orthodox phase, it still fulfills that criterion. What is more significant is that the international "style" of this poem is conveyed through the multilingual list of words meaning *city*, thus tying the poem to the urban imagining contained in the theories of CIAM that Niemeyer and Costa implemented so faithfully in their design for Brasília. It is important to note, as well, that shortly after this poem Augusto de Campos began his "popcrete" phase, which moved away from words and towards symbols and images, often taken from popular culture sources, with conscious reference to American and European pop art. This phase parallels the collapse of the utopian promise of Brasília and the developmentalist

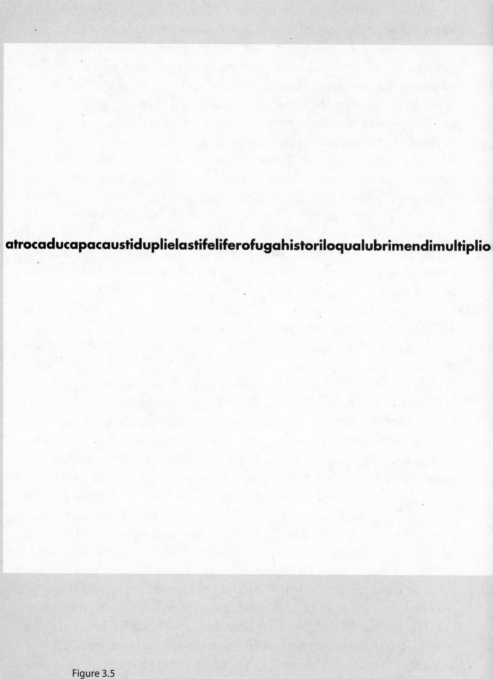

Figure 3.5
Augusto de Campos. "City Poem"

diplastipublirapareciprorustisagasimplitenaveloveravivaunivoracidade
city
cité

augusto de campos (1963)

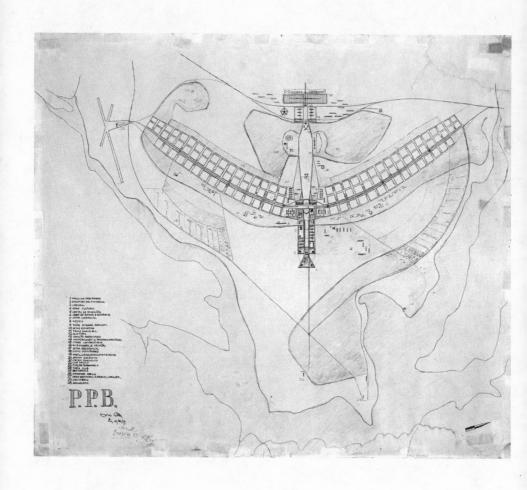

Figure 3.6

Lucio Costa. "Plan for Brasilía"

policies that accompanied it; Brazil, as a nation, suffered an economic collapse, and a military junta took power in 1964. With such a drastic change at the level of government came a shift in poetic strategy. For example, Augusto de Campos produced "Olho Por Olho" in 1964, and "LUXO LIXO" – a poem in which he repeats the word "luxo," printed in an ornate font, in the shape of the word for garbage, "lixo" – in 1965 ("LUXO" 55–6).[9]

Discussing Costa's original sketches for Brasília, James Scott notes that the "monumental axis," as Costa describes it, has alternately been compared to Christ's cross and an Amazonian bow, both of which contribute to the overall mythology of the Brazilian capital and its prophetic origins. Costa distanced himself from such sentimental projections, and Scott sides with him: "Even if the axis represented a small attempt to assimilate Brasília in some way to national tradition, it remained a city that could have been anywhere, that provided no clue to its own history, unless that history was the modernist doctrine of CIAM" (120). But neither Scott nor Holston makes the observation that Brasília is shaped like an airplane, with the Plaza of the Three Powers and Esplanade of the Ministries as the cockpit, the superquadras as the wings, and the sports sector and barracks as the fuselage and tail (in Holston 33; see fig. 3.6). As a symbol of increased connectivity, the airplane would be an appropriate model for Brasília, if a little obvious: flying was the most convenient way for the government workers to travel between the central city and the financial and cultural centres of Rio and São Paulo. But the airplane holds significance for modern architectural design and literature as well. Scott, in arguing against the proportions of the monumental squares and plazas in Brasília, notes that the city is best viewed, "as are many of Le Corbusier's plans, from the air" (121). And Holston begins his chapter "The Modernist Project" with this quote from Le Corbusier's 1933 book *The Radiant City: Elements of a Doctrine of Urbanism to Be Used as the Basis of Our Machine-Age Civilization*:

> Take an airplane. Fly over our 19th century cities, over those
> immense sites encrusted with row after row of houses without
> hearts, furrowed with their canyons of soulless streets. Look down
> and judge for yourself. I say that these things are the signs of a tragic
> denaturing of human labor. They are proof that men, subjugated
> by the titanic growth of the machine, have succumbed to the
> machinations of a world powered by money. (*Radiant City* 341)

Besides the arrogance implied by the imperative "Take an airplane," and the God-like invitation to "Look down and judge for yourself," the perspective from an airplane obliterates the human scale in favour of the monumental. It is a similar view from above that Michel de Certeau, in *The Practice of Everyday Life*, uses to still the agitation of New York City from his perch on the top of the World Trade Center, and allows him to consider the rhetoric of the city using the buildings as letters. It is a pleasurable feeling for de Certeau, but one that he recognizes only provides a partial experience, one that needs to be balanced by walking in the city. It is this realization that never struck Le Corbusier, and kept him ensconced in a regime of scopic pleasures. The implementation of the airplane as planning tool served only to dedifferentiate spaces for living, and there are implications here for poetry as well.

The perspective from the air had its influence on modernist literature, specifically the work of Gertrude Stein, whose writing Décio Pignatari cites as an influence in his 1956 manifesto, "New Poetry: Concrete." In her 1938 book *Picasso*, Stein writes about how the technology of flight altered the "composition of living," and thus required a new mode of literary and artistic composition:

> One must not forget that the earth seen from an airplane is more splendid than the earth seen from an automobile. The automobile is the end of progress on the earth, it goes quicker but essentially the landscapes seen from an automobile are the same as the landscapes seen from a carriage, a train, a waggon, or in walking. But the earth seen from an airplane is something else [...]. When I was in America I for the first time traveled pretty much all the time in an airplane and when I looked at the earth I saw all the lines of cubism. (49–50)

The view from an airplane does away with the earth-bound rules of traditional visual representation, destroying the hierarchy of foreground, middle ground, and background: it replaces depth with breadth. The airplane perspective fascinated the Italian Futurists, as well, and resulted in the genre of aeropaintings (*aeropittura*), to which a state sponsored exhibition was devoted in 1932, linking the work to the mechanical fascism of Benito Mussolini (Cosgrove 237–8). Marinetti also embraced the airplane in his poetry, particularly in *L'aeroplano del papa* (1908), and wrote a 1929 manifesto in support of aeropaintings.

The influence of this view from above is clear in the plans of modernist architects, but it is there in the programmatic statements of concrete poetry, too, including the Noigandres' notion of structure-content, as developed in their "Pilot Plan," and Gomringer's of linguistic "constellations":

> Our languages are on the road to formal simplification, abbreviated, restricted forms of language are emerging. The content of a sentence is often conveyed in a single word. Longer statements are often represented by small groups of letters. Moreover, there is a tendency among languages for the many to be replaced by a few which are generally valid. (Gomringer, "From Line" 67)

Both positions emphasize a stripping down in order to facilitate the communicative potential for concrete poetry in an era of rapid transformation of everyday life, much in the same way that modernist architecture saw technology providing an accelerated path to utopian organization. Concrete was a catalyst technology in urban design; its meaning for poetry was similar.

At a certain point, however, the perspective from the airplane must return to earth. In Brazil, this descent was marked by the shift from concrete to popcrete, in the case of Augusto de Campos, and to semiopoetry in the case of Pignatari. In Europe, concrete poetry had spread from Gomringer's Switzerland to Germany, France, Belgium, Britain, Czechoslovakia, Italy, and beyond. As in Brazil, orthodoxy gave way to a more playful stance. Max Bense in Germany and Pierre Garnier in France became the most vocal theorists of the movement, and the poetic work became less prescriptive and more descriptive; there was less emphasis on structural integrity and more on visual experimentation. The constellations of Gomringer transformed into the technical manipulation of print technology: no more "ping-pong" style compositions, but rather work like Pierre and Ilse Garnier's "Texte pour un architecture," in which the word "cinema" is repeated regularly and in the approximate dimensions of a cinema screen in order to recreate the visual hum of a screen (see fig. 3.7); or the German poet Franz Mon, whose texts appear to have been cut up and mixed with other texts, recalling the images of the French décollagistes of the 1950s and '60s who would cut swathes out of public poster boards and display them as examples of reconstruction-era France's consumerist palimpsests (see fig. 3.8.)

Bense writes in 1965 that "Concrete texts are often closely related to poster texts due to their reliance upon typography and visual effect; that is,

```
cinemacinemacinemacinemacinemacinemacinem
acinemacinemacinemacinemacinemacinemacine
macinemacinemacinemacinemacinemacinemacin
emacinemacinemacinemacinemacinemacinemaci
nemacinemacinemacinemacinemacinemacinemac
inemacinemacinemacinemacinemacinemacinema
cinemacinemacinemacinemacinemacinemacinem
acinemacinemacinemacinemacinemacinemacine
macinemacinemacinemacinemacinemacinemacin
emacinemacinemacinemacinemacinemacinemaci
nemacinemacinemacinemacinemacinemacinemac
inemacinemacinemacinemacinemacinemacinema
cinemacinemacinemacinemacinemacinemacinem
acinemacinemacinemacinemacinemacinemacine
macinemacinemacinemacinemacinemacinemacin
emacinemacinemacinemacinemacinemacinemaci
nemacinemacinemacinemacinemacinemacinemac
inemacinemacinemacinemacinemacinemacinema
```

Figure 3.7

Pierre Garnier and Ilse Garnier. "Texte pour une architecture"

Figure 3.8

Franz Mon. "From et 2"

their aesthetic communication scheme often corresponds to that of advertisements. The central sign, often a word, takes on polemical or proclaiming function" ("Concrete Poetry" 73). Garnier writes in his 1963 "Position I of the International Movement," which was signed by twenty-five other practising concrete poets but significantly not the Noigandres group:[10]

> If the poem has changed It is that I have changed
> It is that we all have changed
> It is that the universe has changed
>
> Men are less and less determined by their nation, their class, their mother tongue, and more and more by the function which they perform in society and the universe, by presences, textures, facts, information, impulsions, energies. (Garnier 79)

The names of modernist precursors like Mallarmé and Apollinaire are no longer included in this moment's manifestos, replaced by the influence of advertisements. The wonders of new technology and the desire to keep artistic pace with it transforms into the pressure to react to its effects, to catch up. Change, which held so many possibilities in the postwar period of development in Brazil and the reconstruction in Europe, was no longer coming but had arrived, and not in the ways that the modernist poets or architects had predicted. There was a new "international style," but one that resulted in the spectacularization of the urban landscape by the commodity and not, to the dismay of Le Corbusier, Costa, and Niemeyer, by that of the technocratic architect. A new understanding of how bodies – sometimes in machines, sometimes not – negotiated the spaces of modernity was complemented by a new understanding of how readers negotiated poetic spaces, sometimes written by machine, sometimes not.

The reaction against the airplane perspective occurred in writing about architecture and urban planning, as well. In 1961, the same year that Brasília was "opened," Jane Jacobs published *The Death and Life of Great American Cities*, in which she adopts the empirical perspective of a pedestrian experiencing first-hand the effects of the urban spaces she analyzes. The first sentence of her book is unflinching in its rejection of what she considered the cold, masculine, rationalist programs of Le Corbusier and his contemporaries: "This book is an attack on current city planning and rebuilding" (5). Where Le Corbusier advocates separate sectors for work and leisure, Jacobs proposes mixed-use buildings; where he calls for cities to be razed and rebuilt in a single, homogeneous style, she sings the praises of old buildings and their power to evoke community history; where he wants to extend roads into expressways through cities for efficient traffic commutes, she sees short blocks for easy pedestrian navigation and increased possibilities for human interaction. She located her critiques in the areas and neighbourhoods she was familiar with, mostly in New York, a method that is not without problems but which, unlike CIAM, sides with the local over the global.

Along the same lines, but from a position of architectural critique, is the study produced out of a Yale Architecture graduate symposium led by Robert Venturi, Denise Scott Brown, and Steven Izenour in 1968, *Learning from Las Vegas*. In this study the airplane is replaced by the automobile, but not the automobile of Stein and Fillipo Marinetti, straightforward and steady. The automobile in Venturi, Scott Brown, and Izenour's study has changed because the road environment had changed. This was an American car, in a uniquely American city:

> A driver thirty years ago could maintain a sense of orientation in
> space. At the simple crossroad a little sign with an arrow confirmed
> what was obvious. One knew where one was. When the crossroads
> becomes a cloverleaf, one must turn right to turn left [...]. But
> the driver has no time to ponder paradoxical subtleties within a
> dangerous, sinuous maze. He or she relies on signs for guidance –
> enormous signs in vast spaces at high speeds. (9)

Their argument proceeds from the explosive growth of Las Vegas in the postwar period into a giant advertisement for itself, and concerns itself primarily with the appearance of the Las Vegas Strip. Fifteen years after Azeredo's "Velocidade" imagined a sonic landscape blurred by acceleration, the automobile had slowed to a cruising speed.

Las Vegas is the reverse image of Brasília, but no less important for developing an understanding of the global forces that can be discovered in analyses of concrete poetry. If the early concrete poets – specifically the Noigandres group and Gomringer – were concerned with what *could be*, following both the Bauhaus faith in the power of design to transform living and its corollary in architecture, then the later poets were concerned with what *had become*. They responded to the new role of the consumer, who had replaced the modernist labourer as the figure of economic development. Walter Gropius's dream of the fusion of artistic forms "rising to heaven out of the hands of a million craftsmen, the crystal symbol of the new faith of the future," was taken up by poets within a global environment where the craftsmen had been replaced by shoppers at the A&P, and creative production no longer hoped to rise to the heavens, but spread, horizontally, to the suburbs (quoted in Guillén 58). The shift in concrete poetry, which is a general shift, not a solid break from one tradition to another, could thus be understood as operating on a hinge between the modernist texts of Le Corbusier and CIAM – *Vers Un Architecture, La Ville Radieuse,* CIAM's programmatic "Athens Charter" of 1933 – and *Learning From Las Vegas,* a text that contributed to the initial understanding of what postmodernism might look like. Whereas the modernists focused primarily on the technocratic control of life through form, the postmodernists focused primarily on the effect of forms, specifically those that were unplanned but which nonetheless had succeeded in infiltrating everyday life on a massive scale, and had turned the urban inhabitant from worker to consumer.

Following this investigation into the transition between modernism and postmodernism, between the worker and the consumer, it is helpful to look at Brasília and Las Vegas as representative cities. Brasília was itself a sign, ideologically weighted by its pristine, monumental architecture; Las Vegas is made up of a collection of smaller signs, constantly changing and littering the roadway with a surfeit of information:

> The rate of obsolescence of a sign [in Las Vegas] seems to be nearer to that of an automobile than that of a building. The reason is not physical degeneration but what competitors are doing around you. The leasing system operated by the sign companies and the possibility of [a] total tax write-off may have something to do with it. The most unique, most monumental parts of the Strip, the signs and casino facades, are also the most changeable. (Venturi, Scott Brown and Izenour 34)

The modernist concept of history is sacrificed to the perpetual present. Efficiency in design has its pinnacle in the hotel casinos that place the check-in desk behind and to the side of the entrance, so that guests walk onto the casino floor before they even see their rooms. Venturi, Scott Brown, and Izenour include in their study a representation of the Strip "showing every written word seen from the road" which looks like it could be a poem by John Furnival (30; see fig. 3.9). The words overlap each other, some in bold fonts, some in small regular fonts in proportion to their actual size. The letters appear to be Letraset, a dry-transfer lettering technology that offers flexibility to the designer, but the depictions of the roadways and medians are obviously done by hand, further distancing the authors' critical methodology from that of their modernist precursors.[11] The authors describe how modern architecture abandoned iconography, begrudgingly including signs such as "LADIES" or "GENTLEMEN" only where regulations or basic efficacy required them, as such images were bound to disrupt the purity of the space. In a passage reminiscent of Le Corbusier's admonishment of architects unwilling to embrace the structural and aesthetic possibilities of reinforced concrete, Venturi, Scott Brown, and Izenour point out that

> Architects who can accept the lessons of primitive vernacular
> architecture [...] and of industrial vernacular architecture, so easy
> to adapt to an electronic and space vernacular as elaborate neo-
> Brutalist or neo-Constructivist megastructures, do not easily
> acknowledge the validity of the commercial vernacular. For the
> artist, creating the new may mean choosing the old or the existing.
> Pop artists have relearned this. Our acknowledgement of existing,
> commercial architecture at the scale of the highway is within this
> tradition. (6)

They do not believe that modernist architects are against technology, but that their technology is outdated. The concrete of Le Corbusier and the steel beams and glass of Ludwig Mies van der Rohe were, after all, consequences of giant leaps in the technology of building, but they were also technologies tied to the industrial revolution. They were no longer symbols of progress, especially in a world entrenched in an ideological schism between the rapidly expanding capitalism of the United States and its allies, and the state socialism of the Soviet Union and its allies.

But simply replacing the airplane perspective of the modernist planner/ architect with the pedestrian perspective of Jacobs and the automobile perspective of the chroniclers of American excess is not sufficient for understanding the global cultural environment of the 1960s. Both Jacobs and the authors of *Learning From Las Vegas* were primarily concerned with conditions in the United States, and while conscious of the importation of architectural style from Europe, they do not pay much attention to the present or future conditions of other nations, or the impact that the invisible hand that had done so much to establish their ways of living might have on the world's inhabitants. The international style of capital was left to its own devices, and its presence in Europe in the wake of the Marshall Plan was

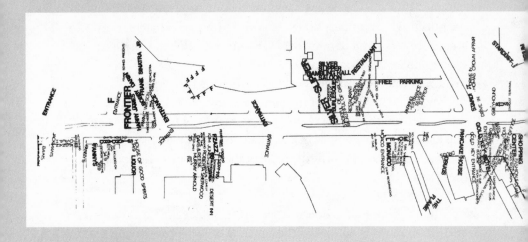

Figure 3.9

Robert Venturi, Denise Scott Brown, and Steven Izenour. Las Vegas Street Signage

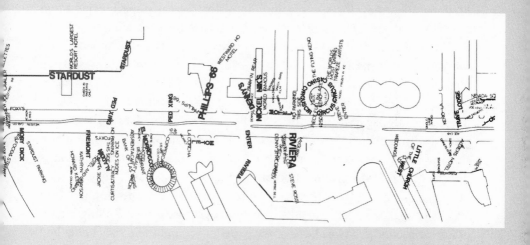

eerily similar. The engineer's aesthetic gave way to that of the social engineer, the advertiser.

Unnational Space

If the first half of the twentieth century was characterized by the spatial shifts rooted in the technologies of the car and then the airplane, the second half introduced a vessel that provided a unique perspective for the understanding of global identities: the space ship. The history of early space exploration overlaps neatly with that of concrete poetry: the Soviet Union's Sputnik satellite was launched in October of 1957 and the last of the Apollo moon missions, which marked the end of the "space race" in most senses of the term, returned to Earth in 1972. Far too many historical accounts of the space program, however, overemphasize the role it played for the United States in the techno-propagandistic battle with the Soviet Union. Not nearly enough place it within a development of a new global imaginary, or the concomitant shifts towards transnational economic organization, a development that is directly linked to the proliferation of imagery within a drastically expanded mediascape. As the twin traumas of the Holocaust and the atomic bomb attacks of 1945 were felt globally, distributed via visual media along a path of horror around the world, the space expeditions and their visual data had a tremendous international effect upon humans' visual comprehension of the Earth, and in doing so altered the way its inhabitants thought about one another. They also contributed to a development of a terrestrial science, one shared and translated into new, programmed languages. Things did not become smaller, in the popular understanding of McLuhan's concept of the global village, but the distances, both on Earth and in outer space, became less of an obstacle. The radio transmitter and domestic air travel made a new level of connectivity possible.

The first image of Earth from space was collected from a camera fitted to the nose cone of a V2 rocket launched from White Sands, New Mexico in 1946. Several V2 rockets – from the same manufacturing plant in Peenemunde, Germany as the rockets that had wreaked havoc on London a year previously – had been captured by the Americans at the end of the war and shipped, along with the team which designed them, back to the United States. The V2 from White Sands reached a height of sixty-five kilometres, just beyond the Earth's atmosphere, before returning to Earth. It was not until Sputnik in 1957, however, that scientists managed to build a rocket powerful enough to launch a satellite into orbit. The polished aluminum spherical satellite emitted a simple pulsebeat as it orbited the Earth. The signal was pure information, without any linguistic character, but information that carried an exciting *message* to its recipients; the pulsebeat operated outside of national language, entirely within scientific communication. The Americans tried to distinguish a code within the emission, but it was nothing more than a simple pattern designed to be received by amateur radio operators around the world, welcoming them to a newly discovered space.

The launch of Sputnik occurred within the International Geophysical Year (IGY), an international cooperative endeavour to use recent advances in scientific observation tools to gather data about the Earth's oceans, weather, polar ice caps and atmosphere. The year was actually eighteen months (1 July 1957–31 December 1958), and was scheduled to correspond with increased sunspot activity and several eclipses. The data collected was guaranteed to be open to scientific organizations from all nations, fostering global exchange using technical data as a universal language. This was the promise of space exploration in general, to discover a territory that superseded the political organization of Earth:

> Amid explicitly imperial tropes of representation, space offered
> the prospect of a renewed form of settlement, this time into a zone
> safely free from human difference. Returning to etymological roots,
> humans could find new domains to culture, together, as a species.
> By considering the earth as a planetary entity, then, fantasies of
> space exploration have presented a "limit case" of one measure
> of scale. Within them – and their potential realization – the
> atmosphere serves as the threshold of human unity. (Redfield 800)

The space race was not simply about the battle between the Soviet Union and the United States for scientific and military supremacy, but was watched by a global community uninterested in the terrestrial political consequences those powers obsessed over. Indeed, as one NASA historian explains, the interest in the space race might have had something to do with the feeling that it existed as a "surrogate for face-to-face military confrontation," and that it had a calming effect on an anxious world that had become accustomed to the idea of rockets carrying nuclear warheads, not scientists and their instruments (McQuaid 392).

The images of Earth transmitted from satellites and astronauts were just that: images of the *Earth*, not of the United States and the Soviet Union alone.

However much the emphasis on the national space programs of each might imply their dominance, the geophysical data did not correspond. As Denis Cosgrove points out, images of Earth from space challenge Western observers' "received notions of continental scale by exaggerating precisely those regions – Africa, the southern oceans, Antarctica – that, through the cartographer's choice of map projections, normally appear so small on world maps, and so correspondingly insignificant in Western geographical consciousness" ("Contested" 278). The images had the effect of recalibrating the visual prejudice perpetuated by even the putatively objective cartographer's instruments. This was the dream of outer space, that it could be a space free of political manoeuvring and trivialities. In an article in the *New York Times* in 1957, shortly following the launch of Sputnik, Andrew Haley of Washington, "one of the few specialists in space law," is reported to have called on the United Nations to declare the moon a "free and independent autonomous area [...] to keep any nation from claiming it as a possession" ("Free Zone Urged" 20). This statement, however utopian in rhetoric, is compromised by the panic some Americans felt in trailing the Soviet Union's rocket technology. It was also not a position shared by Professor Fred Singer of Maryland, who is reported in the article to have proposed turning the moon into a testing ground for hydrogen bombs. His motives were altruistic, though, as using the moon as a target "would eliminate the danger of radioactive fall-out on earth [sic] and would add to the deterrent power of hydrogen bombs by exploding them where all nations could study the results" ("Free Zone Urged" 20).

The spectacle of the Moon, exploding or not, and that of the Earth from space are both part of what was becoming a new technological sublime. The American astronaut Frank Borman is quoted in *Newsweek* in 1968: "When you're finally up at the moon looking back at earth [sic], all those differences and nationalistic traits are pretty well going to blend and you're going to get a concept that maybe this is really one world and why the hell can't we learn to live together like decent people" (quoted in Cosgrove 282). A similar sentiment is present in Mary Ellen Solt's "Moonshot Sonnet," a poem which engages directly with the implications of space travel on the potential for new structures of global communication. She explains her poem:

Made by copying the scientists' symbols on the first photos of the moon in the *New York Times*: there were exactly fourteen "lines" with five "accents." We have not been able to address the moon in a sonnet successfully since the Renaissance. Admitting its new scientific content made it possible to do so again. The moon is a different object today.

Also the sonnet was a supranational, supralingual form as the concrete poem is. So the poem is both a spoof of old forms and a statement about the necessity for new. (307; see fig. 3.10)

Solt's position here resonates with Garnier's "Position I of the International Movement" quoted from earlier: "If the poem has changed / [...] / It is that the universe has changed" (78).

But the photos from Ranger 7 were not the "first" photographs of the moon from space. The Soviets had photographed the moon and its far side in 1959 from their Lunik 3 satellite. What was significant about the Ranger's photographs, besides being produced by Americans, and providing information for a possible moon landing, was the quality of the images. In the *New York Times* article from which Solt composed her piece, the technical gathering of visual data from the satellite is described in detail. The scientists received data from the satellite's six slow-scan television cameras, and used a modified 35 mm kinescope camera to capture the data onto film negatives. The signals, which arrived at ground control in what appeared to human eyes as a light tracking horizontally from top to bottom on a monitor, were also recorded onto magnetic tape, from which another 35 mm print was made. Scientists also used Polaroid cameras intermittently in order to create an instant record of the instruments' functionality. The negatives, upon exposure, were processed "with what was described as 'tender loving care' at one of the finest Hollywood laboratories" (Witkins 8). The four thousand images were one thousand times clearer than images taken by Earth-bound telescopes. The visual interference of the atmosphere only allowed the Earth-bound perspective to gather images from the equivalent of five hundred miles. The Rangers photographs "meant in effect that the 240,000 mile distance to the moon had been shrunk by man's ingenuity to a mere half-mile of what he could see of its topography" (1). This emphasis on the innovation of the imaging process enforces the idea of an expanding, interrelated visual economy determined by shifts in technology. New camera and film technology, used by both NASA and the American film industry, can here be linked to the compositional strategies of concrete poetry.

Figure 3.10
Mary Ellen Solt. "Moonshot Sonnet"

All of these shifts in in how we understood the world and our place in it – spatially, scientifically, visually – allow us to read across texts that we might otherwise assume operate primarily within a literary tradition, or within a visual tradition in art. Denis Cosgrove addresses the ways in which the discovery of new spaces, and the mapping of those spaces, affects not only our understanding of our own positions, but the language we use to describe them, as well. In *Apollo's Eye*, which is a survey of how the globe has been imagined in various regimes of representation throughout history, he stresses the importance of instrumentation in the collection of data by explorers of heretofore unmapped spaces:

> Thomas Jefferson's instructions for Meriwether Lewis and William
> Clark's 1804 expedition into Louisiana Territory emphasized precise
> recordkeeping and surveying and the need to restrict "imagination."
> The explorers' journals indicate a slow fragmentation and eventual
> collapse of language in the face of overwhelming difference in
> the West. Sentence structure, syntax, and descriptive language
> all broke down as the expedition penetrated spaces that had been
> blank on the European map. Such failure of language placed ever
> greater emphasis on nonlinguistic representations – numerical
> tables, graphs and statistics, topographic drawing and painting – as
> accurate registers of vision. (206–7)

This tendency towards the scientific in the practice of exploration and mapping, encompassed in the implementation of numbers and rigidly defined notation techniques, and away from the linguistic or subjective, reaches new heights in the scientists' markings on the Ranger photos, and it is within that realm of restricted imagination that "Moonshot Sonnet" functions with such force. In Solt's composition, the markings reproduce the centering lines associated with camera lenses or telescopes. Each quatrain has a full target, and the finishing sestet has two (this is an Italian sonnet, not an English sonnet).

The poem positions itself within a history of aerial photography, beginning with the invention of the airborne automatic camera by the German Oskar Messter in 1915, which allowed pilots during World War I to photograph large tracts of land in order to map them much more efficiently and accurately:

A new mode of geographical representation was created: "a flattened and cubist map of the earth," which demanded new skills to relate the image to the ground. With increasing altitude, the airborne camera came to replace the human eye in military reconnaissance, and aerial photography evolved into "a new way of seeing in which ... the earth became a target as far removed from the personal experience of the observer ... as a distant planet." (Cosgrove, *Apollo's* 239–40)

Cosgrove points to the famous use of aerial perspective in the opening images of Leni Riefenstahl's *Triumph of the Will*, in which a camera mounted to a plane navigates through clouds, and looks down on the Fuhrer's plane "providing our's [sic] and Hitler's mastering gaze with quasi-cartographic glimpses of the German landscape below." He continues:

The revolutionary perspective afforded by the aerial view of the Earth encouraged balloon photography from the earliest days of the new medium and that view also appealed to the Modernist imagination in the interwar years. This appeal was especially strong in those nations – Italy, Germany, and the United States – that most enthusiastically adopted Modernism's futuristic aesthetic. ("Contested" 279).

But if aerial photography was the apotheosis of the modernist future, what did that imply for satellite photography? The airplane perspective so valued by Le Corbusier and modernist planners, the perspective that allowed them to disregard the human scale in favour of the monumental, seems almost intimate in relation to satellite photography, let alone those photographs taken from the Moon or from deep space. What space photography offered was a near-complete erasure of the human in preference for the geophysical and astronomical. The ordered lines of cultivated earth contain the history of agriculture, and those marks point directly to villages and then cities that represent the pinnacle of human organization. By making the physical marks that were inspirational to the global understanding of modernists invisible or obscured by clouds, images from space elevated the achievement of an apparently disinterested physics to a God's eye view, and began in earnest a way of thinking about the Earth that emphasizes instrumental readings of the geophysical environment over indices of human accomplishment. In Cosgrove's discussion of *Earthrise*, a photograph of the Earth with the Moon's

Figure 3.11
NASA. "Earthrise"

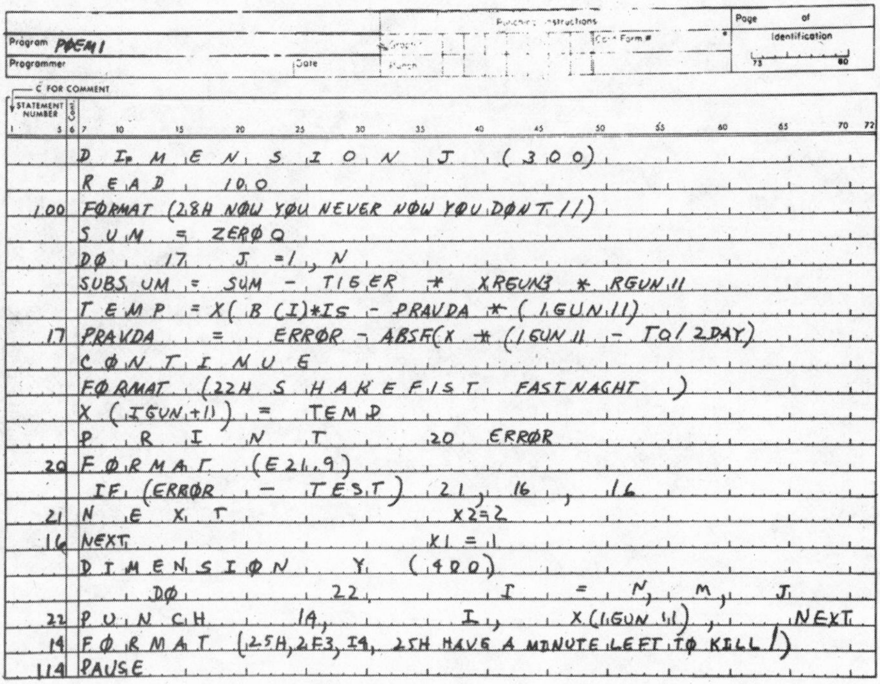

```
C FOR COMMENT
STATEMENT NUMBER | CONT
1        5 6 7   10    15    20    25    30    35    40    45    50    55    60    65    70 72

        DIMENSION J (300)
        READ 100
100     FORMAT (28H NOW YOU NEVER NOW YOU DONT //)
        SUM = ZERØQ
        DØ 17 J = 1, N
        SUBSUM = SUM - TIGER * XREUN3 * RGUN 11
        TEMP = X( B (I)*IS - PRAVDA * ( IGUN 11)
17      PRAVDA = ERRØR - ABSF(X * (IGUN 11 - TO/2DAY)
        CØNTINUE
        FØRMAT (22H S H A K E F I S T  FAST NACHT )
        X ( IGUN +11 ) = TEMP
        PRINT 20 ERRØR
20      FØRMAT (E21.9)
        IF (ERRØR - TEST) 21, 16, 16
21      NEXT                        X2 = 2
16      NEXT                        X1 = 1
        DIMENSIØN Y (400)
        DØ 22 I = N, M, J
22      PUNCH 14, I, X(IGUN 11), NEXT
14      FØRMAT (25H, 2F3, I4, 25H HAVE A MINUTE LEFT TØ KILL /)
114     PAUSE
```

Figure 3.12

Carl Fernbach-Flarsheim. "PØEM 1"

surface in the foreground, taken by astronaut William Anders from the Apollo 8 mission in 1968, he notes that the image "was the subject of immediate commentary and speculation about a reformed *view* of the world" (273; my italics; see fig. 3.11). In Solt's work this comes through in the replacement of the mark of the poet's subjectivity with those of the scientist's purposeful, illustrative marking, and the replacement of all traits of national language by one that could claim to be closer to the literal meaning of *universal*.

The diminishment of the human scale worried Hannah Arendt, whose perspective was shaped in part by the horrors so recently produced by a society in love with technological organization. In her essay "The Conquest of Space and the Stature of Man," which first appeared in 1963, she argues that the space scientists and astronauts were not explorers in the sense previously given to the term as it relates to the European colonizers:

> It was indeed [the scientists'] search for "true reality" that led them to lose confidence in appearances, in the phenomena as they reveal themselves of their own accord to human sense and reason. They were inspired by an extraordinary love of harmony and lawfulness which taught them that they would have to step outside any merely given sequence or series of occurrences if they wanted to discover the overall beauty and order of the whole, that is, the universe. This may explain why they seem to have been less distressed by the fact their discoveries served the invention of the most murderous gadgets than disturbed by the shattering of all their most cherished ideals of necessity and lawfulness. (272)

Solt's poem does not contain this anxiety, though other concrete poems that deal with the technological sublime do. Solt does not mention in her anthology that "Moonshot Sonnet" was designed – which most likely means typeset – by Edwin Morgan, the British poet who wrote a series of poems from the perspective of a computer, all of which end in a glitch.

Carl Fernbach-Flarsheim is another American concrete poet who deals with the intersection of scientific information and everyday life, but, like Morgan, remains within national languages, for the most part, and is concerned with how communication is interrupted or disturbed by conflicting lexicons. His "PØEM 1" from 1967 is composed in FORTRAN, the programming language developed by IBM in the 1950s, and printed by hand onto a programming card. The composition combines technical formulae and instructions: "TEMP = X (B (I) *IS – PRAVDA * (| GUN ||)"; all the Os are switched to Øs (246; see fig. 3.12). A poem he submitted to Solt for her anthology is simply a calendar page with a handwritten note reading "They are setting up new rules – a smaller particle was discovered" (248; see fig. 3.13). Solt adds an explanatory note herself in the glossary: "Here the poet incorporates the calendar page itself as part of the poem, for on the day the scientist makes a revision, the poet knows that he will be called upon to make a revision" (310). While certain concrete poets might be rightly accused of being too technologically determinist, and of being too enthusiastic about the possibilities offered by new discoveries, the relationship between the poetry and the techno-cultural transformations of the period provokes questions about what level of cheerleading readers can accept from a critical literary or artistic practice before it crosses into something else.

Space exploration in its early stage, in spite of its ultra-nationalist politics of aggrandizement, achieved at least in part the supranational character that concrete poetry set as its goal from its first theoretical writings. The American astronaut Michael Collins, who accompanied Neil Armstrong and Buzz Aldrin on the first moon landing in August 1969, recalls:

> After the flight of Apollo 11 the three of us went on a round-the-
> world trip. Wherever we went people, instead of saying, "Well, you
> Americans did it," everywhere they said "We did it," "we, human
> kind ... we the human race ... we people did it." And I had ... I'd
> never heard of people in different countries use this word "we,"
> "we, we" as emphatically as we were hearing from Europeans,
> Asians, Africans, everywhere we went it was "We finally did
> it," and I thought that was a wonderful thing. Ephemeral, but
> wonderful. (Sington)

This moment of togetherness was not a result simply of the reimagining of the Earth prompted by space photography, but of the collective reimagining of the moon as a space belonging to the future potential of humans. In Benedict Anderson's explanation of the emergence of nationhood, he notes that widespread exploration, translation, and expanded literacy challenged the sacred order of empires and dynasties, fundamentally changing the way people "apprehend[ed] the world," and making it "possible to 'think' the nation" (22). The same can be said about new, extraterrestrial exploration, increased translation and expanded literacies that changed the way people "think" the globe. It was not simply the new perspective of Earth from space that held transformative power, but the renewed perspective of space from

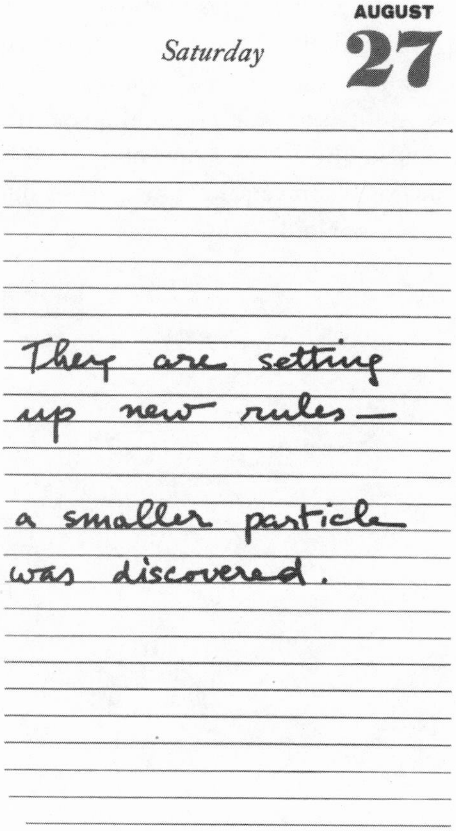

Saturday

AUGUST
27

> They are setting
> up new rules —
>
> a smaller particle
> was discovered.

Figure 3.13
Carl Fernbach-Flarsheim. "Untitled Poem"

Earth. When humans looked at the moon in the 1950s and '60s it had, as Solt argues, become a new object, one that held all the utopian promise that had vacated the modernist city. It was a space, in theory, unencumbered by national boundaries, even after it had been bombarded with American and Soviet satellites and stabbed with a series of stiffened American flags, all of which are as visually insignificant as the ones on Earth as seen from space. It was also a space reachable only through the most rigorous devotion to scientific calculation, and as such represents the second site for concrete poetry's utopian impulse. Both were technologically determined and designed with the dreams of universal emancipation, but one came from looking down, the other, from looking up.

4/

CONCRETE POETRY
AND CONCEPTUAL ART:
A MISUNDERSTANDING

Within the Anglo-American critical tradition, concrete poetry and conceptual art largely disavow each other. When representatives of one speak of the other, it is often to dismiss it or undercut its legitimacy as a poetic or artistic movement. For example, here is Lucy Lippard, in her text *Six Years: The Dematerialization of the Art Object from 1966 to 1972 …* :

> Certainly there are at least twenty people using either words or written things as vehicles for their art, but there is a distinction between concrete poetry, where the words are made to *look* like something, an image, and so-called conceptual art, where the words are used only to *avoid* looking like something, where it doesn't make any difference how the words look on the page or anything. (157)

Here is Joseph Kosuth, quoted in the same text:

Most of the concrete poets are now starting to do theater and getting out of concrete poetry (Acconci, Perreault, Hannah Weiner, etc.). They realize the sort of decadence that follows from that sort of materialism [treating words as *material*]. They are trying to say things about the world that are illogical in terms of language. (132)

Here are Hal Foster, Rosalind Krauss, Yve-Alain Bois, and Benjamin H. Buchloh, in the glossary of their widely assigned textbook, *Art since 1900: Modernism, Antimodernism, Postmodernism* (concrete poetry is not mentioned anywhere else in the book):

As a historical term, Concrete poetry identifies the postwar resurrection and academicization of the linguistic and poetical experiments of the radical avant-gardes of the teens and twenties that had been conducted in the context of Russian Futurism, and the practices of international Dadaism in Berlin, Zürich, Hanover, and Paris. [...] The concrete poets of the postwar period typically emerged in areas that had been both remote and protected from the cataclysms of World War II, both privileged and disadvantaged with regard to the naivety of their early rediscovery of these avant-garde projects. Thus we find early resuscitations named Concrete poetry in the context of Latin American countries and in Switzerland in the forties, often working in tandem with the academicization of abstraction (for example, Eugen Gomringer and Max Bill). Here the celebration of a newfound ludic irrelevance and of typographical gamesmanship displaced both the political, the graphic, and the semiological radicality of the originary figures. (482)

Here is Liz Kotz, in her 2007 book, *Words to Be Looked At: Language in 1960s Art*:

In the postwar era, various types of concrete and visual poetry, in particular, promised to probe the space of the typographic page and link contemporary literature with the visual arts. Yet a reliance on rather quaint illustrational or pictorial modes – as in poems that take on the shape of their subjects – left much concrete poetry out of touch with changing paradigms in the visual arts and the wider conditions of language in modernity. (138)

And here is the Italian poet and critic Sarenco, in a 1971 *Lotta Poetica* editorial co-written with Gianni Bertini, railing against the disproportionate attention granted to conceptual art:

> the recent publications (edition n. 3 of the paris review "vh 101" autumn 1970 – the catalogue of the exhibition "information" at the museum of modern art in new york, in summer 1970) while analyzing the phenomenon of "conceptual art" intentionally missed to mention in any way the visual poetry ...
>
> we intend to exemplify in the next numbers our statements by publishing the product of "conceptual art" showing beside the visual poetic matrix from which it was copied.
>
> for example:
>
> joseph kosuth   copying from timm ulrichs, ben vautier, jean claude moineau etc.
>
> carl andre   copying from all northern concrete poets
> richard artshwager copying from heinz gappmayr
> and so on (12)

The preceding catalogue of slights and slander illustrates a long-standing conflict between concrete poetry and conceptual art, a conflict fuelled by willful misunderstanding and cavalier dismissal on both sides. The purpose of this chapter is to orchestrate a rapprochement, in order that they might begin speaking to each other again. Readers who are confounded by the often artificial separation between poetry and visual art can learn a lot from what each has to say about the other, and the conditions and territoriality that influence their encounters. It should be clear to readers by now that concrete poetry, despite its conventional reception as a postwar poetic eccentricity, and counter to what conceptual artists and art historians claim, is not reliant on shaped language for its poetic and critical force. Recent writing by Jesper Olsson and Antonio Sergio Bessa on the work of Swedish concrete poet and painter Öyvindh Fahlström, and by Claus Clüver and Marjorie Perloff on the Brazilian Noigandres poets, sets out to rescue concrete poetry from its critical purgatory by focusing on its relationship to media, visual art, and the avant-gardes of the early twentieth century.[1]

Conceptual art, similarly, is not simply the placement of words where images once were, nor a completely dematerialized "idea" art. Its critical reception, which differs from concrete poetry's inasmuch as it has seemingly not left art historical discourse since its emergence, is currently undergoing an examination of its relationship to language, as well as how it manifested itself in different geographies and political environments.[2] Conceptual art is also enjoying something of a resurgence in contemporary poetics, particularly in the work of Kenneth Goldsmith, Craig Dworkin, Vanessa Place, and Robert Fitterman, all of whom have described their practice as operating under the rubric of "conceptual writing," relying heavily on the "concept" portion of conceptual art.

As both concrete poetry and conceptual art asked questions about the role of language in identity formation, in structures of power, and in expression, and did so in overlapping historical periods, it strikes me as curious not only that their relationship has yet to be probingly analyzed, but that it has remained so contentious. I propose that the animosity is a consequence of an ongoing case of mistaken identities. Concrete poets, conceptual artists, critics, and chroniclers have been too eager to ascribe the practices of one to the ideas of the other. Both the poets and the artists (and the poets who were artists, and vice versa) worked with the signifying properties of language, but their concerns arose from different geographies, and with different disciplinary goals. Each had a different understanding of what constituted the *global*; the idea was much more radical for poetry, so often limited to circuits of national languages, than it was for visual art, which travels across borders through an established network of galleries and collectors. Conceptual art grew out of New York and England, the headquarters of global capital. Concrete poetry came out of Brazil, Switzerland, and a recently bifurcated, still struggling Germany. Concrete poetry sought to engage a new, global audience. Conceptual art aimed to rewrite the rules of art production.

Another factor in the antagonism between the two groups is the strong possibility that neither knew very well what the other was doing, and assumed a dismissive, reactionary posture in response to a superficial comparison. It is difficult, as a humanities researcher today, to imagine a world without the internet, a world in which international avant-gardes are not meticulously archived and accessible. But even in the heyday of concrete poetry – if there ever was such a day – its poetic influence, especially in North America, was never dominant. In her chapter dealing with concrete poetry in *Unoriginal Genius*, Marjorie Perloff cites a letter that Elizabeth Bishop, who was then living in Brazil, sent to Robert Lowell in 1960, in which she characterizes Brazilian concrete poetry as "pre-1914 experiments, with a little 'transition' & Jolas, and a dash of Cummings," and dismisses it as "awfully sad," despite having "[a] certain nostalgic charm" (quoted in Perloff 56). Bishop's opinion shows two things: first, the condescending gaze of the, for lack of better terms, centre toward the periphery, even within poetic circles; and second, the difficulty in recognizing concrete poetry as a global movement in a discipline so tied to the nation-space. Perloff acknowledges her own earlier misunderstanding of concrete poetry as naively mimetic and overaestheticized in *Radical Artifice: Writing Poetry in the Age of Media*, written in the late eighties, and points to the emergence of the internet and the global cultural networks that flourished in its wake as providing the ground for her new understanding of the work (*Unoriginal Genius* 52). She quotes Kenneth Goldsmith's assertion that concrete poetry was made for the computer screen *avant la lettre*, a conclusion he came to after listening to the Brazilian poet Décio Pignatari speak of interfaces, multi-media, and distribution as the concerns of concrete poetry. In some sense, the international anthologies of concrete poetry that came out in the mid-to-late sixties and early seventies enact the poets' project of international connectivity in a way that anticipated the spatial turn of the internet.

If the print form that concrete poetry found itself tied to was not impediment enough to its wider acceptance, the disciplinary borders between poetry and visual art exacerbated the division. An anecdote shared by Goldsmith in an essay he wrote for a 2008 catalogue for a Brazilian concrete poetry exhibition sheds further light on the condition of concrete poetry in North America in the eighties. Goldsmith admits that, as an emerging artist in the New York art scene, he had never heard of concrete or visual poetry. His work often involved text, and he consciously positioned his sculptures and installations against earlier language pieces, by artists like Joseph Kosuth, Barbara Kruger, and Jenny Holzer, which he considered too cold and confining. It was not until the Miami-based collectors Marvin and Ruth Sackner purchased one of his pieces and invited him to install it in their home gallery that he discovered, in their extensive archive of concrete and visual poetry, examples of the type of work he had been trying to produce himself:

> [At the Sackners'] I encountered an entire history of textuality that I
> never knew existed: concrete and visual poetry. Nowhere, in my dead-
> center position of the New York art world, had I ever heard of this
> stuff. I was floored. Here was a history dating back hundreds of years
> that I – and seemingly the entire New York art world –

was totally unaware of. In it I saw a rich play of semiotic signs and signifiers, uses of letter forms that teased out Wittgensteinian language games, utopian politics, transnational (and transrational) uses of language, all presented with a sophisticated visual elegance. (194)[3]

Upon his return to New York, Goldsmith was dismayed to find his enthusiasm for the history of concrete and visual poetry met with indifference by his artist cohort.

Within this narrative of discovery and dismissal lies a systemic disconnect between poetry and the visual arts that is magnified in the relationship between concrete poetry and the language-centred conceptual art that emerged during the mid-to-late sixties in the United States and Britain. Goldsmith quotes Liz Kotz's description of concrete poetry's reliance on "quaint illustrational or pictorial modes" as evidence that the rift remained, twenty years later (Goldsmith, "Curation" 195; Kotz 138). Referring to Kotz as a "young art historian," and noting that her book had been published by "a top-notch academic press" (194) – by which he means the MIT Press – Goldsmith offers his explanation for the oversight:

> To read poems – any poems – as visual art is a grievous mistake and perhaps is the most common misunderstanding of this genre. While concrete poetry employs visual means, it's the tension between textuality and visuality that gives the work its punch, making it successful poetry. It's like reading Mallarmé as if it was a Monet; although both employ radical ideas of spatiality, to read them through an identical lens would be an inviting confusion of genres, discourses, and intentions. (196)

Goldsmith is half right here, because even if concrete poetry is primarily a poetic project, it does not accept purely literary readings, either. As Goldsmith points out, questions of textuality and visuality come forward through the poems, as well as issues of how language operates in different spaces – formal, geographical, cultural. These are questions that require, if not a confusion of genres and discourses, at least a productive roiling, one that comes through art history and cultural studies as much as from poetics and comparative literature.

It is the disciplinary niche that concrete poetry staked out for itself in the middle part of the twentieth century, combined with its consciously international character, that has likely contributed the most to its general critical neglect. Approaches to national literatures, even when they attempt to deal with concrete and visual poetry, lack the apparatus to deal with its "global" networks. This becomes evident in the limitations of studies examining French concrete poetry, or Canadian concrete poetry, for example, which tend to emphasize form over historical and transnational conditions, conditions which do not remain still within the borders of a nation. Literary scholars, assuming that they find the literariness of the poems intriguing, often lack the lexicon to consider the work within its visual context, and art historians and critics, assuming that they find the presentation of the texts interesting, often lack the literary knowledge to deal with the status of the work as poetry. Consequently, the spatial critiques and relationships between the poetry and emergent technologies have gone largely unrecognized.

A disciplinary disconnect comes through in Kotz's *Words to Be Looked At: Language in 1960s Art* (2007), where poetic experiments by artists such as Carl Andre, Dan Graham, and Vito Acconci are treated within the wider artistic discourse of New York in the sixties. Her study has prompted a renewed interest in how visual art implemented linguistic and poetic structures within an expanded field of cultural production, one that stretched out into performance and music through John Cage, the Black Mountain poets and artists, and Fluxus. But in her focus on American artists in New York, Kotz misses an opportunity to address the role that concrete poetry played in bringing the poetic and the visual together. This link was not simply a formal argument, either; several figures involved in concrete poetry held parallel positions within visual art. Daniel Spoerri wrote concrete poems and was also a member of the Nouveaux Réalistes group in France in the sixties; Emmett Williams wrote concrete poems and published one of the largest anthologies of concrete poetry while maintaining a strong presence in the Fluxus movement; and Dieter Roth and Öyvindh Fahlström both produced visual work while also experimenting with language. Similarly, Kotz neglects to draw a connection between the influence of technology on the artists' language work and the role it played in a number of concrete poems. When speaking of work by John Cage and Andy Warhol, she notes that "the turn to language in sixties art occurred in the wake of new recording and transmission media, as words took on a new materiality and urgency in the face of magnetic sound" (5). Her recognition of a technological shift in language use, when placed beside the implication that technology was used significantly only in New York and its immediate surround, ignores the histories of both sound poetry and *musique concrète* in France, where poets and composers used techniques of splicing and cutting magnetic tape to augment and transform spoken texts. Initiated in 1948 by composer Pierre Schaeffer, musique concrète was very much involved in the recognition and treatment of language and voice as technologically inflected *material*. Kotz similarly overlooks the radio transistor's role in the expansion of culture across the globe. By greatly increasing the range of radio transmission, the transistor resulted in a significant compression of space, bringing disparate regions into contact, a condition that the relatively new field of communication studies took up energetically.

It might seem that I am being too hard on Kotz and participating in the kind of negative criticism that indicts work for having too narrow a scope, even if the work performed within that scope opens up new paths of discovery to a neglected field. But the link between Kotz's topic and concrete poetry is one that she first acknowledges and then dismisses. In a footnote to the passage I quote at the beginning of this chapter, she writes:

> Exceptions [could] no doubt be made here for many poets, including some of Eugen Gomringer's work, as well as for projects by Emmett Williams and Dieter Roth, both of whom were loosely affiliated with the Fluxus group. Yet there is no question that many artists dismissed concrete poetry as deeply pictorial and irrelevant. When Joseph Kosuth describes the work of artists like Graham or Acconci as resembling concrete poetry, there is no question that he means it as a term of derision. (293)

The problem here is not that "many artists dismissed concrete poetry as deeply pictorial and irrelevant," but that this circumstance is overlooked as a site of investigation, and that such a position has reproduced itself over four decades. The questions remain: *why* has art history held an antithetical position to concrete poetry for so long? What was it that the artists in question found so objectionable, and to which poems, poets, and publications were they referring? What did they – and the critics who followed their lead – understand concrete poetry to be?

Poetic Art, Artistic Poetry

The pairing of conceptual art and concrete poetry does not automatically make sense beyond their common practice of *displaying* language: in conceptual art, it was meant as the dematerialization of the art object; in concrete poetry, it was the rematerialization of the word. But such formulations, though conveniently phrased, do not stand up to further scrutiny. Concrete poetry was nearing its end in the late sixties just as conceptual art was beginning to gain momentum, which might explain why the conceptual artists were eager to dissociate themselves from its history while deploying some of its techniques. With concrete poetry's emphasis on commercial design practices and the condition of language within the mediascape of the everyday, it might make more sense to examine the work in relation to pop art, which emerged nearly contemporaneously with that initial meeting between Gomringer and Décio Pignatari in Ulm in 1955. Or, given their stripped down aesthetics and concern with mass production, it might prove germane to mine the similarities between concrete poetry and minimalism. Fluxus, in its international character, language-based experiments, and regular intersection with concrete poetry and poets is an even more likely pairing. Conceptual art's approach to language is different than concrete poetry's. If Kosuth and the other members of the Art & Language group (Terry Atkinson, David Bainbridge, Harold Hurrell, Mel Ramsden, and Charles Harrison, in the early stages) can, however reductively, be designated as the dominant theorists of early, orthodox, language-centered conceptualism, their emphasis on the philosophy of language as dealt with by Ludwig Wittgenstein, and on the structural linguistics of Ferdinand de Saussure and Roman Jakobson, contrasts with the approach of Max Bense, in Germany, and the Noigandres group in Brazil. These latter poets come to language via information theory and computation, in addition to a tradition of poetics built on the work of Ezra Pound and the modernist poets. But what makes conceptual art a valid and productive counterpart to concrete poetry is the fact that beyond its participants' and later critics' near unanimous dismissal of concrete poetry as a significant field, it contains figures who produce work that borrows the techniques of concrete poetry while at the same time denying any line of influence. I am speaking specifically of the work of Carl Andre, Dan Graham, and Vito Acconci.[4]

All three of these artists are firmly set within the canon of conceptual art, despite their practices being so different from one another. And herein lies the problem when choosing representatives for a movement: "conceptual art," like the term "concrete poetry," has both a specific and a vague meaning, as it refers not only to an orthodox form or practice but also to work that responded, and continues to respond, to a shift in art production and discourse coming out of the mid-sixties. But there are specific criteria that mark artists and work as conceptual, the first of which might be a historical position. Some historians locate the beginning of the movement in Harry Flynt's 1962 essay "Concept Art," published in La Monte Young's *An Anthology of Chance Operations* the following year. But Flynt's formulation of concepts *as art* had more in common with the work being done by composers like Young, John Cage, and George Maciunas than they did with the work that would later come to be known as conceptual art. In this Flynt parallels Öyvind Fahlström, who used the term "concrete poetry" in 1953, but in a way that had more to do with musique concrète than with what Gomringer and the Noigandres group would begin to produce two years later. "Conceptual art" proper emerged primarily out of a group of artists and critics operating in New York and England in the late-sixties.

That the work of Joseph Kosuth and the Art & Language group maintains a dominant role in the popular understanding of conceptual art explains the emphasis on *reading* conceptual art as a linguistic exercise. Kosuth and Art & Language, as well as Christine Kozlov and Lawrence Weiner, worked within the category of language-centered conceptualism, drawing influence from logical positivism and structural linguistics. Art, for Kosuth, could no longer be about anything other than the signifying power of art. The title of his influential 1969 essay "Art after Philosophy" played on the double meaning of art produced in the mould of philosophy – as argument, as thought – as well as art as the inheritor of a philosophical tradition gone stale. For the Art & Language group, who through their eponymous journal largely shaped the lexicon and rhetoric of conceptual art during the late sixties and early seventies, a rejection of the plastic arts inspired a rigorous and verbose interrogation of art as language, in both its primary (objects, galleries) and support (critical writings, discourse) languages. Such a position allowed for the near-complete breakdown of art as a category, as the process of analyzing "art propositions" became the *work* of art in place of the material objects to be hung in a gallery or purchased by a collector or museum.

Sol LeWitt represents an alternative narrative to Kosuth and company, and has the privileged position of having written the first manifesto of conceptual art, "Paragraphs on Conceptual Art," in 1967 (although Kosuth later claimed that he himself had used the term in his notes the year before and was thus entitled to the title of "founder"). For LeWitt, whom Alexander Alberro positions as an aesthetic opposite to the tradition represented by Kosuth and Art & Language, conceptual art was an emancipation of the artist from the contingencies and creative vicissitudes involved in the production of actual art work. The artist would create an idea, and that idea would structure the work: "The idea becomes a machine that makes the art" (LeWitt 12).

LeWitt positions this process directly opposite the tradition of expressionist art, in which the genius expressed via the artist's hand and aesthetic decisions are valued above all else:

> It is the objective of the artist who is concerned with conceptual art to make his work mentally interesting to the spectator, and therefore usually he would want it to become emotionally dry. There is no reason to suppose, however, that the conceptual artist is out to bore the viewer. It is only the expectation of an emotional kick, to which one conditioned to expressionist art is accustomed, that would deter the viewer from perceiving this art. (12)

But the art LeWitt imagines as conceptual remains within a gallery and requires a traditional viewing audience to be engaged mentally, if not emotionally, by the work on display. Kosuth and the Art & Language group disparage those viewers, and blame them – and the critics who created them – for the period of stagnation that art had fallen into. Their own artistic-philosophical investigative project was devoted to hauling art out of the emotional bog it had settled in. As Kosuth stated in an interview in 1969, making clear his desire to elevate art discourse to the rarefied sphere of science or philosophy: "The public's not interested in art anyway ... No more interested in art than they are with physics" (quoted in Alberro, "Reconsidering" xx).[5]

The language-centered conceptualists often used language for the presentation of their work as well as for a theoretical model of the works' function. There are important differences, however, between the appearance of language in concrete poetry and its appearance in conceptual art. Kosuth's series of large-format, black-and-white photostats of dictionary definitions, for example, used a medium that was cheap and reproducible in order that they might be thrown away after each exhibition. But such a practice refuses to engage with the materiality of language as it appeared in contemporary culture, with new printing techniques and advances in photography facilitating the expansion of advertising into the everyday. It pretends that language is neutral, disinterested, and ordered by the dominant authority of a dictionary that controls meaning, a structural model more rigid than that of Saussure, who emphasized language's volatility through the idea of language communities. These communities never emerged from dictionaries; it was always vice versa. Language was, for Kosuth and Art & Language, a ready-made, but one which lacked the sophistication and criticality of Duchamp. Even Benjamin H. Buchloh, whose 1990 "Conceptual Art 1962-69: from the

Aesthetic of Administration to the Critique of Institutions" continues to be a landmark essay in the analysis of work from this period, refuses to take them at their word:

> In 1969, Art & Language and Kosuth shared in foregrounding the "analytic proposition" inherent in each readymade, namely the statement "this is a work of art," over and above all other aspects implied by the readymade model (its structural logic, its features as an industrially produced object of use and consumption, its seriality, and the dependence of its meaning on context.). And most importantly, according to Kosuth, this means that artistic propositions constitute themselves in the negation of all referentiality, be it that of the historical context of the (artistic) sign or that of its social function and use. (Buchloh 126)

The language-centred conceptualists presented language as if it were transparent. By contrast, the post-conceptualist artists of the mid-to-late-seventies sought to accentuate the power of language to present itself as *image* and to transmit meaning beyond its semantic character. Alberro explains that the interrogation of the link between text and image moved the work into an examination of how language shapes subjectivity, a position that was more in tune with the post-structural language-based philosophy that emerged in Europe in the mid-sixties from figures like Jacques Derrida, Roland Barthes, and Michel Foucault:

> [There are] distinct differences between [...] post-conceptual art and the linguistic conceptualism of the late sixties. The latter, with its emphasis on a purely formal language, one that correlates historically with the legacies of reductivism and self-reflexivity. By contrast, artists such as [Victor] Burgin, [Jenny] Holzer, [Mary] Kelly, and [Barbara] Kruger theorize language beyond the purely analytic and formal, situating it within a synthetic, discursive practice determined by a system of control and domination. From this perspective, language is perceived as in and of itself the very medium by which ideological subjectivity is always already constructed. In other words, in direct response to the formal neutrality of conceptual art of the late sixties, the post-conceptual work of artists such as Burgin, Holzer, Kelly, and

Kruger in the seventies argues that language is inextricably bound to ideology. ("Reconsidering" xxviii–xxix)

Barbara Kruger's graphic anti-advertisements, for example, expose how the techniques of commercial marketing produce desiring subjects in a hyperconsumerist culture. Jenny Holzer's *Truisms* present text in public spaces in a similar way, playing on the blurred line between conventional wisdom and product slogans and using technologies of commercial display like LED screens, billboards, and posters. Martha Rosler's practice engaged with semiotics and visual language through video, collage, and text in ways that confronted the political control of language in the wake of the Vietnam War.

The interrogation of the links between text and image that characterized much of the post-conceputalist artists' work shifted the discourse into an examination of how language shapes subjectivity, a position in tune with post-structural philosophy. The interest in the relationship between text and image and the weight that correspondence carries in a hypercommercialized global environment is present in concrete poetry from its inception. This is not to say that the practices of Kruger, Holzer, and Rosler are derivative of concrete poetry, but to point out that an approach to language as situated, material, and ideological is something the two movements share. And this points to a curious reversal of disciplinary approaches, as language crosses the boundaries of poetry and visual art. Concrete poetry adhered to the modernist visual art position of the art experience in its emphasis on the immediately comprehensible poem, and on simultaneity. In his 1960 manifesto "The Poem as a Functional Object," Eugen Gomringer writes that concrete poems strive to be "as easily understood as signs in airports and traffic signs" (70). The Noigandres group in Brazil shared a similar utilitarian pose. In their collectively authored, developmentalist-titled "Pilot Plan for Concrete Poetry" (1958), they write: "concrete poetry: tension of things-words in space-time. / dynamic structure: multiplicity of concomitant movements" (de Campos, de Campos, and Pignatari 90). The language-centred conceptualists, on the other hand, refute that position by rejecting the art experience in favour of philosophy, adhering to the modernist literary position that celebrated difficulty and opacity, and demanded sustained and engaged attention from its audience. This position is exemplified by the writing in the journal *Art & Language*, which requires of its readers a pre-education in philosophy and aesthetics

and strives to exclude a mass public. A passage from Lucy Lippard's monumental *Six Years ...* elucidates this position:

> I don't understand a good deal of what is said by Art-Language,
> but I admire the investigatory energies, the tireless spade-work (not
> calling one one), the full commitment to the reestablishment of a
> valid language by which to discuss art, and the occasional humor in
> their writings. The chaos inherent in their reason fascinates me,
> but it is also irritating to be unequipped to evaluate their work.
> I don't know how it is or if it is evaluated by adepts in philosophy
> as philosophy, but I find it infuriating to have to take them on
> faith. I agree with their goal of clearing the air around the "pseudo
> mystique" of art and artists, their demand that observers stop being
> "good catholics." If only they could exorcise the Jesuit in themselves
> at the same time. [...] For all their distaste for formal or "esthetic"
> or "reactive" art, it approaches given conditions analytically (what
> is more "esthetic" than "an inquiry into the nature of art" or into
> the nature of "natural sculpture"?); as well as reactively, inasmuch
> as words, thought, tortuous systems are their material, and they
> emphasize this material and its inherent properties as much as say,
> Carl Andre emphasizes his. (151)

Concrete poetry's approach to language, on the other hand, like that of
the post-conceptualists, is postmodern. Language is tied to ideology and
produces subjectivities, which is why the concrete poets felt that they had to
adapt: they created designed words for a designed world. Recognizing that
language was producing new, global subjects, the poets aimed to intervene.
The *conditions* of language become key: territory, medium, source, and
message. The linguistic conceptualists, conversely, adhered to a modernist,
structural model of language coming out of the first half of the twentieth
century, specifically the work of Jakobson and the logical-positivist writings
of A.J. Ayer. Linguistic context – the historical ground – becomes subordinate
to the concept of a language-system.

While Alberro positions post-conceptualist artists in opposition to
the ideologically disinterested Anglo-American conceptualists, it could be
argued that they were continuing the project of South American conceptual art, which had been active since the mid-sixties. A year before LeWitt
would publish "Some Paragraphs on Conceptual Art," the Argentinian artists Eduardo Costa, Raúl Escari, and Roberto Jacoby wrote "A Media Art

(Manifesto)," which called for the creation of works made up strictly of false accounts of exhibitions and events published in newspapers and magazines. Questioning the manufactured truths of a media-saturated society, the artists claimed, in a manner that both Guy Debord and Jean Baudrillard would have appreciated, "The work would begin to exist in the same moment that the consciousness of the spectator constitutes it as having been accomplished" (3). The work of the Brazilian artist Cildo Meireles concentrated on the commercial transformation of South American society, and one piece in particular addressed the transparency/opacity of language in a politically charged manner. For *Insertion – Coca-Cola* (1970), Meireles printed texts critical of Brazilian politics and imperialism in vitreous white ink on empty Coca-Cola bottles. When the bottles were returned to the factory and refilled, the text became visible, and were distributed commercially by the Coca-Cola Corporation. This was just one in a series of Meireles's *Inerserções em circutios ideologicos* (Insertions into Ideological Circuits), which he describes as rooted in the need "to create a system for the circulation and exchange of information that did not depend on any kind of centralized control," and were transmitted through a variety of alternative "circuits" (Alberro, "Reconsidering" xvii).

Mari Carmen Ramírez emphasizes the interventionist character of Latin American conceptualism, and positions it against the conventional narrative of conceptual art as it was exported both economically and critically from the dominant centres:

> The grounding of artistic languages in extra-artistic concerns has indeed been a constant of the avant-garde in Latin America since the 1920s. It was not only an intrinsic part of the process of tearing apart or recycling forms transmitted from cultural and political centers but a logical step in the act of construction of a tradition with the copy as its starting point. On the other hand, Benjamin Buchloh has suggested that the obsession with "facticity" of North American Conceptual art practices can derive only from the concept of an "administered society" typical of "late capitalism." The absence in Latin America of the social conditions supporting an administered society makes it an unsuitable model, perhaps even antithetical to a Latin American context. The elaboration of a Conceptual art practice aimed at exposing Latin American political and social realities thus involved a series of inversions of the mainstream model of Conceptual art. (556)

Like Brasilia, whose majestic arches are less a design preference than an economic necessity – requiring less concrete, which was an expensive material, and more labour, which was cheap and plentiful – and as such stand as an index to the level of development of Brazil at the time, so, too, does the conceptual art produced in South America offer, in its formal as well as its ideological concerns, an explanation of the relationship of the continent to the cultural centres of North America and Europe.

Accounting for the ways in which post-conceptual practices took up and responded to the concerns of the conceptual artists and their use of language as a mode of intellectual and artistic production has already been performed by critics including Alexander Alberro, Mari Carmen Ramírez, Boris Groys, Miško Šuvaković, and Sabeth Buchmann, as well as many others. Similar investigations of the relationship between Anglo-American conceptual art and dematerialized – though often more strictly politicized and situated – practices in other regions have also helped to reconfigure our understanding of what qualifies as conceptual art.[6] My aim in this chapter, however, is specifically to counter the dismissal of concrete poetry by those who produce the dominant narrative of linguistic conceptualism, and to bring into play ideas about how the artists' and poets' approaches to language carry geographical and disciplinary residue.

Heaps of Language

When speaking of Carl Andre's visual poetry in the introduction to Andre's collected writings, the art historian James Meyer describes the work as "recalling the most radical examples of concrete poetry" (10), but he adds a footnote:

> Although Andre maintains that he took no interest in the international tendency of concrete poetry that flourished in Brazil, Germany, and elsewhere during the 1950s and sixties – his principal inspirations being Pound and Stein – the contemporaneity of these endeavours bears noting. Mary Ellen Solt's observations that concrete poetry stresses the "physical material from which the poem … is made," or that the concrete poem is "an object to be perceived rather than read," may equally be applied to Andre's practice. (21)

Why Meyer places Andre's experiments alongside the "most radical examples of concrete poetry" is likely a rhetorical position determined by the genre of the introduction: considering them alongside the most *conventional* experiments hardly induces a desire to continue reading. But such a suggestion is likely also symptomatic of the belief that concrete poetry is primarily mimetic or shaped poetry. That Meyer should turn to the American Solt for an explanation of concrete poetry is less significant but still appropriate; texts by Gomringer, Bense, or the Noigandres group would have been more authoritative, although *international*.

Andre produced, early in his career, a series of one-word poems, which were printed in the center of a page. About *First Five Poems*, he explains:

> They are not the first poems I ever wrote ... But they are the first
> poems in which I took the English language for subject matter.
> All my earlier poems originated in some conceit or observation or
> sentiment of my own. These poems begin in the qualities of words.
> Whole poems are made out of the many single poems we call words.
> (Andre and Frampton 75)

What is significant here is the modifier "English," which isolates Andre from the concrete poets' explicit aim to deal with *language* on a supranational level; Andre's decision to investigate the constitutive elements of language at the level of the word rather than the letter, or punctuation, also sets him apart. Kotz, in discussing Andre's *One Hundred Sonnets*, a collection of one-word poems repeated in fourteen-line grids, notes that the work "move[s] progressively from pronouns – I / you / he / she / it – to body parts and fluids – head / hair / face / eye [...] blood / urine /sweat – to colors, numbers, minerals, and basic elements of the landscape – sun / moon / star / cloud / rain / as if to assemble a set of basic material properties analogous to those of Andre's sculpture" (146). But this is an unreflexive projection of sculptural techniques onto poetic material, and a major reason for the difficulty art history has had in understanding the project of concrete poetry, or linking visual art to poetics in general. It is also exactly what Kosuth disparages the concrete poets for doing – "treating words as *material*" – although the concrete poets he lists are not really concrete poets (Vito Acconci, John Perreault, Hannah Weiner), but poets attempting to do innovative work with language and space. In conversation with his friend the artist Hollis Frampton, Andre describes his poetic constructivism as the generation of overall designs by the multiplication of the qualities of the individual constituent elements. May I suggest, furthermore, that Ezra Pound in the *Cantos* exploits the plastic and Constructivist quality of words, symbols and phrases. I grant that his purpose is not gained, but enhanced, by this method. Cummings would seem an obvious example, but I would insist that his divisions and eccentricities are more an attempt to reintroduce musical values in poetry than an exploitation of plastic possibilities. (37)

It is difficult to understand how Andre can share the same influences as the concrete poets, and produce similar work, yet consistently refuse to find parallels with any of their poetry. The English critic and anthologist Stephen Bann identified a constructivist strain in concrete poetry in 1967, and the work done by poets like Ian Hamilton Finlay, Dieter Roth, and Hansjörg Mayer, just to name a few, could arguably fit into Andre's poetic desire for the reduction of language to its constituent elements. Unlike Andre, however, these poets took the influence of Pound's fascination with Ernest Fenollosa's research on the iconic Chinese written character to go beneath the level of the word and opened their sphere of influence beyond the American canon to include figures like Stéphane Mallarmé, Guillaume Apollinaire, and Filippo Tommaso Marinetti.[7]

When Frampton challenges Andre on his choice of words for a series of poems – green / five / horn / eye / sound – and suggests a different set might be as poetical, Andre responds:

Yes. Your own blue / six / hair / ear / light follows the method with its own precision. Not even the method is mine but belongs to whomever uses it. Nor do I think that my *Five Poems* are better than yours, but both our sets are radically different from the poem: "*I am a red pansy.*" These latter five words relate most strongly to each other and depart very far from the specificity of their referents. In fact we may presume that the five words together share one super-referent. The five words of my *First Five Poems* very purposely do not share a super-referent. My green is a square of that color or a village's common land. My five is 5 or: ... . My horn is either on the brow of a rhino, or under the hood of a Cadillac. My eye is paired above my nose or founded in my psyche by punning. Sound is Long Island, even. But I have gotten rid of the overriding super-referent. (75)

Andre treats the phrase "I am red pansy," which in itself seems to tap into a specifically American xenophobic, anti-Communist homophobia, as a word, and his disruption of the syntactic order is what, for him, provides a poetic charge. But such a simple disruption is not a new poetic strategy; it had been widely used by the time Andre was writing by figures he lists as influences (Pound, T.S. Eliot, Stein, etc.) and myriad others he neglects to mention. It is strange, however, that, as a sculptor writing poetry, he never addresses the subject of the space of that page, and the function of words within that space.

Robert Smithson, whose writings on language and art have come to occupy a privileged position in the canon of art history, celebrates Andre's poetry in his 1968 essay "A Museum of Language in the Vicinity of Art" for its strategy of demolishing any reference beyond the words themselves. Yet in emphasizing the word, neither Smithson nor Andre is willing to talk about language's material function: how it functions in the space of the everyday, how it marks identities, how it performs, how it *works*. Smithson makes this clear:

> Andre doesn't practice a "dialectical materialism," but rather a "metaphorical materialism." The apparent sameness and toneless ordering of Andre's poems conceals a radical disorientation of grammar. Paradoxically his "words" are charged with all the complication of oxymoron and hyperbole. Each poem is a "grave," so to speak, for his metaphors. Semantics are driven out of his language in order to avoid meaning. (80)[8]

Smithson's grave metaphor operates within Roman Jakobson's formulation of the paradigmatic and syntagmatic axes of language. Smithson sees Andre's poetry as disrupting both axes, as his presentation of single words alone on a page or a repetition of a single word within a grid removes them from their signifying power. But there is a problem with this reading. A grid of the word *green* still refers to the color green, or a park, or money (but most likely the color green), and repeating it on an arbitrarily sized grid does not disrupt that metaphorical axis in any way that differs significantly from the work of Pound and Stein that Andre reveres. Similarly, the works can generally be read aloud quite easily, even if they would be rather dull.

Speaking of a poem he wrote about a rose that he calls a "plastic poem," Andre tells Frampton that the rose "will not be printed in a blooming, petalled pattern" in a thinly veiled reference to the mimetic compositional strategies that Andre associates with concrete poetry (38).[9] In addressing the difference

Figure 4.1
Hansjörg Mayer. "USA"

between his disruptions, or "boiling down" of grammar in order to emphasize words outside of syntax, and the experiments of Stein and T.S. Eliot,
Andre reductively reads their work as developing out of the social constraints
of the time, ignoring Stein's polylingualism in works like *Tender Buttons* that
reflected her experiences with foreign languages – she had a German nanny
as a child and spent considerable time in France – as well as the demographic
shift in the United States, as millions of immigrants entered the country
in the first decades of the twentieth century, bringing their languages with
them. What constraints Eliot worked under are less clear, though it is rea-
sonable to assume that Andre saw the radical experiments in art production
taking place within his cohort as evidence of a liberated cultural sphere.

Examples of poems that implement repetition within a grid form but
which perform a more complex poetic function are not difficult to locate in
concrete poetry. Ronaldo Azeredo's "Velocidade" (1957) is an early example
that treats the word as material – both visually and aurally – while at the
same time referring to the social conditions under which it was written: a
rapidly "modernizing," industrializing Brazilian economy. Hansjörg Mayer's
simple grid poem from 1965, "sau / aus / usa" uses the German words for *sow*
and *out* to identify a political position in the very structure of the initials, or
brand, of the United States. The poem plays on the meaning immanent in the
small words to associate the American police presence in a divided Germany
(police as pigs) with a rising consumerist impulse (pig as a symbol of insati-
able greed). It also refers to the German idiom "die sau rauslassen" ("let the
pig out"), which is the equivalent of "paint the town red" (see fig. 4.1).[10]

Pierre and Ilse Garnier's "Texte pour une architecture" (1965) seems to
have much in common with Andre's techniques in *One Hundred Sonnets*,
but the poem works because of the relationship between the visual effect of
the word's repetition and the meaning of the word at the time of composition (see fig. 3.7). Beyond the fact that *cinema* is a word that functions in
both French and English, the visual composition of the poem in the ratio
of a 35 mm screen simulates a television screen as it would appear on film
(with lines running up and down that would be indistinguishable to the
human eye) or as if the reception were poor. The significance thus comes out
of the meaning of the word *cinéma* in France in the mid-sixties, when television was emerging as a new visual medium through which information
that would have previously been received in public theatres was transmitted. The word "cinema" in the poem also morphs into "macine," which con-
jures the idea of a machine as well as the possessive "ma cine" (excusing the

gender error). The mechanical reading comes out in the vocalization of the poem, the repetition of the word mimicking the sounds of a projector as film runs through it, and the breathlessness and confusion that comes with any attempt at recitation asks questions of the body's relationship to communication media. The title of the poem, "Texte pour une architecture" carries implications for architecture in size, function, and public/private uses. This poem would not work if it were one in a series of grids organized thematically, for instance, if the next poem were to be "popcorn," or "organ," in the way that Kotz notes Andre's sonnets "move progressively from pronouns [...] to body parts and fluids" (146). This type of grouping hardly seems to disrupt the paradigmatic/metaphorical axis in the way Smithson would argue that it does.

Addressing his use of the grid as compositional technique in 1973, Andre writes:

> The grid system for the poems comes from the fact that I was
> using a mechanical typewriter to write the poems, and as you
> know a mechanical typewriter has even letter spacing, as opposed
> to print which has justified lines with unequal letter spacing. A
> mechanical typewriter is essentially a grid and you cannot evade
> that. And so it really came from the typewriter that used the grid
> rather than from the grid to the typewriter. (12)

His emphasis on the ordering properties of mechanical typewriters is rather conventional. Charles Olson develops a similar point in his influential 1950 essay "Projective Verse," although for his purposes the even spacing of the typewriter encouraged a greater control over the breath in the recitation of poetry. Andre talks about his experience with writing his work as a tactile experience, typing with one finger. But it is strange, then, that he does not extend that idea to the page in the machine. The tactility remained at a mediated distance because he submitted to its ordering principle by letting the page be manoeuvred by the machine only. The equivalence of the typewriter and the grid ignores the movement of the page by the poet, or the possibilities created by mechanical failures or alternative features of typewriters (jammed keys, non-uniform letter weight, fading or coloured ribbons).[11] Barrie Tullet's *Typewriter Art: A Modern Anthology* (2014) provides a history of typewriter art that explores the relationship between language, visuality, and the composing hand that proves poets and artists contemporaneous to Andre were very much evading the typewriter's grid. For Andre, language is material, but it is not a social material which goes through changes of meaning in conjunction with historical and technological shifts.[12] Rather, it is a material for the artist to experiment with, to order in unique and creative ways, a position that distinguishes his work from concrete poetry in its insularity.

Andre's poetic works retained the mark of the artist, and would often refer to the region in which he lived. His long poem, *A Short History of King Philip's War*, for example, was produced by mapping a mathematical structure onto a series of texts dealing with the colonization of the United States, specifically the area concentrated around what came to be Rhode Island and Massachusetts. But despite congratulating Frampton on his choice of words to replace his one-word poems, claiming that they are as equally good from a poetic standpoint, the words chosen by Andre are still *chosen by Andre*, and achieve their poetic value from being designated as such. This parallels his sculptural practice, where his sculptures of everyday material such as bricks or bales of hay are granted value by the certificate of ownership that accompanies them when purchased. Alberro describes this practice, which Andre pioneered along with the artist Dan Flavin, as a new form of guaranteeing authorship: "the certificate, signed by the artist, delineates in legalistic language (often complemented by a schematic drawing on standard graph paper) the various components of the work. Given the general accessibility of the materials and Andre's deskilling of the procedures of production, it is primarily the certificate that authenticates his work" (Alberro, *Conceptual Art* 23). At a symposium in 1968, Andre responded to a question about unauthorized reproductions of his sculptural work by comparing them to forged cheques, which implies the only difference between Andre's poems and Frampton's alternatives is the amount of social capital their signatures are able to draw (Alberro, *Conceptual Art* 178). Concrete poetry, on the other hand, never really had the same issues with authenticity or ownership. There are historical, material reasons for this, of course. Poetry, especially avant-garde poetry, has never had as much of a market as visual art so the poets have less to be territorial about than their artist counterparts. Stephen Bann makes this point when discussing his role as an editor in the early sixties, and pointing to the differences between the circulation of concrete poetry versus conceptual art:

> A key reason for distinguishing between the two is that poetry
> and the visual arts work institutionally in very different ways. For
> example, we were at one stage inclined to publish some poems by
> the American artist Carl Andre in *Form*. But then we heard of the

fee he was charging, and as we had never offered a fee to anybody, we decided not to pursue this idea. (13)

Poetry is also primarily distributed through the mass media of books, even within small press editions, and while there are issues of copyright, the modalities of ownership and consumption are vastly different. Concrete poetry, through fine press printing, limited edition folios, and gallery exhibitions strayed from conventional methods of production in order to emphasize the poem as object, but the position of the poet never superseded the demands of linguistic structures of the compositions. From the Noigandres Group's "Pilot Plan":

The poem as a mechanism regulating itself: feed-back. Faster communication (problems of functionality and structure implied) endows the poem with a positive value and guides its own making. [...]

Concrete poetry: total responsibility before language. Thorough realism. Against a poetry of expression, subjective and hedonistic. To create precise problems and to solve them in terms of sensible language. A general art of the word. The poem product: useful object. (A de Campos, H. de Campos, Pignatari 72)

While Andre attempted to boil down syntax to get rid of grammar, the concrete poets sought to boil down poetry to get rid of the poet.

My readings of concrete poems as more complex than Andre might allow for is not intended to reduce the significance of conceptual art's investigation of language and the place of meaning, but to point out that the dismissal of concrete poetry by those artists and their critics is erroneous, and generally born of quick dismissal or a resistance to sustained critical engagement with an international poetic discourse.

Poems for America

The language-based work of Dan Graham provides a counter-example to Andre's poetic work. Graham produced site-specific literary work in the midsixties that sought to intervene in and disrupt the flow of information. His pieces were not explicitly political, but they did perform a critical function in exposing the passivity with which readers of commercial magazines absorb information – the reader as consumer. His project can be traced, in part, to his experience as a young writer in New York, where he moved in 1964 to open up a gallery with friends. The gallery failed after a year, but the lessons that Graham learned from that failure would prove influential:

> Through the actual experience of running a gallery, I learned that if a work of art wasn't written about and reproduced in a magazine it would have difficulty attaining the status of "art." It seemed that in order to be defined as having value, that is as "art," a work had only to be exhibited in a gallery and then to be written about and reproduced as a photograph in an art magazine. Then this record of the no longer extant installation, along with more accretions of information after the fact, became the basis for its fame, and to a large extent, its economic value. ("My Works" 421)

The magazine functioned as a supplement to the gallery system, and the galleries supported the magazines through advertisements. Bypassing the gallery, work like Graham's 1966 photo-essay *Homes for America* in *Arts Magazine* exposed the dependency of each on the other by parodying both the form of the photo-essay, so integral to the reproduction and valuation of visual art, and the advertisement to create what was and still is an all-too-common form – the photo-essay as advertisement (see fig. 4.2). The language Graham uses in the piece is detached; he describes recent trends in housing construction from a quasi-sociological perspective, pointing to the large-scale tract developments that had sprouted up all over the United States. The photographs adhere, for the most part, to a similar objectivity, emphasizing the uniformity of the houses in sequence, as opposed to advertisements trumpeting the mass-produced house as an inexpensive temple to the family. He also implements black and white documentary photography for its putatively objective, truthful character, a technique widely used in conceptual art. Graham's consideration for the space in which his work would operate parallels concrete poetry's interrogation of the book and the page as a site for poetry. Concrete poems came in small press magazines, chapbooks, and ephemera, limited-run large folio works, posters, paintings, audio recordings, and artist books, all of which tested the conventional modes of distribution.

Graham would produce several other magazine pieces, but none on the scale of *Homes for America*. In 1966, he placed an advertisement in the *National Tattler* requesting a clinical description of post-coital detumescence

Figure 4.2

Dan Graham. "Homes for America"

Figure 4.3

Dan Graham. "Figurative"

in males (Graham, *Dan Graham* 98).[13] A list of prices without a total, called "Figurative," was published in *Harper's Bazaar* in 1968, sandwiched in between advertisements for Tampax and Warner's bras (93; see fig. 4.3). There is no indication that Graham considered these pieces as poems, *per se*, although the editor of *Harper's Bazaar*, a friend of Robert Smithson's, published "Figurative" in the poetry section. It would be stretching the comparison of concrete poetry and conceptual art to link the representation of the potential ordering of tract houses represented by letter strings in *Homes for America* to an idea of rhyme schemes, or to the permutational poetry of Haroldo de Campos ("ALEA I – VARIAÇÕES SEMÂNTICAS"; 1967) or Josef Hiršal and Bohumila Grögerová ("Vývoj I"; 1960–62). But a piece that Graham published in the art journal *Aspen* in 1966 invites attention to its status as poetry by his labeling of it as such. The work subsequently has come to be referred to as "Schema," but the program on which it is grounded was titled "Poem / March 1966," and is simply a list of data categories defined by its own presentation: "Each poem-page is to be set in its final form by the editor of the publication where it is to appear, the exact data in each particular instance to correspond to the fact(s) of its published appearance" (Graham, "Poem" n. pag.; see fig. 4.4).[14] Because there are categories that strive for exactitude – percentage of ink coverage, for example – and hence change with every modification of the data, Graham sees the production of the piece as inevitably inaccurate, dependent as it is upon the editor's measurements. He imagines a solution of technological supplantation: "It would be possible to 'compose' the entire set of permutationally possible poems and to select the applicable variant(s) with the aid of a computer which could 'see' the ensemble instantly."

Graham's rejection of the composing subject as insufficient and his emphasis on the materiality of not only the language of the piece but its mode of communication, as well, seems to position it within the same sphere of poetic investigation as the concrete poets, especially in the statistical compositions of Max Bense and the permutational work of Hiršal and Grögerova and Haroldo de Campos. But the conditions of its publication in *Aspen* have perhaps coloured its critical reception: it was in the same issue that Roland Barthes's essay "The Death of the Author" was published for the first time in English. The oft-cited opening of his essay addresses the impossible figure of the author and challenges the artist and poet to reconsider where their "voices" come from:

It will always be impossible to know [the author], for the good
reason that all writing is itself this special voice, consisting of
several indiscernible voices, and that literature is precisely the
invention of this voice, to which we cannot assign a specific origin:
literature is that neuter, that composite, that oblique into which
every subject escapes, the trap where all identity is lost, beginning
with the very identity of the body that writes.

The position of the concrete poets in the decade previous to Barthes' essay
was also sympathetic to this position, though it came more out of a technological determinism than a theoretical response to the ideas of structural-
ism. Concrete poetry sought to undercut the position of the author in order
to compose mass poetry, able to be quickly and collectively consumed. Such
a strategy is articulated in Gomringer's manifestos, but it is also present
in the reduced and often polylingual lexicon of concrete poetry. Adriano
Spatola explains:

Haroldo de Campos says: "Concrete poetry speaks the language
of today's man. It rejects the craftsmanship, discursiveness, and
metaphor that transform the poetry of our age – marked by
technological progress and non-verbal communication – into an
anachronism that causes the divide between poet and public often
deplored in sentimental terms that are anything but objective."
From this perspective, the synthetic/ideogrammatic method that
brings all textual elements (audio, visual, semantic) into play can
be considered an organizational process of the poem in exact
consonance with our civilization's need for as rapid and direct a
message as possible. (92)

For the concrete poets as well as Barthes, it was the figure of Stéphane
Mallarmé who first identified the potential of language to function on its
own, beyond the spectral figure of the author. This fact did not escape the
attention of Brian O'Doherty, the Irish artist who compiled the issue of
Aspen, and who dedicated the issue to Mallarmé. Barthes writes:

In France, Mallarmé was doubtless the first to see and foresee in
its full extent the necessity of substituting language itself for the
man who hitherto was supposed to own it; for Mallarmé, as for

SCHEMA

(number of) adjectives
(number of) adverbs
(percentage of) area not occupied by type
(percentage of) area occupied by type
(number of) columns
(number of) conjunctions
(number of) depression of type into surface of page
(number of) gerunds
(number of) infinitives
(number of) letters of alphabet
(number of) lines
(number of) mathematical symbols
(number of) nouns
(number of) numbers
(number of) participles
(perimeter of) page
(weight of) paper sheet
(type) paper stock
(thinness of) paper stock
(number of) prepositions
(number of) pronouns
(number of point) size type
(name of) typeface
(number of) words
(number of) words capitalized
(number of) words italicized
(number of) words not capitalized
(number of) words not italicized

POEM

35 adjectives
7 adverbs
35.52% area not occupied by type
64.48% area occupied by type
1 column
1 conjunction
0 mms. depression of type into surface of page
0 gerunds
0 infinitives
247 letters of alphabet
28 lines
6 mathematical symbols
51 nouns
29 numbers
6 participles
8" x 8" page
80 lb. paper sheet
dull coated paper stock
.007" thin paper stock
3 prepositions
0 pronouns
10 point size type
univers 55 typeface
61 words
3 words capitalized
0 words italicized
58 words not capitalized
61 words not italicized

Figure 4.4
Dan Graham. "Poem, March 1966"

us, it is language which speaks, not the author: to write is to reach, through a preexisting impersonality – never to be confused with the castrating objectivity of the realistic novelist – that point where language alone acts, "performs," and not "oneself": Mallarmé's entire poetics consists in suppressing the author for the sake of the writing (which is, as we shall see, to restore the status of the reader).

By limiting the reference of language to the actual language, Graham abandons the position of author, abdicating responsibility for not only the meaning of the work but even a portion of its content, as different data is produced with every publication. That he should designate the work a "poem" need not remove it from its status as artwork, but the gesture should be taken seriously. It separates Graham from the dominant American poetry of the time, which operated within the individualized figures and poetry of Robert Bly and the Beat poets, while aligning the piece with the program of concrete poetry to emphasize the materiality of language and the conditions of its expression. As Graham explained in the late sixties:

A page of *Schema* exists as a matter of fact materiality and simultaneously semiotic signifier of this material (present): as a sign it unites, therefore, signifier and signified. It defines itself as place as it defines the limits and contingencies of placement (enclosing context, enclosed content). It is a measure of itself – as place. It takes its own measure – of itself as place, that is, placed two-dimensionally on (as) a page. (*For Publication*)

The fact that it should be placed firmly within the critical history of conceptual art, with no connection to concrete poetry, speaks to the insularity of Anglo-American conceptual art at the time as well as to a persistent refusal to consider concrete poetry beyond an idea of shaped poetry with a visual emphasis. A recognition of how conceptual art overlaps with concrete poetry need not equate the goals of one with the other but could go a long way toward opening a discourse around how and to what end different disciplines implement similar techniques.

Apart from Graham's *Schema*, which is about as material as conceptual art's engagement with language ever gets, conceptual artists used language primarily to critique and subvert the institution of art, specifically the role of the critic and all of his or her apparatuses. Charles Harrison accounts for this antipathy by describing the two voices of post – World War II art production:

the creative and the critical. He argues that the creative voice, which championed the genius of the individual artist and the transformative power of art experiences, dominated the years between the end of the war and the mid-sixties, when conceptual art began to increase the volume of the second, critical voice:

> Conceptual Art worthy of the name was only provisionally and trivially an art without "art objects." More significantly it was an art which was not to be *beheld*, which was not visible – or even conceivable – in any mode which the "adequately sensitive, adequately informed, spectator" was competent to regulate. The initial task was not to invent a form of high art without objects – logically speaking, an absurd enough idea – but rather to evade in practice those predicates which the beholder was wont to attach to the objects of his attention. (50)

This attack on the critic was championed by Kosuth, as well, who wrote in his statement for the 1970 exhibition *Information* that "an artist's dependence on the critic or writer on art to cultivate the conceptual implications of his art propositions, and argue their explication, is either intellectual irresponsibility or the naivest kind of mysticism" ("Statement" 73–4). The beholder was then to be transformed by the exposure of the structures of art production into a reader, a figure who was an active participant in the production of a text's meaning. That concrete poetry emphasized simultaneity and speed of comprehension should not, however, be read as a converse move away from a reader and towards the literary equivalent of the beholder. Such a relationship takes too literally the visual metaphors of both positions. Rather, it is the subversion of the authorial voice in both conceptual art and concrete poetry that ties the projects together. As Barthes argues:

> Once the Author is gone, the claim to "decipher" a text becomes quite useless. To give an Author to a text is to impose upon that text a stop clause, to furnish it with a final signification, to close the writing. This conception perfectly suits criticism, which can then take as its major task the discovery of the Author (or his hypostases: society, history, the psyche, freedom) beneath the work: once the Author is discovered, the text is "explained:" the critic has conquered; hence it is scarcely surprising not only that, historically, the reign of the Author should also have been that of the Critic, but

that criticism (even "new criticism") should be overthrown along with the Author.

Graham's work seems to do a better job of eliminating the author than Andre's poetic work. *Schema* was a model of reproduction, fitting into LeWitt's formulation of conceptual art ideas as machines that makes art. It was even translated for publication in the German periodical *Interfunktionen* in 1972, an event that recognizes its fidelity to language over the composing subject. Andre's work, in spite of its disconnect between the words and the composition of the poem, maintained their original language source, and in doing so retained the character of the conditions of their production. The fact that Andre's "First Five Poems" would always be "green / five / horn / eye / sound," and never "vert / cinq / corne / oeil / son" speaks less about the poem than it does about the poet and his historical and geographic position. Andre's response to Frampton's question about the viability of his poetry, that "not even the method is mine but belongs to anybody who uses it," is not really true: the method belongs to Andre and his group. Certainly no poet other than Andre could ever hope to be published if her/his work simply chose random words and repeated them without any investigation of their visual or semantic structure. The method belongs to Andre in the same way that Tristan Tzara's "How to Write a Poem," which is a set of instructions for cutting up a newspaper article and pulling words and phrases out at random, belongs to Dada. The ignorance of the site of his method is a privilege that comes with the time and space: again, the conceptual artists' retreat into structural linguistics and linguistic positivism are an effect of their position in the Anglo-American political alliance. Austere philosophical investigations were not likely to be received as well in South America, for example. Andre explains:

> The poetry I am trying to write is poetry which eliminates the poet, or at least makes the poet transparent in relation to the light cast upon the object ... What I want to illuminate in my poetry are not those things which only I can see, but those things which any man can see. I am interested in those poems which you can go back to Manhattan and duplicate. (Andre and Frampton 79)

The significant term in this passage, like his unconscious emphasis on "English" in the passage cited earlier when discussing language as material, is "Manhattan." It is an economic as much as a formal issue that he does not express the same position towards his sculpture, despite describing both practices as attempting to perform similar functions with different materials.

Performing the Page

The poetic work of Vito Acconci, like Andre's, maintains a geographical subjectivity as well, although Acconci never adopts the anti-author position to the same extent as Andre or Graham. Acconci was trained as a poet, returning to New York from the Iowa Writers' Workshop in 1964. This background suggests that he would be cognizant of the American contemporary poetry scene, from the New York School to Black Mountain poetics. His emphasis on the space of the page owes much to this tradition, specifically the work of Charles Olson, whose emphasis on the writing of place is fully evident not only in his theoretical writings but also in his epic work *The Maximus Poems*. Acconci's fondness for the typewriter – almost all of his poems appear as typewritten – can also be traced back to Olson, like Andre's. The typewriter is used for its regularity and its disinterestedness, not for any type of compositional agency in the way the concrete poets would have used it; the page is always upright, the margins always set. But the performative aspect of the work is where Acconci departs. Whereas Olson used the typewriter as a tool for scoring the performance of a poem, Acconci records a performance, using the typewriter as a machine to document his performances as poetry. His poem "Page/Pages: Reading the First Page of the *New York Times*, Saturday June 21, 1969," for example, is simply a record of the phrases he comes across at thirty second increments, recorded alongside the page and column of the newspaper where they were found (see fig. 4.5). Craig Dworkin describes Acconci's poetry as "working with the movement of language over the self-enclosed performance space of the printed page" ("Introduction" xi).

But the performance space is not one devoted to the performance of language as much as it is to the figure of the poet. Thus it is less concerned with the appearance of language and its materiality than it is with the disruption of syntax and notation. Dworkin cites a rejection letter written by Acconci for a work submitted to the journal *o to 9*, which he edited with Bernadette Mayer from April 1967 to July 1969: "Not the kind of thing o to 9 is out for; for me, there's too much emphasis on message here, not enough on the space of the page" (quoted in Dworkin xviin6). Here is a document attesting to Acconci's interest in the page as a compositional unit, like that of the concrete

PAGE/PAGES: READING THE FIRST PAGE OF *THE NEW YORK TIMES*,
SATURDAY, JUNE 21, 1969

.30 seconds: and a higher surtax (page 1, column 1)

.1 minute: to settle the war (page 1, column 1)

.1 minute, 30 seconds: total self-confidence (page 37, column 4)

.2 minutes: a bigger setback (page 37, column 4)

.2 minutes, 30 seconds: if things got (page 37, column 5)

.3 minutes: that the politician (page 37, column 5)

.3 minutes, 30 seconds: when Harry S. Truman (page 37, column 6)

.4 minutes: on his experience (page 37, column 6)

.4 minutes, 30 seconds: more and more serious (page 37, ad, columns 7 and 8)

.5 minutes: plus all the other (page 37, ad, columns 7 and eight)

.5 minutes, 30 seconds: send book only (page 37, ad, columns 7 and 8)

.6 minutes: expects to split? (page 37, ad, columns 7 and eight)

.6 minutes, 30 seconds: is becoming a private (page 1, column 1)

.7 minutes: in his first five months (page 1, column 1)

.7 minutes, 30 seconds: along the fairway (page 1, column 1)

.8 minutes: sitting in Texas (page 10, column 4)

.8 minutes, 30 seconds: that he would go (page 10, column 4)

.9 minutes: to try to (page 10, column 6)

.9 minutes, 30 seconds: Johnson School (page 10, column 6)

.10 minutes: Democratic national committee (page 10, column 7)

.10 minutes, 30 seconds: But this best-spent time (page 10, column 7)

.11 minutes: in beautiful interior designs (page 10, ad, columns 1 and 2)

.11 minutes, 30 seconds: Imported from Lisbon (page 10, ad, columns 1 and 2)

.12 minutes: Contract Division (page 10, column 5)

.12 minutes, 30 seconds: by 160,727 to (page 1, column 2)

.13 minutes: to wait for the official (page 12, column 3)

.13 minutes, 30 seconds: may have won this (page 12, column 4)

.14 minutes: sent 25 volunteer (page 12, column 5)

.14 minutes, 30 seconds: become a judge (page 12, column 5)

.15 minutes: that his defeat in (page 12, column 6)

.15 minutes, 30 seconds: "Primaries always leave (page 12, column 6)

.16 minutes: isn't going to enter (page 12, column 6)

.16 minutes, 30 seconds: a term expiring (page 12, column 6)

.17 minutes: repeating the libel (page 12, column 3)

.17 minutes, 30 seconds: Throughout N.Y. State (page 12, ad, columns 5 and 6)

.18 minutes: direct from our factory (page 12, ad, columns 1 and 2)

Figure 4.5

**Vito Acconci. "Page/Pages: Reading the First Page of the *New York Times*,
Saturday, June 21, 1969"**

poets or visual poetry going back to Mallarmé, but one that results in a radically different type of poetry. At this point, in the late sixties, Acconci was already moving toward the medium of performance, for which he is better known. In an interview in 1993, he explained his reasoning:

> It started to *seem* impossible to use on the page a word like "tree,"
> a word like "chair," because this referred to another space, a space
> off the page. Whereas I *could* use words like "there," "then," "at that
> time," ... words that referred to my activity on the page, my act of
> writing on the page. So, in fact, toward the end of the time I was
> writing, I was driving myself into a corner, into a kind of dead end,
> when in order to preserve the literalness of the page the only thing
> I could use on the page were commas, periods, punctuation points.
> (quoted in Kotz 156)

The limitations he outlines are not limitations of language to function as itself, but of language to function as a representation of Acconci, the artist-author – of his desires and movements, of his position in space. The page had become a unit of containment too restrictive for the artist's subjectivity; he wanted it to function as film would, or video, or magnetic audio tape, but language failed to record accurately or disinterestedly enough. His work would eventually become descriptions of performances, which would then be documented by photographs or video. The final issue of *o to 9* would testify to Acconci's shift away from poetry, including as a supplement a series of Street Works, propositions for or descriptions of performances by artists and poets such as Adrian Piper, Hannah Weiner, and John Perreault, among others, including Acconci.[15]

Marketing Language

Although Acconci and Mayer published writings by international authors, the journal was very much a New York publication. In this way the poetry mimics the larger tendency of early conceptual art, with considerations of the international primarily located in its pursuit of a market. For Benjamin Buchloh, the evacuation of the authorial voice from conceptual art, along with all remnants of a transcendent aesthetic experience, was a formal reaction to the "operating logic of late capitalism," manifested in a "rigorous and relentless order of the vernacular of administration" (143; 142). In this way, the satisfaction that Lucy Lippard feels in being able to contain and transport an entire exhibition in a manila envelope becomes caught up in the shift from the heavy infrastructure of modernist art production – gallery spaces, museums, art movers and shipping companies – to the slick, portable infrastructure of the knowledge economy, and the Xerox reproductions and electronic communication that came with it.

Alexander Alberro takes Buchloh's position further by proposing that the work of the conceptualists was less a reaction to than an adoption of that logic. Unlike Kotz, Alberro justifies his decision to focus his study *Conceptual Art and the Politics of Publicity* primarily on work coming out of New York City by arguing that not only the form of the work but also its distribution was determined by the economic position of New York at the time. It is through Alberro that an explanation of the formal decisions of Anglo-American conceptual art might be developed in parallel with concrete poetry's concern with a global shift in communication and consumption, and of why, perhaps, the artists were more reluctant than the poets to frame it as such.

Alberro identifies gallery owner and curator Seth Siegelaub as a major figure in the success of conceptual art, and the list of artists that Siegelaub represented confirms it: Carl Andre, Joseph Kosuth, Lawrence Weiner, Robert Barry, Sol LeWitt, and Douglas Huebler are just some of the artists who would go on to become the dominant representatives of the movement. Siegelaub was twenty-three years old, one year younger than Dan Graham, when he opened up his gallery on Fifty-Sixth Street in New York, eight blocks south of Graham's. Seth Siegelaub Contemporary Art, which also sold oriental rugs and had couches to encourage potential purchasers to experience the gallery as an art environment, would last a year longer than Graham's John Daniels Gallery, but in 1966 the gallery did not close so much as it evolved. Siegelaub moved his operation to a two-bedroom apartment near Madison Avenue, the center of the booming advertising industry, and from this location began to function as a gallerist at large, claiming, "you don't need a gallery to show ideas" (Siegelaub 38).

It was Siegelaub more than any of the artists he represented who transformed the language surrounding art, and he did so in a manner that, like the concrete poets, took advantage of material shifts in communication in order to expand the reach of his message. If the concrete poets addressed the appearance of language as it is designed in advertising in an attempt to hijack or *détourne* its style towards a poetic end, Siegelaub adopted the language of public relations and corporate press releases towards a commercial end: selling the work of the artists to an expanding market of newly affluent Americans. In a pamphlet he drafted for the art consultation company Image, which he founded along with Jack Wendler, a wealthy businessman and collector, Siegelaub writes:

> Fine Art? Why should we get involved with art? ... Because Fine Art is good business. The contemporary corporation has much to gain from the identification with the positive virtues the Arts possess ...

> Specifically, an identification with the Arts will do the following: a. Improve the image of your company by making your public more aware of what you are doing in the community. b. Assist in developing a more fully rounded personality for your corporation by adding a Cultural dimension. c. Provide a bold, unique and exciting element in the presentation of your products and services. d. Promote greater public acceptance of your corporation and its products and services by making yourself more attractive and visible in the marketplace. (quoted in Alberro, *Conceptual Art* 14)

The transformation of language is not material here, but generic. The gallerist-curator becomes the publicist, the entrepreneur who unashamedly fuses the world of commerce and high art in a manner as radical as the conceptual artists' rejection of the critic as middleman.

Though Joseph Kosuth was never as explicit about his entrepreneurial spirit as Siegelaub, Alberro makes a case for his being every bit as strategic, noting that he operated as his own public relations representative by ensuring that he could always be "found at the 'right' places, speaking to the right people," and accumulating the cultural capital that would attract investors (*Conceptual Art* 26).

It is perhaps against this spectacularization of the artist as commercial rather than social figure that Sarenco, the Italian visual poet, critic, and publisher, launched a serial attack on conceptual art in his journal *Lotta Poetica* at the beginning of the seventies. In several articles printed between 1971 and 1972, all titled "Poesia visiva e conceptual art / un plagio ben organizzato" (Visual Poetry and Conceptual Art / A Well-Organized Plagiarism), he attacked language-based conceptual work produced by figures like Kosuth, Andre (in his poetry), and Richard Artschwager. Sarenco largely avoids examples of their work, however, instead opting to disqualify the entire conceptual art movement as derivative and socially corrupt. Support for his position came from Paul de Vree, the Belgian concrete and sound poet, who wrote the opening article of *Lotta Poetica*'s first issue, in which he laments the proliferation of individualistic, conformist poets at a time of increased mechanization of society. The French concrete poet Jean-Francois Bory provides a note of thanks to Sarenco's exposé in *Lotta Poetica* 3, claiming: "i hope you will go on in this way because all the conceptual artists have, in fact, copied from the visual poetry and i saw things directly stolen in my books by linde burkhardt (germany), cordioli (italy) and many others. the list would be too long to enumerate it here" (quoted in Sarenco, "Poesia," *Lotta Poetica* 3: 12). And Dick Higgins, the American poet, visual poetry historian, and proprietor of Something Else Press, which published Emmett Williams's *Anthology of Concrete Poetry* in 1967, wrote a supportive letter in 1972, taking the view that Harry Flynt's original formulation of "concept art" lacked the "sick brouhaha of fashionable, marketable 'concept art.' [...] But it makes it crystal clear, since it's where the term originates, that the 'newness' of 'concept art' is artificial" (Higgins n. pag.).

All of these positions are polemical and lack any engagement with specific conceptual pieces or their artistic functions. But they are useful in understanding how much attention conceptual art received from the international art market at its peak. In one article Sarenco takes aim at Giancarlo Politi, the publisher and editor of *Flash Art*, for refusing to recognize the lineage of linguistic conceptual art in the history of concrete and visual poetry – a concession that might devalue the work as *innovative*, in the entrepreneurial sense – and hits upon a material reality that helps explain the reason why concrete poetry is at a disadvantage in a historical dialogue: "the reason why politi backs up the conceptualists with drawn sword is fairly obvious: his review is entirely paid by the galleries art [sic] whose 'stables' are composed by 'conceptualist race horses'; [*Flash Art*] is not an information periodical but a publicity magazine from the first to the last page" (*Lotta Poetica* 9: 12; lower case in the original). Despite concrete and visual poetry's emphasis on keeping up with technology, and on maintaining pace with a rapidly changing society, they never adopted the language of capital in the same way as conceptual art, and continue to suffer the discursive ramifications.

Without initially referring to Kosuth by name, Sarenco does point to his series of photostat dictionary definitions:

> the conceptual artist reproduces [a definition] as is, making it
> bigger, [...] its linguistic abstractionism, that is revalueing [sic] it as
> an apex of the splendour of the bourgeois intellectualism. the poet is
> not satisfied to [...] ascertain how a dictionaru [sic] definition is well

made: he wants to know whom and what there is behind it, who
commands behind that language, what class situation it represents.
(*Lotta Poetica* 7: 16; lower case in original)

Because Sarenco's language comes out of the radical Italian poetic avant-
garde, his position is foreign to many of the concrete poets who came before
him, who were less interested in the class criticism than they were in the
material conditions of language (see fig. 4.6). Although Eugen Gomringer,
Henri Chopin, and the Noigandres Group were all concerned with politics
on some level, and with the politics of the left, specifically, none of them can
be placed on the same footing as the Italian visual poets, who saw their work
functioning alongside social revolution. But Sarenco's critique of the politics
of conceptual art is significant, and one that mirrors the kind of dismissal
that visual art and its critics have adopted toward concrete poetry: that it is
disengaged, simply a formal exercise, that it is depoliticized.

As it turns out, both positions are wrong, and they are both right. While
Kosuth's definitions are not as politically engaged as Sarenco's poems, or
as the Brazilian concrete poems that deal with American imperialism or
developmentalist economic policies, Anglo-American conceptual art's radical questioning of the structure of art production, specifically what a gallery
can be and the role of the critic, did result in work that engaged directly
with issues of class, gender, and imperialism in the seventies, particularly in
the work of artists like Hans Haacke and Martha Rosler. A South American
conceptual artist such as Cildo Meireles might be a better precursor for the
work of Haacke and Rosler, but it was the highly publicized, market-shifting
artists including those represented by Siegelaub who created the spaces and
critical infrastructure for the acceptance of their work. That same infrastructure, however, maintained and protected the dominant narrative of conceptual art as a language-based, Anglo-American phenomenon at the expense
of work from different, peripheral disciplines and terrain. But the impulse in
Kosuth and Art & Language to make art more of a philosophical exercise, to
be circulated and understood by artists alone, is in direct opposition to concrete poetry's project, whose practitioners sought to expand the circuits of
reception for their poetry through the development of a method that would
compete for attention in a world where the *viewer* was beginning to take the
place of the *reader*. The idea of the *international*, for conceptual art, was not
of a global audience, as it was for the concrete poets, but of a global market-
place, and recognizing that difference moves critical readers from both literary studies and art history toward a new space of understanding.

Figure 4.6

Sarenco. "Poetical Licence"

5/

INFORMATION IN FORM: "THE TENSION OF THINGS-WORDS IN SPACE-TIME"

Spaces of Concrete

In 1955, the Swiss artist and poet Andre Thomkins began collecting words that carried meaning in two or more of the German, French, and English languages. A member of the Darmstadt Circle of experimental poets and artists, a group that included the American Emmett Williams, the Icelandic Dieter Roth, the German Claus Bremer, and the Romanian Daniel Spoerri, Thomkins was used to operating in a polylinguistic environment. Much in the same way that Augusto de Campos, in his "City Poem" (1963; see fig. 3.5), took up the Latin roots shared by words in English, French, and Portuguese that can be completed with the suffixes "city / cidade / and cité," Thomkins implemented the list as form, and used words that infiltrate and occupy different national languages, though with different pronunciations and meanings, as a way to address both the impediments and opportunities created by an increasingly connected international cultural sphere. The poem appears in Williams's anthology as a simple list of words, six per line, but Williams's gloss describes a different form: "'Dogmat-Mot' is a mobile composition of 120 words arranged on mobile discs which present the reader with ever-changing phrases" (n. pag.). The poem-as-object, a triangular arrangement of ten hexagons with words printed around their edges and trisectionally, all of which hinge on a central pivot, allows readers to operate the poem as program, and to speak and read "several languages simultaneously – with all the attendant ambiguities" (Williams n. pag.) (see fig. 5.1).

Thomkins's poem-object is evidence that the combinatorial and permutational approach to language as material that operates across borders was a concern of concrete poetry from its earliest days. I have already pointed to similar concerns in the work of Haroldo and Augusto de Campos as well as that of Eugen Gomringer and Josef Hiršal and Bohumila Grögerová. In relating concrete poetry to its historical position within the emergence of a technologically produced global imaginary, I have connected permutational and polylinguistic compositions to the feelings, both optimistic and anxious, stemming from the mechanical approach to language, specifically how it developed out of Alan Turing and other mathematicians' code-breaking efforts during WWII. What is especially interesting about Thomkin's poem-object, then, is less the poetry of it than its objectness. Williams says that it was "published" by Galerie der Spiegel in Cologne in 1965, but is *published* the correct term? The poem is not on a page, or at least a page as it is conventionally understood. Nor is it a book, though an argument could be made that the structure contains the potential for various poetic permutations, and is therefore more like a book than a page. Should it be framed? Should it be shelved?

The lesson I want to draw from Thomkins's piece, to which I will return later, is that concrete poetry operates within a space that is particularly difficult to locate. Its poetic form is inextricable from its distributive form, and its method of circulation is by no means homogenous: it manifests as sculpture, as painting, as poster; as handwritten, mechanical, or photo-printed; on pages of mass-printed editions and small-press books, folios, and ephemera. It is certainly true that previous poetic movements, specifically the historical avant-gardes, also challenged standard disciplinary categories, but not to the extent of concrete poetry. The Dada poets were close associates of the Dada painters, but the poetry of Hugo Ball, Tristan Tzara, and Kurt Schwitters was designed to function on a page or a stage. The Futurists' words were liberated from the line but not the page, even if that page was not always a standard size. The Surrealists, as well, though experimental with images and

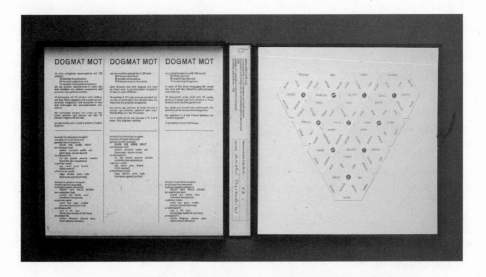

Figure 5.1

Andre Thomkins. "Dogmat Mot"

psychology, were less so with form. Isidore Isou's Lettristes might come closer to concrete poetry's elusive distributive form, as they branch into painting and film, but the Lettriste movement was not a poetic movement as much as it was a self-consciously avant-garde project. The concrete poets, however – perhaps because their experience of space in the second half of the twentieth century had shifted so far from that of the poets and artists of the first – slide between the gallery and the book, the poster and the page, the mass-printed anthology and the fine-art press edition. The tension between the word and the image, and the possibilities for distribution that each historically adopts, is part of what has kept concrete poetry out of dominant cultural discourse for so long, but is also a large part of what makes it so significant as a twentieth-century poetic experiment. By looking specifically at the shift within the work from an aesthetics of production to one of distribution and reception, I argue that it enacts an understanding of space that has implications for poetry, visual art, and culture on a global scale within its period and beyond.

Concrete poetry's dispersed geography, although paradoxically integral to its cohesion as an international movement, sometimes accentuates its incongruities and makes mapping the work difficult. The movement's chronological development is also an impediment; the period between 1955 and 1971 provides a convenient bracket, but it is a considerable span, and encompasses the transformation of the work from an early orthodoxy to a more experimental practice. The period and movement also occupies a precarious historical position on the hinge between modernism and post-modernism and as such demands to be read against the spatial characteristics of both.

Traditionally, approaching the concept of space within literature evokes Gotthold Ephraim Lessing's *Laocoön*, the eighteenth-century essay which attempts to outline the formal imperatives of literary and visual representation. Literature, Lessing argues, operates temporally, through narrative. The plastic arts operate spatially, as there is no order in visual representation: foreground and background function in simultaneous relation to each other. It is with reference to this text that the literary critic Joseph Frank opens his 1945 essay "Spatial Form in Modern Literature," which deals with how modernist writers attempted to refute Lessing's criteria by forcing their readers to experience texts outside of the temporality of narrative. Frank deals with the major modernist authors – James Joyce, Virginia Woolf, Marcel Proust, Gustav Flaubert, Ezra Pound – and outlines how their practice of shifting narration and disjointed syntax attempted to spatialize literature, disrupting the idea of a narrative linearity. He positions the techniques and concerns of the Imagists in opposition to the verbiage of the Victorian era, and locates a possible explanation for such a shift in the work of the early twentieth-century German critic Wilhelm Worringer, who theorized that the spiritual stability of an era can be determined by the degree to which its cultural production adheres to naturalistic representation. Worringer's argument, although reductive, posits that naturalistic representation, particularly in the plastic arts, arises from cultures that have a harmonized relationship with the cosmos, and thus delight in representing the order they find themselves in. Example periods cited are ancient Greece, the Italian Renaissance, and Western Europe at the end of the eighteenth century. Non-naturalistic representation, conversely, springs from cultures with a confused relationship to the cosmos, and who thus delight in the transformation of nature into lines and planes; simplified, if not scientific, representation allows them an escape from the external world. Examples of art from these perturbed periods are Egyptian monumental sculpture, Byzantine art, and most of the work produced during the twentieth century. Naturalistic style is characterized by perspective and depth; non-naturalistic style is characterized by shifting vantage points and surface (Frank 71). Geoffrey Cook makes a similar point when he argues that examples of visual poetry throughout history seem to arrive on the cusp of an episteme (141).

Frank cites Pound's *Cantos* to argue his point about the obliteration of the conventional idea of time-space, as the work juxtaposes ancient, Renaissance, and modern references in no discernible progressive order. Languages – Greek, French, Italian, and Chinese – appear beside each other in a collapsing of geography and tradition. This technique is a disruption of the literary analogue of Renaissance perspective, as is the work of Woolf, in a text like *To the Lighthouse*, or Joyce, in a text like *Ulysses*. The unfolding of a narrative does not, in these works, follow an order that allows for the comfortable positioning of a reader:

> Past and present are apprehended spatially, locked in a timeless
> unity that, while it may accentuate surface differences, eliminates
> any feeling of sequence by the very act of juxtaposition. Ever since
> the Renaissance, modern man has cultivated both the objective
> visual imagination (the ability to portray space) and the objective
> historical imagination (the ability to apprehend chronological time);
> both have now been abandoned. (76)

Modern literature aims for a space of simultaneity rather than one of causal progression, what Marshall McLuhan has argued is an acoustic space rather than a visual space (see, in particular, *Verbi-Voco Visual Explorations*; 1967). In a footnote at the end of his essay, Frank notes that some critics' objections to his argument insist, in lockstep with Lessing, on the time-based nature of literature. Frank responds: "I could not agree more. But this has not stopped modern writers from working out techniques to achieve the impossible – as much as possible" (76).

Concrete poetry's space complicates Frank's space. Its resistance to standard ideas of poetry and the book position it somewhere beyond modernism – in spite of the explicitly stated influence of writers such as Ezra Pound, James Joyce and Guillaume Apollinaire – functioning within what Rosalind Krauss might refer to as an "expanded field" of poetry. But examining concrete poetry in light of Frank's understanding of how space functions in literature allows us to situate the work historically. If non-naturalistic representation is a sign of a confused relationship to the cosmos, it is easy to identify in a literature that departs so drastically from conventional form the anxiety that came in the wake of the nuclear bomb and cold war posturing. On a different level, the degree to which the disruption of the literary analog of Renaissance perspective – the poetic line, and to a lesser extent, the page – appears in concrete poetry to be beyond the most radical time-space experiments of Pound's *Cantos*. The Austrian concrete poet Gerhard Rühm's 1958 placard poem "Jetzt" is an example of a poem that deals explicitly with both visual and literary perspective, and of the connection between time and space that Lessing's *Laocoön* attempts to treat programmatically (see fig. 5.2). The poem presents the word "jetzt," which is German for *now*, in various different font sizes and typefaces, some beginning with an uppercase *J*, some with a lowercase, some with serifs, some without. The idea of a stable present is confounded by the spatial understanding of *now* as a fleeting, shifting time index, one that contradicts itself as soon as it signifies: *now*, once read, becomes *then*, in a constant coming into being and passing away that the layout of the poem encourages. As such it evokes the experience of simultaneity in a more effective manner than Pound or his contemporaries, although in this case with a more explicitly temporal reference.

Like the blank middle in Gomringer's "silencio," which performs the silence that the presentation of the word destroys, the blank space in Rühm's poem enacts the *now* that the repetition of "jetzt" annihilates. Making use of both the idea of perspective, in the larger words occupying the foreground and the smaller words the background, as well as the idea of font size

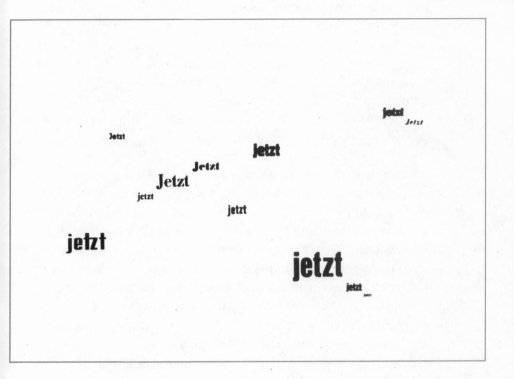

Figure 5.2

Gerhard Rühm. "Jetzt"

corresponding to volume, a strategy implemented by the poetic and graphic avant-gardes of the early twentieth century, the poem refuses to provide the reader/viewer with a fixed position in the way that a conventional poetic line would, or a photograph or perspectival painting would: no representation of "jetzt" could be any more *now*, or *present*, to use a pun, than any of the other representations. Depending on how the reader imagines the movement of the poem, the larger words can either be closer to the present – a less stale now – or further from it, if it seems like the text grows from the smaller text, rather than vice versa. Both of these readings suggest progressive movement, rather than a simultaneity of nows, just in different intensities, producing alternative and equally fruitful readings. How can some nows be of more importance, or of different characters than others? And what is the blank space out of which the nows emerge? In an age of globalization and uneven development, and for what I have previously referred to as the poetry of the Marshall Plan, the answer seems to be that there are places that are now and places that are then. In the commercialization of culture as well as the tyranny of progression in modernization, trends that meet intensely in the postwar period of affluence and reconstruction, the emphasis on now, in whatever language, carries within it a political character that would not have been there had this been a Futurist or Dadaist poem.

The various typefaces in Rühm's poem position it within a culture of the increased visualization of language, particularly in relation to advertising. Language in advertising was no longer meant to function transparently, but to communicate a disruption of standardized lines and representation. Stephen Bann makes this clear when he says: "Concrete poetry thematizes the operation of language in general, the way it affects us, and the way we communicate with it. Concrete poetry thus operates in a way that is comparable to how advertising works, utilizing the various types of graphic signals that we react to in everyday life" (Schaffner n. pag.). Words referred to themselves, in an attempt to stand on their own, creating a new poetics that was put to great use by developers of *brands*. In this sense the term "jetzt" gains greater meaning by parodying the consumerist desire to be up to date – the modernist "make it new" comes to ground in post-WWII consumer culture as "buy it new." The dizzying assault of the various "jetzt"s performs the anxiety of the consumer, to whom history simply means out of style.

The drastically altered mediascape that arose at mid-century alongside electronic media is what led Marshall McLuhan to theorize the experience of space as acoustic rather than visual. As the media critic Richard Cavell puts it:

"To combine a notion of space as socially produced with an inquiry into the technologies of spatial production is to work towards a social theory of the production of space. McLuhan sought to examine not only how society produces space but also how technologies of space produce society" (Cavell 30). People live on Earth but in different worlds. How are those worlds produced? McLuhan's position is that the technology of the book since Gutenberg, and the rise in literacy the printing press allowed for, has emphasized a visual understanding of space, as ordered and linear. With the development of electronic media, however, ideas of spatial order are destabilized, resulting in a collapsing of time and space.[1] Voices become disembodied via telephony and sound recording; bodies become disarticulated by photography and film. Renaissance perspective and the printed page are replaced by a media environment that demands a new proprioception.

While it might seem counterintuitive to apply the term "acoustic" to visual poetry, it becomes appropriate when referring to the understanding of space on which the work relies. McLuhan's work was known and engaged with by various concrete poets. Décio Pignatari, significantly, translated McLuhan's *Understanding Media: The Extensions of Man* (1964) into Portuguese in 1969.[2] The Noigandres group's embrace of McLuhan should not come as a surprise, as their own project was also concerned with the transformation of *space* at mid-century. The "Plano-Piloto" [1958] refers to this new spatial understanding:

> concrete Poetry: product of a critical evolution of forms. assuming that the historical cycle of verse (as formal-rhythmical unit) is closed, concrete poetry begins by being aware of graphic space as structural agent. [...]
>
> concrete poetry: tension of things-words in space-time.
>
> dynamic structure: multiplicity of concomitant movements.
> (de Campos, de Campos, and Pignatari 90)

The "Plano-Piloto" outlines a development of space beyond that of the line of verse and emphasizes ideas of movement and simultaneity in place of fixed perspective and progressive, causal relationships. Rühm's "Jetzt," also written in 1958, shares a similar excitement and suspicion of the new spaces, and how they are to be implemented and felt.

The emphasis on space, and its transformation from the rigid and ordered to the floating and fluid, comes out in the cultural criticism that engaged with shifts in both production and consumption that overlapped the most active period of concrete poetry. And although it might at this point in time seem out-dated, a discussion of how postmodern approaches to culture account for compositional shifts and conditions of circulation in concrete poetry opens up a range of illuminating questions, largely due to concrete poetry's historical position at the height and then cusp of modernism. The poets worked in a moment characterized by post-colonial uprisings, massive national reconstruction projects, the rise of the superpowers, and the initiation of the cold war. All of these factors influenced culture on a global scale, and help us understand postmodernism less as a style of literary or art production than a dominant mode of culture. Such an approach pre-empts any protest that the techniques we might identify as characteristic of postmodern cultural production – such as the use of popular culture in high art contexts, or the fragmentation of the subject – have already been put to extensive use by modernist writers and painters; this is the type of protest that usually results in the separation of the work from its historical contingencies. A similar reasoning might be offered in response to those who claim concrete poetry is as old as the first written symbol, or that it remains a viable poetic category for contemporary poets. These positions, as I argue in my introductory chapter, serve to elucidate a literary style, but impede a greater understanding of the movement's reasons for coming into being, or for its expiration.

As Fredric Jameson points out in his early essay "Postmodernism, or The Cultural Logic of Late Capitalism," in the section dealing with his theories of cognitive mapping, humans' perception of the world changes over time, and those changes have material effects on culture and the organization of living. It is a point that might seem obvious, especially for a historical dialectician, but Jameson makes an effort to shift attention away from the temporal and toward the spatial, performing a critique Marshall McLuhan had spent much of the 1960s and '70s enacting extensively in his theories and book work. Jameson uses developments in cartography – from maps of coastlines to larger regions, to the globe in its entirety, and then to the representation of curved lines on a flat map – as examples of technological advances that shift the way people relate to their spaces, or "how technologies of space produce society" (Cavell 30). The time period Jameson identifies as the emergence of postmodernism is marked not only by a rapid increase in communication, but also by a new visual representation of the globe in the form of photographs from outer space. This visualization has the double effect, as I argue in chapter 3, of drastically altering the human scale so integral to the modernist imagination, while developing a new understanding of the Earth's geography.

If modernism as a cultural dominant was marked by a consideration of time, specifically the march toward some better, mechanized future, postmodernism is defined by space. Grand narratives become grand spectacles; the synchronic overtakes the diachronic. Jameson's primary metaphor for the postmodern space is the Bonaventure Hotel in downtown Los Angeles, and he foregrounds his inability to critique the structure in the lexicon with which he is accustomed to speaking about architecture: volume, line, order, etc. What he speaks about instead is a deracination of the hotel visitors' spatial understanding, how they become disoriented and confused within the interior, and are unable to see into the building from the exterior thanks to its reflective glass surface. Jameson's understanding of the influence of postmodernism on culture comes out of his observation of architecture, a form that he argues is more than any other cultural sector tied to the economical shifts from the realm of the nation and its industries to the accelerated wealth production of multinational corporations within finance capital. He points to the headquarters of multinational corporations, whose architectural style, though hardly homogenous, carries the residue of their moment better than other media, and it is these buildings' aesthetic opposition to modernist styles that Jameson reads onto other cultural artefacts: the rise of photography as a fine art medium, for example, or the linguistic disjunction found in language poetry representing the breaking down of a unified subject position (Jameson 63–4). A similar experience of deracination and frustration of disciplinary tools of analysis greets the literary critic in her/his encounter with concrete poetry. Ideas of language are imploded; there is no standard measure of meter, form, or syntax. Imagery becomes image, literally. The modernist subject disappears, and national and linguistic borders become blurred.

David Harvey, in his book *The Condition of Postmodernity*, continues Jameson's trajectory but emphasizes how both the economic and cultural sectors contribute to a particular historical understanding of the world. He recognizes how space and place can often become confused, and sympathizes with those critics who resisted postmodernism's global perspective in favour of local conditions of production and the urgency that those conditions often call out for. But he warns against positioning it in opposition to the new modes of post-Fordist capitalism: "The assertion of any place-bound

Figure 5.3

Décio Pignatari. "Cr$isto é a solução"

identity has to rest at some point on the motivational power of tradition. It is difficult, however, to maintain any sense of historical continuity in the face of all the flux and ephemerality of flexible accumulation" (303). He offers a similar refutation of other critics' emphasis on cultural representations of postmodernism by warning against the fusion of aesthetic and social understanding of space, noting that it is not just in architecture that we can identify the effects of new forms of global capital in the very transformation of urban infrastructure to attract investment, and that postmodernist space also produces geographies of uneven development.[3]

A characteristic of postmodern cultural production that also seemed to irritate those with a modernist sensibility is the presence of a populism where a rigorous aesthetic order once ruled. In architecture, Jameson notes that the buildings take on a form that is meant to impress and entertain rather than shape and motivate. The postmodern architects, he argues in agreement with Denise Scott Brown, Robert Venturi, and Steven Izenour, did in fact learn from Las Vegas. The paradigm of the architect/artist as genius is replaced by the market as genius; the idea of history as linear and progressivist is refuted. Similarly, in concrete poetry there is a tension between the popular and austere styles that makes it difficult to position as either modern or postmodern; it is much better approached as both. There is a general trend in the Brazilians' work, at least, that moves from clean, ordered works that approach the popular by using the poster form, or by referring to consumer goods, like Décio Pignatari's "Bebá Coca Cola" or "LIFE," towards poems that implement photographic printing techniques or more illustrative methods, utilizing structures beyond the semantic possibilities of verbal language.

Examples of the latter type of poem are Augusto de Campos's "Olho Por Olho" (1964) and Pignatari's "Cr$isto é a solução" (1966; see figs. 2.12 and 5.3). Pignatari's poem, which folded out to 16" x 6.5" from *Invenção* No. 5, whose dimensions were much greater than the dollar bill it references at 10" x 7," ties the fervour of the market to that of religion in a very stark way, replacing the portrait of George Washington on the American one-dollar bill with that of a heavenward gazing Christ, wearing a crown of thorns. Printed on the back is the phrase "Cr$isto é a solução" and a legend, in English, explaining that "cr$" is the abbreviation for the cruzeiro, the Brazilian currency, "isto" is Portuguese for *this*, and "é a solução" means *is the solution*. The meaning of the work is not difficult to access: the worship of the market, represented in the paired iconography of Christ and the American dollar, produces a power structure similar to that of the church, who for millennia have been comforting the poor and disenfranchised with assurances that God, or Christ, is the answer. The poem's message is not nuanced, but its boldness and transparent political message is an indicator of a particular cultural shift.

The relationship between poetry and advertising becomes even clearer at this point than it was in the early part of the movement, especially in the poet's use of photo-based printing techniques. Pignatari worked in the advertising sector, and has talked about how, at the same time he was writing concrete poems, he was creating word designs and acronyms for corporations and governmental departments. *LUBRAX*, for example, is a word he came up with for the Brazilian national oil corporation Petrobras, and that refers to a type of motor oil ("Entretien" 451). He also used concrete poetry methods to compose an advertisement for a pharmaceutical company's antidiarrheal medicine in which the phrase "PERTURBAÇÕES INTESTINAIS" (Digestive Troubles) is gradually squeezed together into a cohesive lump before being replaced by the encroaching brand name of the medicine, "DISENFÓRMIO" (1963) (see fig. 5.4). In an interview in 1992, Pignatari claims with some pride that he and fellow concrete poet Luis Angelo Pinto were the first poets to work in the advertising industry in Brazil ("Entretien" 451). It was not necessarily rare for graphic designers to produce concrete poetry: Marcel Wyss and Dieter Roth, Eugen Gomringer's collaborators on *Spirale*, a proto-concrete journal, were both trained and practising graphic designers, as were various Italian and Russian Futurists. However, the movement of a poet in the opposite direction speaks to the relationship concrete poetry wished to develop with the spectacle of contemporary global culture, even in its basest forms.[4] In this way the networks of communication and lines of transportation that information and commodity exchange travelled through became something concrete poets aimed to emulate, piggybacking on the expansive routes' capital.

It would be inaccurate to accuse concrete poetry of a cynicism or capitulation, especially given the history of the Brazilians' political work, but it would be just as irresponsible to believe that all reference to the lexicon of advertising is oppositional in the modernist tradition of the avant-garde. The poem "$ kill" (1969), by the British poet John Sharkey, is visual in the simplest terms, mimetic and obviously positioned against the American imperialist state and its wars in Indochina (see fig. 5.5). There is little else to see in "$ kill" than a reduced politics of protest that activists in growing antiwar and anti-imperial movements implemented with the same verve and strategies of corporate advertising. One could talk, perhaps, about the regularity of repeated words as lines of visual composition, especially the bold letters

PERTURBAÇÕES INTESTINAIS

N PERTURBAÇÕES INTESTINAIS F

EN PERTURBAÇÕES INTESTINAIS FÓ

SEN PERTURBAÇÕES INTESTINAIS FÓF

ISEN PERTURBAÇÕES INTESTINAIS FÓRI

DISEN PERTURBAÇÕES INTESTINAIS FÓRM

DISENFÓRMIO

Neomicina
Antibiótico de pequena absorção e de poderosa ação no combate aos diferentes agentes da infecção intestinal.
Ftalilsulfatiazol
Sulfa de baixa solubilidade e de grande ultilidade na redução da flora patogênica.
Sulfadiazina
Completa a terapêutica atingindo os focos de origem das infecções intestinais, bem como os bacilos disentéricos localizados profundamente na mucosa intestinal.
Pectina
Hidrato de carbono obtido de frutas cítricas de efeito antitóxico (diminue a obsorção de toxinas) e sintomático (atua como constipante).
Homatropina
Antiespasmódico eficaz nas manifestações dolorosas decorrentes das infecções intestinais.

Disenfórmio pediátrico
Neomicina 25 mg; Ftalilsulfatiazol 125 mg; Sulfadiazina 125 mg; Pectina 20 mg; Homatropina 0,1 mg; Veículo para 5 cm³.

Disenfórmio comprimidos
Neomicina 50 mg; Ftalilsulfatiazol 250 mg; Sulfadiazina 250 mg; Pectina 30 mg; Homatropina 0,5 mg.

Procienx

Instituto Farmacêutico de Produtos Científicos Xavier
João Gomes Xavier & Cia. Ltda.

Figure 5.4

Décio Pignatari. "Disenformio [advertisement]"

$$$$$$$$$$$kill   kill   kill   kill   kill   kill
$$$$$$$$$$$maim maim maim maim maim maim
$$$$$$$$$$$$kill   kill   kill   kill   kill   kill
$$$$$$$$$$$maim maim maim maim maim maim
$$$$$$$$$$$$kill   kill   kill   kill   kill   kill
maim maim maim maim maim maim maim maim
kill kill kill kill kill kill kill kill
maim maim maim maim maim maim maim maim
kill kill kill kill kill kill kill kill
maim maim maim maim maim maim maim maim
kill kill kill kill kill kill kill kill
maim maim maim maim maim maim maim maim
kill kill kill kill kill kill kill kill

Figure 5.5

John Sharkey. "$ Kill"

in "kill" against the regular letters in "maim" which is meant to evoke the red and white lines of the American flag. The negative space in "kill," though, specifically the gap between the *k* and the *i*, make it formally difficult. If the word were printed in uppercase, as "KILL," the problem is still not solved, as the distance between the horizontal lines in the *L*s produce a similar problem with spacing. Similarly, the visual energy of the $ in place of the stars might distract the reader from noticing there are fifty-five dollar signs replacing the fifty stars, but I suspect that it is more a question of composition than a political statement: would it be a comment on the perceived colonial project of American-style capitalism? The title of the piece, which could be pronounced "skill," certainly refers to how efficient the United States' military had become at warfare, and ties the poem directly to the anti–Vietnam War movement. Sharkey's technique likely responds to what he saw as the blatant crimes of a military and economic superpower, and takes advantage of a simplified, spectacularized good (socialism) versus bad (capitalism) politics. In this way the "skill" referred to in the title of the poem might also denote a shift in poetic or artistic "skill," from the carefully constructed, formally balanced verbi-visual composition, to the advertising techniques of the poster, though designed to resist the conditions those advertising methods sought to exploit. This poem was designed to reject close reading, to communicate an obvious and polemical message quickly and effectively. The renunciation of the reader's time and engagement, and also the reader's skill, is a significant characteristic of concrete poetry's project, and one that points directly to the conditions of language and communication in an emergent consumerist moment.

While it is true that the process of reading and comprehension had accelerated beyond early twentieth-century practices by the time of Sharkey's work, and that part of the project of concrete poetry from its early theorizations was to facilitate quick comprehension of poems across languages, a reduced poetic language was never meant to result in a reduced understanding of the complexity of ideas. For an example of a protest poem that follows a more complex strategy of concrete composition, one need only look at Augusto de Campos's "LUXO LIXO" (1967) or Hansjörg Mayer's "USA" (1965), both of which use the structures of words to extract immanent critiques of social and geo-political power relations, the former dealing with the unequal distribution of wealth in developmentalist Brazil, and the latter with the cultural, economic, and military presence of the United States in post-WWII Europe (see figs 5.6 and 4.1).

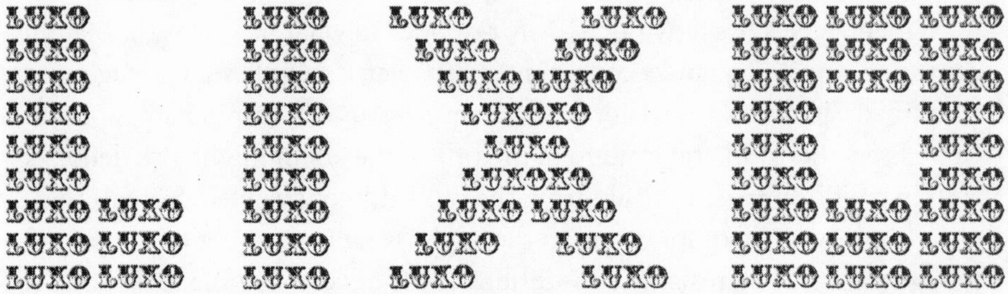

Figure 5.6
Augusto de Campos. "LUXO LIXO"

Technology Art

There is a diagram in David Harvey's *Condition of Postmodernism* that illustrates the relative size of the Earth to the technologies available to physically navigate it. Referring to annihilation of space through time, Harvey makes the blunt point that the methods we use for moving through space qualitatively alter our experiences of what is possible in the span of human life. While concrete poetry is not a supersonic jet, it is not completely divorced from that technology, either. What concrete poetry performed so well across its various iterations was the interrogation of not only the poetic line, but the literary page and the letter, as well. Spatially, all of those factors functioned differently than before; the context in which they were uttered and distributed, the cultural community on a grand scale, had changed drastically in relation to new modes of electronic communication. Kenneth Goldsmith, in his short essay "From (Command) Line to (Iconic) Constellation" (2001) argues that the attention that concrete poetry received at the turn of the twenty-first century – referring primarily to the Yale Conference in honour of Haroldo de Campos in 1999, and the exhibition *Poetry Plastique*, curated by Charles Bernstein at the Marianne Boesky Gallery in New York in 2001 – can be understood by its proximity to the development of the internet, a cultural mode of transportation that delivers on concrete poetry's promise of a global, networked space.

Goldsmith says the idea of the connection between concrete poetry and cyberspace came to him while listening to Décio Pignatari speak about the project of concrete poetry in Brazil and realizing that the lexicon Pignatari was using was similar to that which is often used to describe the experience of the internet: interface, delivery, content, multi-media, distribution, etc. (Goldsmith n. pag.). He notes that we, as readers and subjects in many ways produced by the internet, are now used to seeing texts in different formats, and on different machines (standard monitors, cell phones, public information screens, e-book readers). More people now pay attention to fonts because of the rise of the computer; anyone who has had to create an event notification now knows how fonts and layout contribute to meaning. Both students and teachers are likely conscious of how language can be manipulated visually to adhere to a specific page length, either via spacing, kerning, or font selection. To visually stretch an argument to appear longer, replace Times New Roman with Courier. To condense an argument into a determined page length, switch to Arial Narrow. The same strategies are often achieved, in ways that were once the trade secrets of typesetters, graphic designers and contract writers, by the manipulation of font size. This is a relatively recent body of knowledge for a word-processing public, but the emphasis on the space of the page and the shift between typesetting was at the fore of concrete poetry. Goldsmith points to the ways in which poems were published in several forms in different publications as anticipating the manipulation of language experienced by citizens of the computer age. Décio Pignatari's "LIFE", for example, appeared over six pages in Emmett Williams' anthology, on a single page in Mary Ellen Solt's, and as an eight-page pamphlet in *Noigandres*. Likewise, Ronaldo Azeredo's "Velocidade" appears in an ornate, serifed font in Williams', but in Solt's is presented in a font much closer to its original, Futura.

On the occasion of the the New York-based publishing house Primary Information's reissuing of Williams's *An Anthology of Concrete Poetry* in 2013, a tweet from UbuWeb, the indispensable online archive of art and poetry that Goldsmith founded in 1996, makes the connection between concrete poetry and contemporary internet culture clear: "Just so ya know, UbuWeb was founded, based on, and inspired by that anthology of concrete poetry. It's still the fuel that runs the site" (Goldmsith [ubuweb]).[5] Elsewhere, Goldsmith cites Max Bense's argument, from his 1965 manifesto "Concrete Poetry," that concrete poetry does not separate languages, but unites them, as having specific relevance to the current global, cyberspatial condition. He notes that "Bense's insistence on a combinatory universally readable language predicts the types of distributive systems that the web enables. It insists on a poetics of pan-internationality or non-nationality, which finds its expression in the decentred, constellation-oriented global networks where no one geographic entity has sole possession of content" (n. pag.). Goldsmith's optimism here – though it sounds dated, just over a decade later, coming before the monetization of the internet and debates over net neutrality and digital piracy – argues forcefully for the re-examination of concrete poetry within larger cultural and historical contexts. In this sense concrete poetry parallels the concerns and conditions of a similarly neglected form within visual art, and one which operated contemporaneously with it: technology art. An examination of how technology art operated within its own spatial parameters will aid in understanding how cultural spaces operated differently at the end of a particular formulation of modernism.

While concrete poetry took up the nascent shift from the page to the screen in its composition, technology art made a similar transformation in the realm of visual art. The work poses difficulties for critical reception in much the same way as concrete poetry, deracinating the gallery visitor and confounding discourses of composition and sites of meaning. The critical project of Edward Shanken, an art historian who focuses on the intersections of technology and art, recuperates the electronic, or cybernetic moment in art production that has been overshadowed by the contemporaneous, much more successful language-based conceptualism. In his essay "Art in the Information Age: Technology and Conceptual Art," Shanken points to an exhibition not often mentioned in discussions of art and technology, *The Machine: As Seen at the End of the Mechanical Age*, organized by Pontus Hultén at the Museum of Modern Art in 1968, an exhibition Hultén described "as a simultaneously nostalgic and futuristic exhibition on art and mechanical technology" (433). The impetus for the show was the collective feeling that the machine was giving way to electronics, and thus the space the machine occupied – traditionally the factory, farm, or some other specific geography of production – was being phased out in favour of a more dispersed, "post-industrial" space. This shift, from the mechanical to the electronic, operates as another popular metaphor for the spatial hinge between modernity and postmodernity.

The same year as Hultén's show, Jasia Reichardt, who had curated the *concrete poetry britain canada united states* exhibition at the Institute for Contemporary Art in London in 1966, organized *Cybernetic Serendipity*, a show that included poets, artists, and engineers, and which would travel to Washington, D.C. and San Francisco in 1969–70. Reichardt's show would prove to be a primary influence on the two major exhibitions of technology art that were mounted in New York in 1970: Kynaston McShine's *Information*, at the Museum for Modern Art, and Jack Burnham's *Software*, at the Jewish Museum. It is Burnham's show that Shanken sees as the most interesting of them all, however, specifically in its embrace of software as a model for human interaction. He writes:

> *Software* was predicated [...] on the ideas of "software" and
> "information technology" as metaphors for art. Burnham conceived
> of "software" as parallel to the aesthetic principles, concepts or
> programs that underlie the formal embodiment of actual art
> objects, which in turn parallel "hardware." In this regard, he
> interpreted contemporary experimental art practices, including
> conceptual art, as predominantly concerned with the software
> aspect of aesthetic production. (434)

This passage offers an entrance into the relationship between technology art and conceptual art, both of which have significant crossover and engagement with concrete poets and poetics. All three movements interrogated the ideological structures of the reception of art and literature within modernist discourse, and sought to reposition the relationship: technology art in the metaphor of electronic networks, conceptual art in the realm of linguistic positivism, and concrete poetry in the treatment of language as material.

In an essay in *Artforum* in 1968, Burnham writes of his concern over the growing polarity between high art and what he refers to as unobjects, or information-technology based artworks, and how each fits into an increasingly information-saturated culture. He compares the "'new car' of the automobile stylist" with the "syndrome of formalist invention in art, where 'discoveries' are made through visual manipulation," emphasizing that repetition was passing for innovation at a time when technological innovation, in the form of software language, offered a real opportunity to alter the language and production of culture. As evidence he points to the practices of the artists Ad Reinhardt and Donald Judd, and the writer Alain Robbe-Grillet, all of whom practice a style of writing that attempts to describe their work as completely as possible, in spite of the risk of banality or loss of a literary style. Burnham connects that instinct towards completeness to the language that programmed the modern computer. Locating the root of this descriptive practice in Judd's writings between 1962 and 1965, Burnham argues that it "resembles what a computer programmer would call an entity's 'list structure' or all the enumerated properties needed to *physically* rebuild an object" (31). He gives the example of Robert Morris's contribution to the 68th American Exhibition at the Art Institute of Chicago in 1966, comprised of two sans-serif L-shaped forms that had shown in New York the previous year. Burnham explains that the fact that Morris sent the plans to the Chicago museum's carpenters instead of shipping the forms, which would have been more expensive than rebuilding them, proves that "in the context of a systems esthetic possession of a privately fabricated work is no longer important. Accurate information takes priority over history and geographical location" (31). Although Morris is closely connected to conceptual art, minimalism, and performance art, not technology art, it is his mode of production in this instance, rather than the actual work produced, that Burnham links to a call for future art production which would emphasize greater technological interaction between artists and institutions, as well as audiences.

Such a radical break in art production would face serious opposition. Even Sol LeWitt's definition of conceptual art, as an idea machine that makes the work, still has as its ultimate embodiment a physical work of art. Likewise, as I outline in chapter 4, even those artists who made nothing were still able to sell their ideas via gallerists like Seth Siegelaub, who marketed objects of mass production (xeroxed pages, for example) as limited editions. On the whole, conceptual artists resisted computer technology as a site for their ideas, although they widely utilized the contemporaneous shifts in technologies of reproduction: the photocopier, telex, and snapshot photograph were all central to the distribution of much of the work. There are various concrete poems which occupy a middle ground between technology art and conceptual art methods, as composition that begins in a systematic approach ends up in a physical work, and encourages the production of further work: Haroldo de Campos's "ALEA I – VARIAÇÕES SEMÂNTICAS" is one example; Thomkins's "Dogmat-Mot" is another. In Thomkins's final poem-object, which relates directly to the kind of cross-linguistic computational methods of Alan Turing's codebreaking project during WWII, though on a much smaller scale, the meanings of the words become detached from their signifiers, and the words are reduced to their linguistic material, full of information in the way Weaver and Shannon use the term: it is all potential meaning, no message. The poem does not even have a proper orientation that would allow the reader-operator to feel oriented towards the work, just as it has no ground-level language to allow the construction of a lexical key. It is an international abdication of authorial intent, a removal of the composing subject that operates at the same time as an exclusion of the reading subject. It gestures towards the fantasy of inter-linguistic communication via a frustration borne from indeterminacy.

Johanna Drucker is enthusiastic about Burnham's understanding of material as giving way to the systemic, and about his development of a "sculptural practice grounded in relationships" ("Interactive" 43). She agrees with Shanken about Burnham's approach to software, arguing that the difference between Burnham and McShine's exhibitions is that *Software* was about participation, while *Information* was about control (44). Perhaps unsurprisingly, *Information* was better funded and had more institutional support. Its roster of artists drew heavily from the current stock of conceptual artists. *Software* was more experimental, and suffered for it; the exhibition ended up grossly over budget and had technical difficulties. As Shanken observes, the reception of both shows at the time and throughout much of the interim, is of a certain character:

Critics opined that [technology-based art] was dominated by the
materiality and spectacle of mechanical apparatus, which was
anathema to the conceptual project. Technical failures of art and
technology exhibitions, like *Software* (which, ironically, was plagued
with software problems), contributed to waning public interest,
just at the moment that a succession of large, successful exhibitions
of conceptual art were mounted. Widespread skepticism towards
the military-industrial complex after May 1968 and amidst the
Vietnam War, the Cold War and mounting ecological concerns all
contributed to problematizing the artistic use of technology – and
the production of aesthetic objects in general – within the context
of commodity capitalism. ("Art in the Information Age" 436)

But there is something in Burnham's approach and in much of technology
art that is worthy of recuperation. There is something fascinating about an
exhibition of art literally *not working*, instead of just having theoretical or
curatorial deficiencies.

And it is important to realize that the institutional blitz of the 1970 exhibitions were neither the beginning nor the end of the movement. The British
painter and educator Roy Ascott had been trying to fuse painting and cybernetics since the 1950s, and had by 1966 developed the Cybernetic Art Matrix
(CAM), a network of artists and thinkers that would be regulated by a sort of
social feedback between the members:

CAM was intended to provide a variety of functions, such as
facilitating interdisciplinary collaboration between *geographically
remote* artists and scientists, providing a pragmatic art education
curriculum for the young, and enriching the lives of "the new
leisured class" by enhancing creative behavior and providing
amenities and modes of aesthetic play. (Shanken, "Cybernetics" 274;
emphasis added)

A similar impulse is present in Reichardt's exhibition *Cybernetic Serendipity*,
where displays of poems created by computers and of formulae created to
create images are presented side by side, with no distinction made between
the disciplines of the contributors: poet beside scientist, philosopher beside
programmer.

In relating the work of this period to the innovations, both social and
technological, brought about by internet, Drucker points to Ted Nelson and

Ned Woodman's contribution to *Software*, *Labyrinth*, an interactive catalogue of the exhibition that allowed viewers to determine their own path through an interlinked database of texts, thus choosing their own non-linear narrative that would then be printed out for them (Drucker, "Interactive" 35). This early use of hypertext heralds the postmodern shift towards ideas of hyperspace: having replaced the single authorized text with a possibility of exponential texts within a compositional system, the rules of analysis become frustrated. This shift is an important one in the difference between modernism and postmodernism. Whereas modernist literature might have juxtaposed disparate scenes within a narrative structure, the *order* was still determined by a single author, and made solid by authorial intent. In postmodernism, such authority is abandoned to the vicissitudes of a program or system of meaning production, and a certain level of *uncontrol* is aimed for.

The form of Nelson and Woodman's project is not in the record of the printouts, but in the program for the potential production of the texts; it is written in a language that is at once quite simple, from the perspective of a computer programmer, and at the same time inaccessible to everyone else, going far beyond the modernist notion of difficulty in literature. As a result, work such as Nelson and Woodman's cannot be archived in the way that a traditional catalogue of an institutional exhibition might be, in book form with an essay by the curator and photographs of the installation. It challenges our understanding of where art or literary work exists, and consequently our concepts of access and authorship. Although there are images of the software exhibition available, they are insufficient for documenting the participatory character of the exhibition, the very point of which was to challenge the print- and image-based dominance of art production and criticism. The challenge, it can be argued, was successful inasmuch as the critical legacy of the show has been relatively small. But that can only be of minor comfort to the participants.

The Mathematical Way of Thinking

Computer language therefore becomes one kind of technological Esperanto for a newly imagined community of mechanical subjects. The modernist subject is mathematicized by what Max Bense refers to as the project of "generative aesthetics" in an essay he contributed to Reichardt's exhibition. Bense, a professor of science and philosophy in Germany and a major figure in the Stuttgart concrete poetry scene since 1961, describes generative aesthetics as the "artificial production of probabilities, differing from the norm using theorems and programs" ("Generative" 58). It is, he argues, "an aesthetics of production which makes possible the methodical production of aesthetic states, by dividing this process into a finite number of distinct and separate steps which are capable of formulation" (58). Highlighting the wider culture's relationship to the expanding emphasis on automation and the role of machines in information production and control, Reichardt reprints an American newspaper article on the page preceding Bense's essay that is dated 1 April, 1950, and that describes the Washington, DC, unveiling of a machine the Americans captured from Nazi Germany during the war. Called the *Müllabfuhwortmaschine*, it is referred to as "Hitler's most deadly secret weapon," and functions by matching up semantic "entities," "operators," and "entity phrases" to develop sentences like "Subversive elements were revealed to be related by marriage to a well-known columnist," or "Capitalist warmonger is a weak link in atomic security." The source of the information on the machine is a relocated Nazi scientist whose name, Dr Krankheit, in its similarity to Walter Cronkite, along with the date and absence of any specific newspaper citation, signals the article is a prank; but it is significant for its display of the types of anxiety around the production of meaning through the development of new, mechanical languages (Reichardt, *Cybernetics, Art* 56).

Bense's "Statistical Poem" (1966) puts the aesthetic of mechanical production into action by taking a series of basic German words and running them through a system of repetition. The complete poem appears as a block of text that does not adhere to ideas of line breaks or order beyond the compositional system. The poetic value, or the aesthetic of the work, is disinterested, cold, and ordered. The words, "es" (it), "ist" (is), "wenn" (if), "aber" (but), "doch" (still), and "nicht" (not) are first presented as a list, then in combinations of two, then three, etc., until the final line, which uses all the words together in a phrase that translates as *but if it is still not* (Bense, "Statistical" 264). There is a tension in the poem's generative process that engages with the expectation of language to express coherent, syntactical meaning, and the last line participates in the interrogation of language's function. If language can produce meaning without the human, or at least with the human in a reduced form (creating a formula, choosing the material, then implementing the formula), how does that meaning function, and what philosophical implications might it have? The process becomes metalinguistic, and the power of the work comes from not only the reader's frustration with the impeded meaning, but in the desire that impediment produces in her/him to complete the phrases, and thus become an active participant in the production of the poem.

The basis for Bense's approach to composition can be found, like that of the early concrete poets, in the ideas of the concrete artist Max Bill. In Bill's 1949 essay "The Mathematical Way of Thinking in the Visual Art of Our Time," he is not so explicit as to require the fusion of mathematic/mechanical and literary/artistic production, but he does call for a recognition of the role mathematical thought plays in modernist creativity and aesthetics. He responds to those critics who claim that mathematics lacks the emotional charge of aesthetics by emphasizing the need for reason to accompany feeling in art. In an almost cartoonish statement of the ideals of modernist rationalism, he argues that "It is mankind's ability to reason which makes it possible to coordinate emotional values in such a way that what we call art ensues" (7). He points to the paintings of Piet Mondrian as a model of the successful removal of what is alien to the medium, specifically the "mere naturalistic replica of [a] subject" through perspective and figurative representation (5). He identifies the flourishing of the mathematical way of thinking in the twentieth century in the work of the Constructivists, which developed alongside the proliferation of aerial photography and blueprints related to what Le Corbusier would call the "engineer's aesthetic." At the same time, he notes, "mathematics itself had arrived at a stage of evolution in which the proof of many apparently logical deductions ceased to be demonstrable and theorems were presented that the imagination proved incapable of grasping" (8). Einstein's Theory of Relativity would be the famous example of this type of mathematical shift; Bernhard Riemann, N.I. Lobatschewesky, and Janus Bolyai's refutation of Euclid's Fifth Postulate, which deals with parallel lines and terminal space, would be an earlier, lesser known but no less significant contribution (Whittaker 34). These approaches refute an idea of ordered, rational space, arguing that lines, when experienced on a scale beyond the human – on the level of the cosmos, for example – do not adhere to a conventional understanding of space, much in the same way that electronic media, by connecting disparate geographies, alter the understanding of space produced by the technology of the book, or the alphabet before that. Mathematics had become a metaphor of order and control as well as chaos and fluidity, and brought with that shift a transformation of what had been previously thought possible. It was no longer the math of factories, and of scientific management. It had become the math of the computer, and the space ship, the math of the atom and all its potential and terror.

For Bill, mathematics provides a primary mode of cognition that determines not only spatial understanding, but emotional understanding as well. It allows for both individuation and collectivity. It allows subjects to apprehend their relationship to their physical surroundings, and therefore influences their appraisal of the "interactions of separate objects, or groups of objects, one to another. And again, since it is mathematics that lends significance to these relationships, it is only a natural step from having perceived them to desiring to portray them. This, in brief, is the genesis of a work of art" (7). However suspicious any claim to identify a genesis of a work of art might seem, Bill's ideas nevertheless had tremendous influence not only within the field of concrete art, but concrete poetry, as well, both through the work of Eugen Gomringer, his secretary at the Hochschule für Gestaltung in Ulm, and his influence on the visual artists associated with the Noigandres group, including the "pualistas" Waldemar Cordeiro and Hermelindo Fiaminghi, who were accused by the Rio de Janeiro neo-concretists of being too rigid in their devotion to Max Bill's teaching (Mammí 22). While his examples are heavily weighted toward the visual realm, it is clear that certain poets followed his position, replacing the syntactic line with a grid and emphasizing the geometry of letters and their relationships to each other beyond semantic meaning. Bill's presentation of mathematics as a universal language made its way into the transnational impulses of various poets' critical writing, as well, most explicitly – unsurprisingly – in the early texts of Gomringer.

There is a difference, however, between the production of texts via mathematical formulae or mechanical programs and concrete poetry: the former does not automatically result in the latter. While Bense's "Statistical Poem" is, at its base, a programmed presentation of language, there is an aesthetic sensibility that works backward from the final line, "but if it is still not," to parse the various arrangements of its semantic elements. The poem could have worked backward from "is if not still it but," and the effect would have been reduced. It would be likewise lessened if it worked backward from "his are till gut lit by," to engage in a simplifying exercise. Bense's aesthetic is not present in the same way in work that depends on a computer program to produce the final text, though the distinction is at times difficult to identify. Some of Edwin Morgan's poems, which are written from the perspective of a computer, and which include imagined difficulties like key jams and programming errors in order to illustrate how computer technology and human creativity might influence and struggle with one another, need to be distinguished from projects like that of Robin McKinnon Wood and Margaret Masterman, who offer as an example of a computer poem a text that resulted from a programming bug that they could not replicate. It came out of a program meant to combine the physical with the literary to produce poetry mechanically: the program was meant to divide "continuous text into 'Phrasings' corresponding to the rhythmic divisions of speech or spoken prose. These units usually include two stress-points and a terminal intonation feature, forming breath-groups which are also sense-groups" (Wood and Masterman 55). This type of experiment is perhaps better positioned within the history of automata and linguistic standardization than an aesthetic sphere. Friedrich Kittler, in *Discourse Networks 1800/1900*, traces this history as far back as a competition held in 1779 by the Academy of Sciences in St Petersburg that commissioned engineers to develop a machine "capable of purely pronouncing the five vowels" (36). The Academy of Sciences hoped these machines would do away with regional accents and dialects, those pesky markers of history, class, and geography that stood in the way of "enlightenment" culture. The difference between the inventors of automata in the late eighteenth century and the programmers and engineers of the mid-twentieth, though, was that they were now imagining the machines not so much as models but as artists. Johanna Drucker identifies the habit

> of engineers developing pleasing or curious results (more commonly in digital imagery, but also in language) and determining it "art." Artists and poets, though they might use technology, are aware that aesthetics is a discourse within history, and their work relies upon that knowledge. (Drucker, "Interactive" 40)

For early technology artists, it was the metaphor of software and networks that offered more promise and excitement than the images or texts the process produced.

In a text that examines the history of the computer in humanities research and artistic production, Drucker expands on her distinction between the engineer and the artist, identifying two related methods of knowledge production: *aesthesis* and *mathesis*. *Aesthesis* refers to the role of the human in digital environments, and describes the influence of human thought and behaviour on the design of digital environments and vice versa. *Mathesis* is a term meant to describe an assumption of objectivity or autonomy from culture: "Knowledge forms are never stable or self-identical but always situated within conditions of use. Knowledge, then, is necessarily partial, subjective, and situated. Objectivity, we have long recognized, is the wish dream of an early rational age, one that was mechanistic in its approaches" (*Speclab* xiv).

Bill makes a similar distinction in his call for a nuanced understanding of the connection between mathematics and creative production, rejecting the work that tries to fuse (computer) science and art, and which received so much opposition from the artistic sphere for its apparent lack of emotion or spirit. The scientific aleatoric, of which Wood and Masterman's work is an example, does not represent Bill's theory, and fits more in the category of *mathesis*. Bense's "Statistical Text," de Campos's "ALEA I," and even Josef Hiršal and Bohumila Grögerová's "Developer" series, all of which begin with an investigation of the poetic relationship between deliberately chosen words and semantemes and use procedural methods to extract them, are examples of the use of the mathematical way of thinking that results in *aesthesis*.

A poem that straddles the divide between the programmatic and the poetic, between the aleatoric and the composed, and combines the fields of concrete poetry and technology art, is Stephen Scobie's "Instructions for Computer Poem 3 – Night and Day." The piece, which was installed in the University of British Columbia's 1969 exhibition, *Concrete Poetry: An Exhibition in Four Parts*, is presented as a sheet outlining the rules of the piece, a series of computer printouts hung on the wall, and a printer installed in a room with a pile of paper collected at its base (see fig. 5.7). The poem's "rules" begin with two lists, labelled "List A – night" and "List B – day," each of which is made up of words that describe the concepts of night and day, but also contains words that are only slightly related. The list for night, for example, has words such as "night," "black," "darkness," and "midnight," but also includes words such as "dies," "under," "waste," and "far." Likewise, the list for day has "sun," "blue," and "radiant," but also includes "become," "leap," and "together" (Scobie n. pag.). Though setting up a binary between day and night, Scobie recognizes that language, even when selected from a condensed list by a computer, adheres to meanings which have been socially constructed, and which have aesthetic associations that are at times rooted in common use but are also subject to the whims of the user, in this case one who is interested in the poetic possibilities of language. The curiosity of his word choice in his lists is contrasted with the calculated, mechanical language he uses to describe the production of the work.

Without including the actual programming data that would be entered into the machine, as Carl Fernbach-Flarsheim might do, or displaying potential failures of the computational approach to poetic composition, as Edwin Morgan might do, Scobie's poem adopts a style that becomes opaque in its attempt at transparency. It challenges the reader, in its description of the computer's function, to imagine the poems from a mechanical perspective.

The reader is therefore required to shift her/his expectation of what poetry should be: first in the negotiation of the lists describing night and day, where poetry would likely be expected to be neither as binaristic nor as exhaustive or banal, and then again in trying to envision which words would or could be randomly selected from the list and positioned in lines that would potentially have some movement between the concepts of night and day, but also that might end up being obscured by overprinting:

> One complete poem will consist of four "runs." These four runs are all to be shown on one print-out sheet, over the same area. Thus it will be necessary to store the first three runs until all the selection is complete. The runs are to be superimposed: overprinting is allowed. Runs 1 and 2 will be from list A; runs 3 and 4 from list B – thus, in the event of any overprinting, list B words will always be printed over list A words. (Scobie n. pag.)

More detailed description follows, prompting the question: where is the poetry located? And what is the relationship between the poet and the computer as creative subjects? The poem is arguably the lists and description of the potential work, which would satisfy a reader who demands creativity be located in a thinking, human subject. But Scobie's language complicates that position, positing that a "complete poem" only comes into being after it has been mechanically composed and printed. This is a shift from the aleatoric practices of Fluxus experiments with language, and even from Tristan Tzara's method for writing a Dada poem – cutting up a newspaper article and then extracting the words one by one – in that it emphasizes both the human and the mechanical. Scobie chooses the concepts and the lists of words, and designs the software (in collaboration with a computer programmer), but the computer chooses and arranges the words as well as prints them onto a page: a level of composition and material production that departs significantly from previous experimental, procedural poetics, even those of Augusto de Campos, Bense, and Hiršal and Grögerová.

Situating Concrete Poetry

Having outlined the shifts in conceptions of space that influenced the production, or poetics, of concrete poetry, I now want to emphasize the spaces in which the reader-viewer experiences the work: the spaces of distribution.

```
Computer Poem 3.      Night and Day

The basic material of the poem is the following lists of words:

      List A - night                    List B - day
      night                             day
      moon                              dawn
      darkness                          sun
      forest                            blue
      stars                             seed
      ocean                             waken
      lantern                           become
      black                             bright
      far                               singing
      fear                              butterfly
      gloomy                            sundials
      mirk                              laugh
      stumbles                          together
      shadows                           beyond
      fell                              white
      sang                              loves
      moan                              golden
      owls                              wonder
      darker                            radiant
      darkens                           happiness
      death                             shine
      dies                              daisychain
      below                             welcome
      under                             noon
      mystery                           enchanting
      wild                              soft
      groans                            leap
      weeping                           runs
      nightingale                       meadows
      waste                             waterfalls
      stifle                            cloud
      midnight                          above
      sunset                            green
      prowl                             river
      blind                             arise
```

One complete poem will consist of four "runs". These four runs are all to be
shown on one print-out sheet, over the same area. Thus it will be necessary
to store the first three runs until all the selection is complete. The runs
are to be superimposed; overprinting is allowed. Runs 1 and 2 will be from
list A; runs 3 and 4 from list B - thus, in the event of any overprinting,
list B words will always be printed over list A words.

In each run, the computer will randomly select 10 groups of words from the
opposite list. Each group will consist of between 1 and 3 words, the number
to vary randomly. No word may be used twice in one run.

In each run, these groups are to be placed at random among the eligible spots
in the designated area, which is a print-out sheet 60 spaces wide and 45 lines
deep. Only every third line may be used for printing.

Eligible spots are as follows:

    for list A, beginning at spaces 0, 10, 20, 30, 40 of every third line,
    for list B, beginning at spaces 15, 25, 35, 45, 55 of the same lines.

This provides 75 eligible spots for each list, only 10 of which will be used
per run. There should be, as a result, a general shift from left to right
from list A words to list B words. In the unlikely event of one run overprinting on itself, the group chosen second will overprint on the group
chosen first.

Figure 5.7

Stephen Scobie. "Computer Poem"

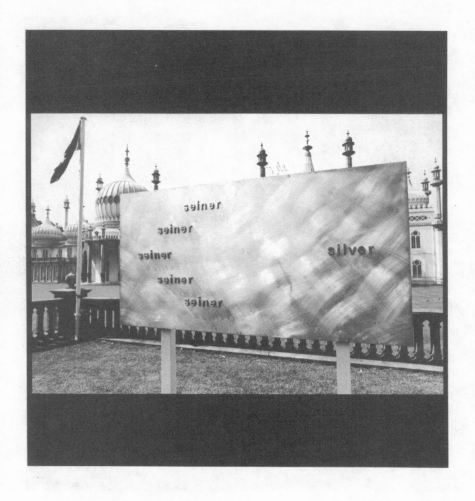

Figure 5.8

Ian Hamilton Finlay. "Purse Sein"

Scobie's poetic proposition in itself disrupts ideas of poetic and linguistic material and meaning, but the form the work takes in the gallery offers an example of an equally radical gesture, and one which opens up questions of where concrete poetry belongs, and which borders it can cross or blur before it becomes something different. The installation photograph included in the exhibition catalogue shows Scobie's work in a semi-chaotic state: a dot matrix printer sits on a high (reading level) plinth with paper cascading down from it, collecting on the floor where it looks like people have picked it up to view it then dropped it down again, crumpled and loose. Poems in sequence have been torn from the printer and hung on the wall, with notices and explanatory texts interspersed. The image recalls the first time we see Peter Sellers' character, Group Captain Lionel Mandrake, in Kubrick's *Dr Strangelove*: reinforcing the film's critique of communications technologies and a surfeit of information as diminishing, rather than increasing, people's ability to understand each other, Sellers appears from behind a long sheet of paper he is reading, which he then lets fall to the floor in a heap.

Poems that, like Scobie's, require photographic documentation in order to be circulated are commonly found in concrete poetry publications. The work of Ian Hamilton Finlay, to whom Scobie is connected as a critic and scholar, often takes on site-specific, sculptural form (see fig. 5.8). The garden at his home, called "Little Sparta," in Stonypath, Scotland, functions as a site for a collection of his sculpture poems. The series of "plastic poems" by Kitasono Katue, which are photographs of crumpled pages and other objects, is also an example. The necessity for a work to be documented by photography is standard for visual art, but is rare for written poetry as it has taken form since the development of the printing press. Much of concrete poetry took advantage of new techniques in printing and design to depart from the authoritative line of typesetting, a compositional strategy which emphasized the visual material of language over its syntactic function, and it was a small but natural progression from the disruption of the line to that of the page, and then the book. The placement of concrete poetry within a gallery therefore makes sense. The space of the gallery allows for the juxtaposition of work in ways that the book – either fine-press portfolio or mass-printed anthology – is unable to perform. It allows for a simultaneity and disorder that consecutive pages confound.

This is not to say that the gallery is somehow superior to the book for the distribution of concrete poetry, but simply that the presentation of the work it makes possible contributes to the function of the work. And it should also be noted that the idea of the gallery is neither stable nor free from historical context, having undergone significant transformation within the twentieth century alone. The exhibition catalogue, which is also a twentieth-century development, though it in some ways documents an exhibition, is less an accurate representation than a recognition of the limitations of available spaces of distribution. The poetry anthology, and more specifically the international anthology, which has arguably been the dominant form of concrete poetry's distribution, performs a similar function in that it both increases access to the work while at the same time accentuating its spatial impediments: small print runs, poster poems, small editions or unique texts, sculpture-poems, and so on. Gomringer's manifesto "Concrete Poetry" was written as an introduction to a planned anthology in 1956, and there were several anthologies published during the years of the movement's peak activity, including the retrospective and mass-printed anthologies of the late 1960s and early '70s. In a footnote to one of his many essays on concrete poetry, Claus Clüver offers this impressive list:

The anthologies by year are: Max Bense and Elisabeth Walther, eds., *Konkrete poesie international. Roth* (Stuttgart, 1965) no. 21; *Poesia concreta internacional*, catalogue of exhibition at Galeria Universitária Aristos, March-May 1966 (Mexico City: Universidad Nacional Autónoma de México, 1966); Stephen Bann, ed., Concrete poetry issue, *Beloit Poetry Journal* 17,1 (1967); Stephen Bann, ed., *Concrete Poetry: An International Anthology* (London: London Magazine Editions, 1967); Eugene Wildman, ed., "Anthology of Concretism," *Chicago Review* 19,4 (1966); Emmett Williams, ed., *An Anthology of Concrete Poetry* (New York: Something Else Press, 1967); Mary Ellen Solt, ed., "A World Look at Concrete Poetry," *Artes Hispánicas / Hispanic Arts* 1, 3–4 (1968); Adriano Spatola, ed., "Antologia della poesia concreta," *Il peso del concreto*, ed. Ezio Gribaudo (Torino, 1968); Carlo Belloli and Ernesto L. Francalanci, eds., *Poesia concreta: indirizzi concreti, visuali e fonetici*, catalogue of exhibition organized by Dietrich Mahlow and Arrigo Lora-Totino, Ca' Giustinian, Sala delle Colonne, 25 September–10 Ocotber 1969 (Venezia: Stamperia di Venezia, 1969); Max Bense and Elisabeth Walter, eds., *Konkrete poesie international 2. Roth* (Stuttgart, 1970) no. 41; Liesbeth Crommelin, ed., *klankteksten / ? konkrete poëzie / visuele teksten* (Amsterdam: Stedelijk Museum, 1970). The earliest international anthology using "Concrete Poetry" as the collective

title was Eugen Gomringer's "Kleine Anthologie konkrete Poesie,"
Spirale 8 (1960): 37–44. (Clüver, "Concrete Poetry" 54–5)

The concrete poetry anthologies, so central to the works' distribution and historical context, have contested the book form in varying ways, challenging the linear organization of information as well as their own ability to contain a work in its original form, or, like an exhibition catalogue, simply to reproduce it. The anthology becomes what the French author and Minister of Culture André Malraux, who was an active cultural figure in Europe around the mid-twentieth century, championed as a "museum without walls." Malraux developed this term to describe the proliferation of books utilizing photographic printing techniques that opened up the experience of cultural artefacts to new, larger audiences who would benefit from the privilege that had previously been limited to populations of the grand urban centres of the west. Malraux's vision was pragmatic, certainly, but also ideologically inflected. For him, the beautifully printed, full-colour books were a tool to continue European imperialism via culture. At a moment when a beleaguered French colonial power was being challenged in the First Indochina War — the first of several anticolonial struggles to follow in the 1950s and '60s — Malraux was imagining a way for Europe's power to shift modes, another example of the collapsing of time and space instigated by technological advancement in the twentieth century. Though Malraux had the masterpieces of European painting and sculpture primarily in mind, the idea that works functioned better via wider distribution than within a designated space of observation applies to the impulse found in the anthologies of concrete poetry. Concrete poetry anthologies departed from previous anthologies in their embrace of the visual and international characteristics of the work. In the way that Brian O'Doherty, in *Inside the White Cube: The Ideology of the Gallery Space*, argues that a gallery "viewer" is one who looks but also who is *looked through*, like a camera's viewfinder, in that s/he is produced by the gallery space, the reader of concrete poetry is *read through*, or produced by the space of the anthology: a space that aims for globality and hypertextuality to match the shifting spatial order at mid-century (O'Doherty 55; 61).

The anthology form is an ancient one; the word has its root in the Greek *anthologia*, the verb for flower gathering. Contemporary students and instructors may not associate such bucolic imagery with the term, having likely had the experience of reading heavy and standardizing literary anthologies, and discussing the canonizing practices of the anthologies' compilers.

Leah Price locates the print-based anthology, as we understand it today – as opposed to the oral collection of poems referred to in the Greek context – within the rise of the printing press, which in combination with the defeat of perpetual copyright in 1774 resulted in an exponential increase in the amount of writing that *could* be printed and accessed by a wide public (4). As early as the 1700s, there was a concern that the sheer amount of printed information available to the public might contribute to the dilution of high culture. Expansive novels such as George Eliot's *Middlemarch* or Samuel Richardson's *Clarissa*, themselves products of the print revolution, were popular sites for extraction, the implication being that a skilled anthologist can provide a more efficient experience of reading long texts, selecting choice passages to function synecdochally, and preventing the vast expenditures of time required to consume the entire work. Price cites the eighteenth-century British anthologist Vicesimus Knox defending his practice: "the art of printing has multiplied books to such a degree, that ... it becomes necessary to read in the classical sense of the word, LEGERE, that is, to *pick out* ... the best parts of books" (quoted in Price 4). Francis Turner Palgrave described his authoritative 1861 anthology, *The Golden Treasury of the Best Songs and Lyrical Poems in the English Language* – the text Ezra Pound loathed and at one point tried to replace with a collection of his own choosing – as a project which aimed to improve a culture in which "everything is to be read, and everything only once" (quoted in Price 4). The anthologists of the nineteenth century, like their contemporaneous urban planners, played the role of cultural surgeon, bleeding literary works in order to save them from being subsumed into some grand agglomerated literary corpus.

Friedrich Kittler writes that in Germany in the early nineteenth century, the anthology was used as a way to *reduce* reading. The accumulation of texts since the invention of movable type had resulted in a reading mania, where women, in particular, were reading *too much*. Anthologies such as *Education and Instruction for the Female Sex*, by Betty Gleim, an instructor at an all-girls school, were specifically produced in order to narrow the scope of consumption, and to form taste in the reader, rather than to develop creative powers. Gender was not the only terrain that was to be managed by anthologies, however. The Bavarian Minister of Education, Immanuel Niethammer, sought to create, once and for all, an anthology that would end the reading mania for both sexes, and which would interpellate the readers into a grander cultural order: "Only because 'the Bible has ceased to be a unifying point for the education of all classes' and 'can hardly be expected to attain that position again, given the kind of thinking now in ascendancy' was there 'the need for a *National Book*'" (Kittler 149). No less grand a figure than Johann Wolfgang von Goethe was charged with collecting work for Niethammer's grand vision, but his choices turned out to be too historical-empirical, and the text failed to live up to Niethammer's expectations for an anthologist's poetic: the works seemed flat placed against each other, and the arrangement displayed little of the energy and inspiration of Goethe's talent for language.

The responsibilities of the concrete poetry anthologists were not so grand, but they were still substantial, and might perhaps be compared more aptly to the figure of programmer than that of surgeon. Like Dudley Fitts's 1942 anthology, *Contemporary Latin American Anthology* – which was funded in part by the United States' Office for the Coordination of Inter-American Affairs, and which placed English translations alongside Spanish and Portuguese poetry in an attempt to foster a Pan-American identity that would link Argentina to Alaska – the concrete poetry anthologies were tasked with producing a global connectivity. And, again like Fitts's anthology, the works presented suffer for their breadth. In this way, the concrete poetry anthology becomes a kind of material contradiction. Works that are composed on a typewriter lose the indentation that the letter makes on the page; poster poems lose their scale. Booklets like Pignatari's "LIFE" are reduced to consecutive pages; longer poems, like Emmett Williams's "Sweethearts," are excerpted. Three-dimensional works appear as a single, authoritative photograph;[6] works in colour sometimes end up in black and white. The whims of an editor or publisher, who might not appreciate the significance of design or layout to the meaning of poems, might also get in the way. In a recent interview Gerhard Rühm complained that Dick Higgins, "the congenial but over-eager publisher" of Something Else Press, reproduced some of his texts "in a graphically incorrect way" ("Interview" n. pag.). Rühm absolves Williams, the editor of the Something Else Press anthology, of responsibility for the errors, noting that he was also dissatisfied with aspects of the final text. But the issue of collecting and reproducing polylinguistic, multiformed work in the standardized and regulated space of the anthology challenged some of the basic concerns of the movement. Poetry that emphasized the materiality of language and the alterations it had undergone during the emergence of a new global imaginary ended up contained within a book, the very space of the poetic tradition against which much of it was positioned. Some of the anthologies gesture toward recognizing the limitation of the book and the black and white page, most significantly in the use of colour in Solt and Bann's anthologies, and in the inclusion of Augusto de Campos's fold-out poem "LUXO LIXO," in Solt's text, but these are exceptions. Williams's and

Wildman's texts are all in black and white, as is Bory's, though his contains considerably more photographs than the other two. These mass printed, Anglo-American texts differentiate themselves from the large portfolios published by fine arts presses such as Eugen Gomringer Press in Switzerland, Edition Hansjörg Mayer in Germany, and the Noigandres Press in Brazil. Ian Hamilton Finlay's Wild Hawthorn Press in Stonypath, Scotland produced ephemera and small runs, resisting the urge toward massification and the compromises it requires.

The order of the poems in the mass-printed anthologies is curiously varied. All of the texts seem to advocate a hypertextual approach, as do most anthologies; the reader is not expected to consume the text from start to finish, but to follow her/his interest. The binding of the pages prevents an experience similar to that Nelson and Woodman created for the Software exhibition catalogue, however. Readers might flip through Solt's or Bann's texts, but even a basic engagement of the poetry would inform them that it is organized by nation or language group. Williams's text is not paginated, but the poets appear in alphabetical order, which privileges linguistic ordering versus that of numerical ordering. Wildman's editorial presentation is more content-based, and seems to be organized by his taste, with the poets and their nations listed at the beginning, and then before each contribution. Bory's is similar, but he lists the poets and the poem titles at the end and, as the title *Once Again* implies, he positions concrete poetry and the examples of *poesia visiva* within the ancient tradition of visual literature, in a manner similar to that of the visual poetry collections that were typical of the early 1970s (particularly Klaus Peter Dencker's *Text-Bilder: Visuelle Poesie international*, Berjouhi Bowler's *The Word as Image*, and Massin's *The Word as Image*).[7] Adding to this ahistoricity is his and Wildman's decision to present all of the texts without dates.[8]

A text that enacts concrete poetry's critique of the book in its content as well as its form is British-Canadian poet Steve McCaffery's *Carnival: The First Panel, 1967* (see fig. 5.10). Considering the time of its composition, it is difficult not to locate in the visual character of the work the stylistic influence of John Furnival and Henri Chopin. Furnival's *Tower of Babel* (1964) displays a busyness similar to McCaffery's text, and Chopin's regular use of the black and red ribbon on a typewriter to create patterns out of repeated words and letters is a precursor. The tendency to mix passages of more conventional, lined poetry amongst that pattern, especially with alternative spellings based on sound, gestures toward the work of the western Canadian concrete and visual poet bill bissett. McCaffery also includes as an epigraph a passage from the De Stijl manifesto (1920) that outlines what concrete art and concrete literature should be:

> the duality between poetry and prose can no longer be maintained
> the duality between form and content can no longer be maintained
> thus for the modern writer form will have a directly spiritual
> meaning
> it will not describe events
> it will not describe at all
> but ESCRIBE
> it will recreate in the word the common meaning of events a
> constructive unity of form and content. (McCaffery n. pag.)

The inclusion of this passage in combination with the apparent influences of previous concrete poets positions the work firmly within the concrete poetry genre, but in other ways McCaffery's text can be seen as a departure from the tradition. Like bissett, who, despite producing visual-based poetry and publishing other visual poets in his Vancouver blewointment press since the early 1960s, went largely unrecognized by the International Concrete Poetry movement, McCaffery produced work that was more expressive than what concrete poetry had come to be known for. This poetry was visual, but not shaped, and for the most part the images that the letters, words, and symbols developed could not be related back to the subject of the poem as easily in a Furnival text, for example. Caroline Bayard has noted that the difference between Canadian concrete poetry and the work of the international movement, dominated by the Europeans and South Americans, was that Canadian poets approached concrete poetry without the sophisticated printing techniques available to those poets who were trained as graphic designers, and thus were less likely to emulate the type of visuality that linked the work to the altered linguistic landscape that came with the rise of advertising and communication networks. Canadian concrete poets were more likely to arrive at concrete poetry via poetic communities, and had more of a DIY aesthetic than those poets who produced fine art press editions. bpNichol is the only Canadian concrete poet to have had any real recognition by the international community, appearing in Solt's and William's anthologies and participating in the retrospective, movement-culminating exhibition at the Stedelijk museum in 1970. Though Nichol's style was varied, utilizing typewritten, handwritten, and cartoon-like language, it is only his cleanly printed work that appears in the anthologies and catalogue.

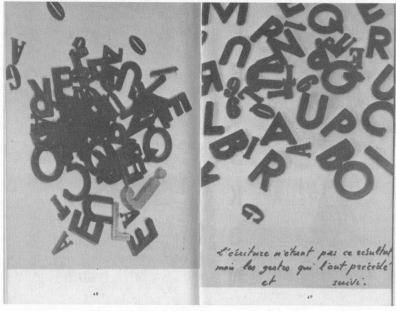

L'écriture n'étant pas ce résultat
mais les gestes qui l'ont précédé
et suivi.

Figure 5.9
Julien Blaine. "Breuvage épandu"

Figure 5.10

Steve McCaffery. From *Carnival: The First Panel: 1967–70*

Where McCaffery's *Carnival* departs from concrete poetry most, however, is in its demand for the participation of the reader. The book, or pad, as it might be called, comes with the pages bound at the top but perforated; in order to experience the composition of the piece as a whole, a reader must tear the pages out and arrange them. In this way the contradiction of the presentation of concrete poetry – a genre that emphasizes simultaneity – within book form is revealed, and the reader becomes active in the tactile refutation of the book, a physical analogue of the poetic line. Previous concrete poetry publications have performed a similar rejection through refusing to bind their pages, instead collecting them within a folding cover, specifically the large format portfolios printed by Edition Hansjörg Mayer and Eugen Gomringer Press, and the catalogue for the UBC exhibition, but none has performed the critique so effectively as McCaffery's, which forces the reader to choose: either keep the book intact, but know that the experience of it is impeded by the technology of the book, or destroy the book in order to respect the poetry, and in doing so reject the physical benefits of the book form, such as containment, order, and stability.

Moving Beyond Concrete

McCaffery continued his critique of the book over a period of years, most productively in collaboration with bpNichol under the name of the Toronto Research Group (TRG). McCaffery, who had come to Canada from England to do graduate work at York University, only met Nichol in 1969, and much of the research that they performed together took place in the 1970s, the publication of the TRG's manifesto coming in the spring 1973 issue of the journal *Open Letter*. This historical positioning places McCaffery and Nichol at the end of the International Concrete Poetry movement, and when considered alongside their poetic work of the same period, argues for treating them as initiators of a post-concrete poetics. McCaffery's 1970 *Transitions to the Beast*, published by Nichol's Ganglia Press, was written in direct counterposition to the semiotic poetry that came out of Brazilian concrete poetry circles in the mid-60s, and distributed primarily through *Invenção*. The short essay printed on the back of McCaffery's text identifies Pignatari and Pinto's work in particular, and diminishes its attempt at an alinear and nonlexical poetry inasmuch as it is dependent upon a lexical key for decoding its meaning. For McCaffery, the work of the Brazilians is too strictly semiotically influenced. His work rejects a direct relationship between his imagistic work and previously existing concepts. Whereas the Brazilians, in both the semiotic poems as well as the more orthodox concrete work, were concerned with the creation of new, collective language that can communicate quickly, a language to function in the new, rapidly developed world, McCaffery sought to frustrate equivalence:

> the semiotic form acted only as the initial impulse to search for a
> nonlexical sign language   increasingly [...] im feeling
> the need for a more rawly human & a less technocratic approach to
> borderblur for a greater perceptual system entry in short of more
> personal feeling & due attention to our more simplistic responses to
> & in front of language. (McCaffery n. pag.)

The insertion of an idiosyncratic poetic subject is something that McCaffery shares with Nichol and bissett, both of whom developed a highly personalized poetic style that often utilized hand drawn letters and figures alongside or overtop of text. All of their work countered the distanced, technologically determined subject of much of concrete poetry: the procedural had given way to the performative. There is nothing more contrary to the tradition of concrete poetry as it sprang from Max Bill than the reference, let alone a transition, to a beast (see fig. 5.11).

This emphasis on the creative subject runs counter to not only the dominant poetic theories around concrete poetry at the time, but also the reception of concrete poetry exhibitions within art criticism. A year before, in an essay published in the catalogue that accompanied the UBC exhibition, Ian Wallace hailed concrete poetry as the final step in literary modernism, one that emphasized the opacity of language. He celebrated the work as doing what conventional literature was no longer capable of: "challeng[ing] the imagination in an era charged with powerful electronic media whose effects are most strongly felt in the appearance of things and our emotional identifications with these appearances" (n. pag.). The emphasis on the work is still on the material conditions that produce it. In a review of the show for *Artforum*, a twenty-two-year-old Jeff Wall emphasizes how intelligent the work is, picking out Hansjörg Mayer's *Alphabetenquadratbuch* as an example:

> The fact that the finished product tells us a great deal about
> the medium in which [Mayer] is working, and the method of
> manipulation he employs upon the medium, and very little

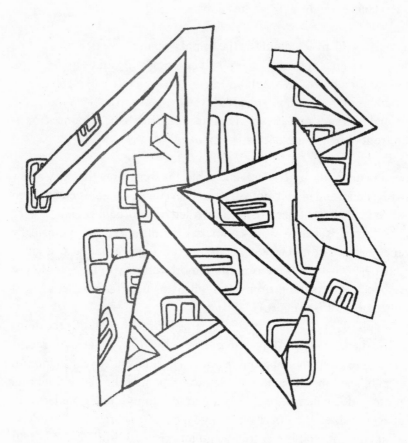

Figure 5.11

Steve McCaffery. From *Transitions to the Beast*

"about" the artist himself is a result of the artist's realization of the
most intelligent and valuable means of making contact with his
audience. (71)

Following this passage Wall places Mayer alongside the American conceptualists as a figure who is doing intelligent, philosophical work around
language. But Wall's approach, like Wallace's, seems to come out of a
Greenbergian emphasis on the expression of *form* that would soon be challenged by the post-structural theories of language McCaffery and Nichol
were beginning to read, theories which elevated play and contingency, and
the agency of the reader, over structural ideas of communication and form.
While Wallace and Wall positioned concrete poetry at the end of modernism, McCaffery and Nichol located it in the beginning of something else.

McCaffery and Nichol were perhaps the first concrete poets to engage
with the critical theory around writing and language that emerged in the
mid-1960s. Though claiming literary references similar to those of many
concrete poets, specifically the grand modernist figures of Gertrude Stein
and James Joyce, as well as those belonging to the tradition of shaped or
visual literature like that of Rabelais or Madeline Gins, they also claimed
inspiration from the ideas of Roland Barthes and other continental theorists (McCaffery and Nichol 15). In his introduction to the collected research
reports of the TRG, McCaffery emphasizes how "important [it] is to realize
the scope and context of our readings: [Edmond] Jabés, [Jacques] Derrida,
Barthes and [Jacques] Lacan had all been read by 1974" (17). Their investigations into post-structural and postmodern theory contributed to their
suspicion of the order implied by much concrete poetry, and specifically the
mechanistic approach that resulted from engagements with new computer
technology. In their 1972 "TRG Research Report 2: Narrative – The Book
as Machine," an excerpt from one Nichol's notebooks is printed as a mathematical formula Nichol composed in order to measure a reader's "ability to
gain access to the book / machine" (75). The sardonic algebra is presented
as hand-written in the midst of a typeset book, with variables representing
the "degree of adherence to or antipathy towards traditional book / machine
values on the part of the reader" and "the degree to which the book / machine
is utilized traditionally or in a non-traditional way by the writer" (75). The
pages following apply the formula to various texts using playful hypothet-
ical readers and texts, with all the calculations done in Nichol's distinctive
handwriting. The resistance to the technological determinism comes out as
well in their response to Kitasono Katue's self-portraits, in which the poet

crumples a page of his own writing and then photographs it, offering the photo-documentation as a poem. McCaffery and Nichol argue that the poems participate in that modernist photographic mode of 'exact reportage,' and claim that it would have been more effective if the reader were asked to tear the page out themselves: "It is precisely because Katué does *not* choose to bypass photo-documentation and use the page as instruction leaflet or the subject-goal of intervention that his work is less effective than it might have been and remains allied to traditional, reified 'art'" (72). Their idea of concrete had become softer; they had inserted the subject back into the work in the forms of the writer as well as the reader, insisting on the practice of an engaged reception of the work to counter the early, orthodox concrete ideal of efficient, reduced language communicating across geographies. Concrete poetry aimed to create a reader; McCaffery and Nichol aimed to have readers create the work.

McCaffery positions the work he produced with Nichol as not limited to their national environment. After an anecdote about the Canadian poet Dorothy Livesay poking McCaffery in the stomach with an umbrella and accusing him, an English immigrant, of taking publishing space from Canadian writers, McCaffery defends the TRG's perspective: "Through the several intellectual differences of our writing lives both [bp] and myself maintained a common subscription to Gertrude Stein's credo that the writer's responsibility is to be contemporary. Contemporary for TRG was non-canonic and international" (18). But the TRG's internationalism is different than what the International Concrete Poetry movement knew as international, just as their post-structural theoretical base was different from the cybernetic and communications theory of the concrete poets. For McCaffery and Nichol, internationalism was not so much the recognition of new networks of communication and cultural exchange opening up terrain, an internationalism that was closely tied to the ideals of modernist development, but rather it was a non-nationalism, a theoretical space that was separate from the material conditions of global citizenry, and as such leaned more towards the cosmopolitanism that Timothy Brennan sees as incompatible with the political project of internationalism (see chapter 2). The internationalism that defined the experience of a figure like Eugen Gomringer, who left Bolivia as a child and moved to Switzerland, itself a polylinguistic space, or of Emmett Williams, an American living in Germany and collaborating with Daniel Spoerri, a Romanian, and other Europeans in the Material Group, is different than that of McCaffery, who moved from England to Canada, one of its colonies. Though Canada is bilingual, there is no evidence that McCaffery or Nichol were interested in the politics of national or international subject formation. In fact, the emphasis by Canadian poets in the late '60s and early '70s on the creation of a national identity was part of what Nichol and McCaffery were actively writing against. But antinationalism is not the same as internationalism. What they considered concrete poetry, as well, was not the same as what had been, up until then, the dominant understanding of the form. It is appropriate that the bulk of their theoretical and poetic output comes within the period I have identified as the terminus of concrete poetry as an international project.

McCaffery and Nichol's work can therefore be viewed as completing the transition from modernism to postmodernism that the international concrete poetry movement had begun in the mid-1950s, switching from a modernist internationalism to a postmodern globalism, and inserting the human subject and its accompanying need for contingency and play into a space where order and structure had previously ruled. The value of reading concrete poetry within postmodernism and the post-structuralism that often gets lumped into the same category is not to claim that it was performing a postmodern function *avant la lettre*, but that its function as a movement, and the conditions which brought about its methods, are both linked to a cultural and economic historical position hinged between modernism and postmodernism. This obfuscating, uncomfortable position is the same one they occupy formally, between poetry and visual art, and between the corresponding distributive forms of the book and the gallery.

/

CONCLUSION:
DESIGNED WORDS IN THE WORLD

Approaching concrete poetry as "designed words" for a "designed world" provides a ground for reading the work spatially. By this I mean that by striving to understand the way the concrete poems signify across forms, nations, languages, and disciplines, readers come up against aesthetic characteristics that cannot be subsumed into a particular formalist or disciplinary discourse, and which require them to shift their critical terrain. Concrete poems are not fixed – rooted to a page or site – but neither do they float. They have histories and functions. They have weight. They *mean* within a larger critical network, and the process of positioning them within a field of understanding has political implications. The modifier "designed" implies that the words are meant to serve a purpose, and challenges critics to question the technological and cultural bases of the work. How are the words instrumentalized in whichever space or sphere they operate? In the case of concrete poetry, the design of the work carries within it the residue of a moment that encountered a radically new way of imagining the world and its inhabitants.

My critical project, one that emphasizes the poetry's historical, social, technological, and artistic contexts, is *designed* to re-signify the term "concrete poetry." My ambition is to prevent readers who encounter the work from understanding it simply as a mid-twentieth-century poetic eccentricity, or as synonymous with visual poetry in its various forms across history. While it might sound bleak, I hope readers will now associate concrete poetry with the effects of nuclear weapons on a world consciousness: how the threat of terrestrial annihilation might have produced new forms of international identity beyond whichever side – American, Soviet, non-aligned – a nation might be on. I hope readers will be unable to avoid linking concrete poetry's compositional strategies to the mathematical approaches to language made possible by early computer technology, or the connection between the International Style of modernist architecture, as it came to ground in Brasília, and the international ambitions of the Brazilian Noigandres group, whose preliminary output was greatly affected by their discovery of a formal compatriot in the figure of Eugen Gomringer, halfway across the world in Switzerland. I hope readers will no longer be able to ignore the relationship between concrete poetry and visual art, and not just the concrete art of Max Bill and the De Stijl group. Concrete poetry is intertwined with the work of the language-centered conceptual artists, as well as that of technology artists who sought to insert their work into new spaces, where the responsibility of the receiver would stand on equal footing of that of the sender. Readers will have to consider the form in which concrete poetry comes to them – by book (mass printed anthology, ephemera, or fine press edition), gallery, or sculpture – and remember that each has historical and spatial ramifications.

In Sianne Ngai's introduction to *Ugly Feelings*, she warns readers that they might be thrown of balance by her willingness to read texts within what she calls "jarring juxtapositions": Martin Heidegger and Alfred Hitchcock with Herman Melville, for example. She defends her practice by arguing that "this method of disjunctive alignment is intended to allow the texts to become 'readable in new ways' and thus generate fresh examinations of historically tenacious problems" (8). This is a political position that stakes its ground against the disciplinary categories that continue to dominate the production of knowledge. Rosalyn Deutsche articulates a similar strategy in her work on the politics of space:

> Radical interdisciplinary work [...] takes account of its own spatial
> relations. It interrogates the epistemological basis and political
> stakes of disciplinary authority. Less interdisciplinary than
> postdisciplinary, such work is based on the premise that objects
> of study are the effect rather than the ground of disciplinary

> knowledge. How these objects are constituted – through which
> exclusions or repressions, is itself a political question that
> conventional forms of interdisciplinarity disregard. Instead, they
> grant their objects of study an independent existence and therefore
> take for granted the existence of absolute foundations underlying
> distinct, specialized areas of knowledge. Mere exchanges of data, of
> course, leave disciplinary identities intact. (208)

Figuring out how culture is designed within spaces which are also designed – that is, created by forces with a function *in mind*, be it the transformation of urban life by architecture or political influence via the imaging of terror – takes on the challenge of thinking across disciplinary and geographical spaces.

There is a risk that departing from disciplinary categories too enthusiastically might result in a generalized, reduced field of knowledge. David Harvey warns of this in his critique of contemporary discourses surrounding cosmopolitanism. He does so by effectively juxtaposing Immanuel Kant's writing on cosmopolitanism, specifically his essay "Perpetual Peace," in which he calls for a "universal law of humanity," against his lesser-known *Geography*, which Harvey cites as an example of a text that fails to understand its subject, and which traffics in generalized racial stereotypes ("Cosmopolitanism" 532). Harvey draws from this example the conclusion that all cosmopolitanism has within it "an embedded geopolitical allegory," and expands on that point to advocate situated geographical research for analyses that stretch across disparate spaces (557). When dealing with poetry that comes out of Italy, France, Brazil, Canada, the United States, Czechoslovakia, Austria, Germany, Switzerland, the United Kingdom, and several others, and that seeks to operate in an international exchange, Harvey's warning would produce significant anxiety in even the most worldly critic. Franco Moretti, who works on a global scale, defends his practice of following forms across national and linguistic boundaries through the concept of "distant reading," a structural approach that uses literature as data in order to elucidate a systematic understanding ("Conjectures" 57). However, there is also a value to a macro perspective that does not seek out a system, but rather critically juxtaposes cultural material in spaces that are not fused completely with physical locations: cultural geographies. Concrete poetry, in its explicit desire to function globally, calls out for such an approach.

Determining how designed words function within a designed world, as a critical approach, offers a method for understanding contemporary poetic and artistic production, as well. The world and its words are not any less designed today than fifty years ago, although different strategies have appeared which allow for new paths of investigation. The work of Kenneth Goldsmith, for example, occupies a curious intersection between poetry and art, explicitly in his designation of it as "conceptual poetry," after Sol LeWitt's formulation of "conceptual art," but also in relationship to Andy Warhol's films and pieces by other artists that deal with information technologies. His *Day*, which is a transcription of the complete *text* – including page numbers, stock quotes, and any words found in advertisements – of the September 1, 2000 edition of the *New York Times*, has a connection with Vito Acconci's "Page/Pages: Reading the First Page of the *New York Times*, Saturday, June 21, 1969." Goldsmith's text, I am sure he would argue, is far less interesting: Goldsmith himself admits to using boredom as a strategy; he aims for boredom (Goldsmith, "Being Boring"). He achieves this in part through collecting and archiving expired information, information that at one point was vital enough to be printed or broadcast, but which loses its charge almost instantly. This strategy is clear in *Day*, but also in his American Trilogy: *The Weather*, in which he transcribes and arranges a year's worth of weather reports from a New York radio station; *Traffic*, in which he transcribes a twenty-four-hour period of New York traffic reports, broadcast every ten minutes; and *Sports*, in which he transcribes the commentary from the longest nine-inning Major League Baseball game on record, between the Boston Red Sox and New York Yankees on 21 August 2006.

What are we to make of these texts' attitude toward information in the initial years of the twenty-first century? How does Goldsmith's approach to language as excess relate to the conceptual artists' understanding of language as transparent? And what is a reader to take away from the centrality of New York City to Goldsmith and the production of conceptual art, considering the dramatically altered global context surrounding that city? How does Goldsmith's New York differ from Warhol's? Goldsmith's work is readily available on the internet as well as in book form: how should we read them differently? Each has its particular material effects, especially considering the literary limbo created by e-book readers and online publications, a condition that has ramifications for ideas of intellectual property, distribution, and access. Where do we read, now? What are our languages, and how are they conditioned? How do we define literary space at this moment, and how does that allow us to theorize how we defined it in the past, when the question seemed less pressing?

The digital poetry of Brian Kim Stefans poses related questions in different form. He describes, in the introduction to his poem "The Dream Life of

Letters," how he was dissatisfied with a poem he had written in response to a poem presented by the poet Rachel Blau DuPlessis. He composed a poem that transformed DuPlessis's work; he re-ordered all its words alphabetically, implementing a compositional strategy that has links to the statistical treatment of language in Max Bense's work. But, as Stefans points out in the introduction to the final version of his poem, he became dissatisfied with the work as it aged, and how it stubbornly insisted on a settled, still form: "as it was in a sort of antique 'concrete' mode, it resembled a much older aesthetic, one well explored by Gomringer, the De [sic] Campos brothers and numerous others in the past fifty years, and so it wasn't very interesting to me" (Stefans). He transformed the text by animating it with Flash, a program that the vast majority of internet users encounter on a daily basis without knowing it. In this way he goes a step further than a poet like Carl Fernbach-Flarsheim, who composed work in Fortran, the programming language developed by IBM in the 1950s, or the hypertextual experiments of Ted Nelson and Ned Woodman in their catalogue for the *Software* exhibition in 1970. The work that Stefans produces is visual, but it is not concrete. It would be better described as a parallel infrastructural material: broadband. The conditions required to view Stefan's eleven- to fourteen-minute Flash-video-poem are recent, but no less significant than those which the development of reinforced concrete produced for the modernist project.

A similarly productive roiling occurs when approaching the work of Christian Bok, specifically *The Xenotext*, his attempt to create a living, self-replicating poem using a chemical alphabet to compose a DNA sequence to inject into bacteria. Like the computer poetry of the 1960s and '70s, but more complex, and tied to the body, questions come up about where the poetry exists. In which processes, in which media, in which contexts and moments does the act of poetic production manifest, and from which subjectivity? Are these even the correct terms anymore? When Darren Wershler and Bill Kennedy refer to themselves as "compilers" rather than poets in their role as developer-programmer-authors of *Apostrophe Engine*, a text comprised of "you are" phrases that completely transforms itself into all new "you are" phrases when a user/reader clicks on a phrase, notions of authorship, subjectivity, and algorithmic identity all tumble into the foreground. Although categorized under the rubric of "conceptual writing," these works demand approaches that move beyond models of the literary, or of the historical avant-garde, and are best served by multi-disciplinary, polyvocal engagements. These works are invitations to methods.

The dominant initial critical experience I feel when "reading" these contemporary texts is that, despite their familiarity, I lack the lexicon to engage them. I had the exact same experience when I first encountered concrete poetry. In the case of "The Dreamlife of Letters," to adequately engage with it I would have to learn more about Flash animation, and the way language has developed and is still developing on the internet. But a satisfactory reading would require a more expansive approach, one that would take into account the internet's demographic (literally, a writing of and by the *demos*, but a specific and exclusive *demos*), as well as the policies, both political and economic, that define what we commonly understand as an unmappable – to borrow a term from computer coding – space. There are new spaces in this world, but there are also old spaces. Words perform in both. How should we read them, and what can our reading do?

NOTES

Chapter 1

1 Fahlström was born in São Paulo and lived in Brazil until he was ten, but I have never come across a reference to him as a Brazilian-Swedish poet. Eugen Gomringer, however, is often referred to as Bolivian-Swiss, which likely has to do with the amount of time he spent as a child in Bolivia as well as his practice of composing poems in Spanish as well as German and English.

2 Haun Saussy provides a list of critiques of Pound and Fenollosa's approach: "for an account of the 'ideogram' that classes it among fallacies of translation, see [Jean] Paulhan, *La preuve par l'étymologie*; for a thorough-going polemic against the idea of ideography, see [John] DeFrancis, *The Chinese Language*. For an overall (if partisan) account of Pound's 'invention of Chinese,' see [Hugh] Kenner, *The Pound Era*" (Saussy, 177n).

3 Kostelanetz actually includes two different Hinde photographs of Piccadilly Circus, each equally full of advertising, on pages 9 and 34. The one described here is on page 9.

4 There are exceptions to this rule. Figures such as the East German poet Carlfriedrich Claus developed a very distinctive, handwritten style that was widely anthologized, and the American Carl Fernbach-Flarsheim often used handwriting in his poems, but for the most part the concrete

poetry is produced mechanically. Canadian concrete poets like bill bissett and bpNichol, who largely operated outside the scope of the International Concrete Poetry movement, and who were prolific in the 1970s, also composed much of their work by hand.

5 According to Kathleen McCullough's nearly exhaustive bibliography of concrete poetry, Andre was not published as a concrete poet until 1978, in Alberto Pimenta's *Il silenzio dei poeti* (15).

6 "Il y a comme un point aveugle de notre histoire des idées et des arts : l'attention légitimement portée sur les avant-gardes fait oublier tout le reste, au risque de fausser notre perception historique en déséquilibrant le point de vue."

7 There have been studies in other languages, as the Portuguese, Spanish, German, Italian, and French have been much better at recognizing the importance of the work, though primarily within their national traditions. Most recently it has been the art world that has worked to reconsider concrete poetry and position the work within its historical moment, with exhibitions in Brazil (*Concreta '56: a raiz da forma* at the Museu de Arte Moderna and *Poesia Concreta: o projeto verbivocovisual* at the Instituto Tomie Ohtake and the Fundação Clóvis Salgado), England (*Poor. Old. Tired. Horse.* at ICA), and Canada (*Letters: Michael Morris and Concrete Poetry* at the Morris and Helen Belkin Gallery).

8 Canada warrants three lines, devoted to the single Canadian participant, bpNichol: "Canada's leading concrete poet is B.P. Nichol [sic], one of the editors of GRONK. From his text we learn that 'love' is also a beautiful word to look at" (47).

9 Of the four major anthologies in English – Stephen Bann's, Emmett Williams's, Eugene Wildman's, and Solt's – only Solt's maintains a rigid nationalist division. Bann's is divided into three sections based on language, the Brazilian and the German (including in it the Swiss and the Austrian) poems representing the first wave, and the English (including British and American) representing the second wave. Williams's is organized alphabetically by poet, and Wildman's seems to be organized by the aesthetics of the editor.

10 The FRG was officially recognized in September 1949 but did not achieve full sovereignty until 1954. The GDR was created in October 1949 (Gumpel 3).

11 This conflation continues in the remainder of the quotation: "Such poetry reflects a consciousness of concrete qualities and has played a role in the more or less continuous tradition leading from the origins of writing to

the sort of poetry which this book is about. The term 'concrete' will thus be used, from time to time here, to refer to aspects of earlier work within the tradition" (2).

12 She cites Gomringer's statement that concrete poetry is supranational, as well as his proof that it developed simultaneously in Switzerland and Brazil, and then quotes his statement "I am therefore convinced that concrete poetry is in the process of realizing the idea of a universal poetry" (12). But she attributes this to his 1954 manifesto "From Line to Constellation," when, in fact, Gomringer did not apply the term concrete to his poems until 1955, and the text she is actually quoting from is his 1956 manifesto "Concrete Poetry."

13 Bayard misses the opportunity to defend her position as it relates directly to Canadian concrete poetry, however. A significant amount of critical writing around Canadian concrete poetry was developed with such language-centered or, to use Bayard's terminology, postmodern theory in mind, coming as it did in the 1970s, and much of it out of bpNichol and Steve McCaffery's Toronto Research Group (TRG), a collaboration known for its engagement with contemporary theoretical (often continental) texts.

14 Cf. Mary Ellen Solt (254) and Mike Weaver (101), who both present the poem in its social context.

Chapter 2

1 The original printing of the poem, in *Noigandres* 5, was black ink on white paper, and did not include a translation. In Emmett Williams's anthology, the poem is also not printed in red, and a gloss is offered that provides similar information to Solt and Quieroz's translation, but without any explanation of "cloaca." The font of the poem in Williams's is also different than the original Futura used by Pignatari.

2 The term "coca-colonization" gained renewed popularity in the antiglobalization movement of the 1990s and 2000s, likely spurred in part by the publication of Reinhold Wagnleitner's 1994 book, *Coca-Colonization and the Cold War: The Cultural Mission of the United States in Austria After the Second World War* (University of North Carolina Press).

3 The Japanese artist Isao Hashimoto's video work *1945–1998* (2003) displays the locations of the 2,053 nuclear tests carried out by various nations between the years of 1945 and 1998, and is a powerful representation of how pervasive nuclear weapon testing was in the latter half of the twentieth century.

4 See the catalogues for Serge Guilbaut's *Be-Bomb: The Transatlantic War of Images and All That Jazz, 1946-56* (2007), and Paul Schimmel's *Destroy the Picture: Painting the Void 1949–1962* (2012), and John O'Brian's *Camera Atomica* (2015).

5 In *The Code Book*, Simon Singh suggests that Rejewski's machine was called the "bombe" because of the regular ticking of its sifting through messages, and the force that its discoveries could have in the outcome of the war. Or, he also suggests, it might be named so because Rejewski came up with the concept for the machine while in a café, eating a hemisphere of ice cream known in Poland as a "bombe" (156)

6 Translated by Edwin Morgan as "ALEA I – SEMANTIC VARIATIONS (a mock-pocket-epic)" (de Campos 106).

7 "as possibilidades de permutação entre dez letras diferentes dus palavras de cinco letras cada ascendem a 3.628.800" (de Campos 179).

8 Janet Flanner, writing under the pseudonym Genet for *The New Yorker*, points out that in 1961 alone, the organization who considered Charles de Gaulle a traitor for negotiating with the Front de Libération Nationale (FLN) towards Algerian independence, had set off one hundred and ninety-one bombs in Paris, and one hundred and sixty-one in the provinces (151).

9 It is significant that Fiore was a student of the German artist George Grosz, who, along with John Heartsfield was one of the first practitioners of photomontage, and who used the technique to great effect in criticizing the political environment in Germany under the National Socialists (Cavell 127).

10 For an in-depth analysis of how time and space have changed with advances in industrial and economic organization since the early modern period, see Part III of David Harvey's *The Condition of Postmodernity: An Enquiry into the Origins of Cultural Change.*

11 Henri Chopin is sympathetic to the position of Garnier and McLuhan and Fiore: "In short, the Word is responsible because instead of making it a way of life we've made it an end. Prisoner of the Word is the child, and so will he be all his adult life" ("Why I Am" 81).

12 Canadian concrete poets bpNichol and Steve McCaffery, in their collaborative form as the Toronto Research Group, reproduced Quentin and Fiore's thumb photographs in their "TRG Report 2: Narrative Part 1 – The Book as Machine," published in *Open Letter* 6 (Fall 1973): 113–20 (McCaffery and Nichol 80–1). The thumbs they use belong to the same hand, however.

13 For a well-researched and fascinating contextualization of McLuhan and Fiore's book experiments within photo-printing technology and design, see Jeffrey T. Schnapp and Adam Michaels's *The Electric Information Age Book: McLuhan/Agel/Fiore and the Experimental Paperback*.

14 Kittler introduces his book *Gramophone, Film, Typewriter* (originally published in German in 1986) with a discussion of the (at the time) rather new technology of fibre optic cable networks, which he notes are impervious to the electromagnetic interference that would result from a nuclear explosion, and which he also notes is of major concern for the Pentagon, who count on such networks for reliable communication during wartime (1). Strengthening the link between the H-Bomb and Turing's Bombe, Kittler goes on to discuss the development of computer technology by Turing and his group in their attempt to crack the Enigma code (17–19).

15 Appadurai tempers some of his optimism in *Modernity at Large* in his subsequent book, describing *Modernity's* approach as "too harsh in its criticisms of the modern nation-state and naively cheerful about the benefits of global flows" (*Fear of* 3).

16 For an attempt to characterize concrete poetry as a primarily South American poetic form – by designating Gomringer, the son of a Swiss father and Bolivian mother, and who lived in Bolivia as a child, and even Öyvind Fahlström, who was born in São Paulo to Swedish parents and lived there until he was 10, as South American poets – see David Colón's "'Now what the DEFFIL can that mean!': The Latin American Roots, Rhetoric, and Resistance of Concrete Poetry."

17 This passage by Goethe, and Marx and Engels' mention of world literature in *The Communist Manifesto* (1848), form the two originary moments for the field of world literature. Interestingly, the passage in which Marx and Engels refer to world literature is also the passage in which they bring about an idea of cosmopolitanism (476–7).

18 "Area studies were established to secure US power in the Cold War. Comparative literature was a result of European intellectuals fleeing 'totalitarian' regimes. Cultural and Postcolonial Studies relate to the 500 percent increase in Asian immigration in the wake of Lyndon Johnson's reform of the Immigration Act of 1965. Whatever our view of what we do, we are made by the forces of people moving about the world" (Spivak 3).

19 Spivak shares a suspicion of the emphasis on the novel as the primary genre for imagining the routes of global culture, and indeed sees it as an impediment to understanding cultural responses to globalization.

In her essay for Robbins and Cheah's collection *Cosmopolitics: Thinking and Feeling Beyond the Nation*, she writes, in reference to Jean-François Lyotard's model of the "oral formulaic epic tradition" ("Cultural" 331):

> Incidentally, this particular tradition, through long historical transmogrification, is alive and well in counterglobal revolutionary theater (indeed, the theater for political mobilization is the most stylized end of all politics of counterdiscourse), not necessarily in the hegemonic language, owing little or nothing to the European novelistic tradition, about which Benedict Anderson et al. go on endlessly. This phenomenon falls out of benevolent definitions of world literature, produced in the North. Cultural politics. (332)

20 The connection between poetry and mathematical computation is usually associated with the OULIPO group, which was founded by Raymond Queneau and François Le Lionnais in 1960. Unfortunately, critics rarely connect their practice to the communication theory of the time, with most accounts categorizing them as inheritors of Surrealism.

21 Gumpel identifies a strong concrete poetry tradition in East Germany but explains that it did not have the same meaning as in the west. "Concrete" in East Germany referred more to an emphasis on the everyday lives of citizens and their work than a concern for the philosophical or social ramifications of an emphasis on the visual character of language. In this way it has more in common with previous socialist realist movements than what most critics would today refer to as concrete poetry. And although I argue that concrete poetry was very much a Western poetry, many poets practiced within Soviet bloc countries such as Poland and Yugoslavia in the 1960s and 1970s.

Chapter 3

1 Although the Plano-Piloto was published in 1958, it was actually assembled writings by members of the Noigandres group that had been published between 1950 and 1958.

2 For an in-depth analysis of the relationship between the Noigrandres poets and concrete art in Brazil, see Claus Clüver, "The Noigrandres Poets and Concrete Art."

3 Gerhard Rühm is unflinching in his condemnation of Döhl's work as bad concrete poetry: "[Döhl's poem] belongs on the joke page of a magazine

rather than in a serious literature lexicon or an anthology of concrete poetry" ("Personal" 223).

4 Some public buildings in England were made from concrete as early as the 1880s: "This allowed the public to become to some extent familiar with the general characteristics of the method, and enabled great advances to be made in structural techniques; but it did not force architects to study the aesthetic potentialities of the material, and it was precisely these which the public, having seen the factories and railway sheds, most distrusted" (Collins 78).

5 "Art Nouveau, born, or at any rate baptized in 1896 (when it received its name), obviously needed a new plastic material if its buildings were to be organically constructed; ferro-concrete, which had been patented by François Hennebique only four years earlier, and used in his first factory the previous year, urgently required an appropriate and original architectural form if it were not to be merely a means of stylistic imitation. Instead therefore of carving solid ashlar into intricate rounded shapes, what could be a more obvious solution of both problems than to utilize this new plastic structural system in its most logical way, by moulding it with all the *élan* which modern fashion required?" (Collins 121).

6 This is excepting poets such as the East German Carlfriedrich Claus or the British John Furnival, both of whose poems are usually intricate images made up of handwriting or fields of type.

7 Read begins his essay with an account of how civil service demonstrators in Brasília in 2003, who were protesting against the drastic reduction of pension benefits, began smashing the large plate glass windows of the Congresso Nacional. The poignancy of the image comes from the fact that the pension benefits were part of the very social package that included the construction of Brasília as a modernist utopian project. Their attack on the very architecture of Brasília as a symbol of failed promises is therefore especially apt, particularly against the large glass in particular as it was meant to function as both a metaphor for truth and transparency but also as a representation of reinforced concrete's ability to provide such structurally sound *openness* "with its soaring spans and uncommon cantilevers" (Niemeyer, quoted in Read 262).

8 "The relationship between design, advertising, and typography, in particular, was firmly established at the beginning. The Bauhuas concept of 'good form' had a decisive influence, and we generally chose sans-serif, non-decorative fonts for their clarity and precision. The microgeometry of the letters contributed to the macrogeometry of the poetry during concrete poetry's initial phase."

9 "'Popcretos,' c'est une terminologie que j'ai créée un peu comme par jeu, car nous n'avions pas à cette époque l'intention de créer un nouveau mouvement. C'était à la fois un peu de jeu par rapport aux orthodoxies de la poésie concrète, et un peu d'autocritique. Et ces expériences incorporaient un peu de pop art, de vie quotidienne. [...] Ces poèmes et ces travaux avaient bien sûr un certaine direction politique parce que c'était le moment de la dictature militaire au Brésil; les poèmes offraient une sémantique politique, essayaient, un peu sous l'influence du concept de Maïakovski, d'établir une connexion entre une position politique révolutionnaire et un art révolutionnaire" (de Campos "Entretien" 377).

10 The only signatory from Brazil was E.M. de Melo e Castro. There is a note at the end of the text that Ferdinand Kriwet agrees with parts of the declaration, and that Henri Chopin could not sign it for reasons that "are discussed within his poetry" (Garnier, "Position I of the International" 80; 1968). A note on an earlier, unpublished version claims that the Noigandres group preferred to remain within the formulation of concrete poetry in their 1958 "Plano-Piloto Para Poesia Concreta," and that Garnier had yet to hear back from the Stuttgart group, comprised of Bense, Reinhold Döhl, Ludwig Harig, and Claus Henneberg (Garnier "Position I du Mouvement"; 1963).

11 The dry-transfer lettering known as Letraset came onto the market in 1961 and was instantly successful. Although there is no evidence that it was widely used amongst concrete poets, who preferred, for the most part, the typewriter, letterpress, and hand-lettering, it is likely that it contributed to at least some of the work, specifically those pieces that use irregular fields of orientation, like Mary Ellen Solt's flower series. The popularity of Letraset amongst graphic designers, a profession amongst which several concrete poets can be counted (Pignatari, Gomringer, Roth) is well documented (Consuegra 265).

Chapter 4

1 See, for examples, Jesper Olssen's "Kneaded Language: Concrete Poetry and New Media in the Swedish 1960s" (*Modernism/modernity* 18.2 [2011]) and "Writing through the Data Banks: A Note on Poetry and Technology in the Swedish 1960s" (http://www.dichtung-digital.com/2003/4-olsson. htm); Antonia Sergio Bessa's *Öyvindh Fahlström: The Art of Writing* (Northwestern University Press, 2010); Claus Clüver's "The Noigandres Poets and Concrete Art," (Pos 1.1 [2008]; and Marjorie Perloff's *Unoriginal*

Genius: Poetry by Other Means in the New Century (University of Chicago Press, 2010).While much recent critical work has concentrated on the output of specific poets or groups, or even national traditions, the ideas discussed can translate easily across national and formal boundaries to open up questions of distribution and reception as they relate to concrete poetry in its global milieu.

2 Liz Kotz's *Words to be Looked At: Language in 1960s Art* (MIT Press, 2007) follows Simon Morely's *Writing on the Wall: Word and Image in Modern Art* (University of California Press, 2005) in attempting to account for language use in visual art. For work on how conceptual art manifested in different geographies, see Alexander Alberro and Sabeth Buchmann's *Art After Conceptual Art* (MIT Press, 2006) and Alberro and Blake Stimson's *Conceptual Art: A Critical Anthology* (MIT Press, 2000).

3 It is worth noting here how rare it is to come across "collectors" of poetry, especially collectors who display work in a gallery. It is the unique character of concrete and visual poetry – as distinguished, at times with difficulty, from "text art" – that opens that discursive space between book and gallery, page and poster. The value of the Sackner collection to critics and practitioners of concrete and visual poetry cannot be overstated.

4 On at least one occasion, conceptual art and concrete poetry were exhibited beside each other. One of Joseph Kosuth's Photostat dictionary definitions – in this case for the word "abstract" – appeared in the University of British Columbia's 1969 exhibtion, *Concrete Poetry: An Exhibition in 4 Parts*.

5 Although there has been much written recently about the relationship between conceptual art and poetry, almost entirely as a result of the designation of certain contemporary compositional techniques as "conceptual writing," much of the work takes a rather narrow approach to conceptual art. When Kenneth Goldsmith consciously plagiarizes Sol LeWitt's "Paragraphs on Conceptual Art," substituting "Writing" for "Art," and "writer" for "artist" throughout, he enacts a technique that has more to do with current technologies of literary and cultural production than engaging with conceptual art. Similarly, Craig Dworkin, in his introduction to his and Goldsmith's edited anthology *Against Expression: An Anthology of Conceptual Writing*, at times moves too easily between conceptual art and conceptual writing, and the anthology itself collects an extremely diverse sample of literature under the rubric of "conceptual writing." For a more complete analysis of the relationship between conceptual writing and conceptual art, see Judith Goldman's "Re-thinking 'Non-Retinal Literature'" in *Postmodern Culture* 22.1 (September): 2011.

6 This dialogue intensified around *Global Conceptualism,* a collaboratively curated, large-scale international exhibition at Queens Museum of Art, New York, in 1999.

7 Meyer points out that Andre's background was working class, but his family was literary, and as a child adults would often recite poetry to him, even on a jobsite where they might be working together: "His father, an immigrant from Sweden, had not learned English until the sixth grade. While Andre's mother and uncle were his earliest instructors in the rhythm and meter of poetical language, his father taught a different lesson: the semantic specificity of the word. The English lexicon, hard won, was greatly prized in the household on Moffat Road, and not only the diction of the great poets" (11). For what it is worth, this biographical anecdote might provide some understanding of Andre's fixation on English and the American tradition, and perhaps his rejection of a parallel poetic project, that of the concrete poets, who also understood the power of English, but who addressed it as a potentially imperial force, and dealt with it through translation, formally simplified language, and by paying attention to the transformation language was undergoing at mid-century.

8 That Smithson should laud Andre's poetry for its displacement from the political and temporal that necessarily accompany dialectical materialism is not surprising given Smithson's own practice, in which measurements of the human are often subordinated to those of the earth or the universe. But Smithson's fixation on geological time is often too close to theological time, which extracts itself from the human scale. The critical success of such a position speaks loudly of the privileged site of production that both Smithson and Andre were working out of at the time.

9 Andre's statement would prove prophetic, as a few years later, in 1966, Mary Ellen Solt would produce a series of poems in which the names of flowers and plants were arranged into shapes that mimicked the shapes of their referents. Her decision to put one of these poems, "Forsythia," on the cover of her 1968 anthology, *Concrete Poetry: A World View,* perhaps the most widely referenced of the concrete poetry anthologies in English, is likely a contributing factor in the sustained link between concrete poetry and mimetic, decorative compositions. There is more to this poem, however, as each of the "stems" is comprised of Morse code symbols for the corresponding letters, linking the tradition of pastoral poetry with the new understanding of nature in contemporary communication theory.

10 The poem suggests a possible reference to the North American colloquial verb phrase "to pig out," but the OED locates the phrase's first usage only

as early as 1978. Thanks to Jeff Derksen for bringing this phrase to my attention.

11 The Brazilian concrete poets were more likely than any other group to work with colours in their compositions, but it was not as a result of forsaking the typewriter. Augusto de Campos's "Poetamenos" series from 1953, for example, which consists of fragmented speech and syntax in coloured fonts arranged on coloured pages, was composed using a typewriter and coloured carbon paper (*Poesia Concreta* 18).

12 At this point in his career, much of Andre's poetic output had become primarily prose printed in blocks, as in *Still A Novel* (1972), which disrupted reading by repeating letters and eliminating spaces, but which could still be decoded by the reader in the way that a word-search grid puzzle might function, a technique he was still using in 2001, though with handwriting instead of a typewriter. The shapes or appearance of the puzzles have no relation to the meaning of the statements or words, but function strictly as an impediment to reading. There are a few examples of poems from earlier in the sixties where words are illegible because of over-inking, or of a work that uses only punctuation to create an op-art type pattern via page adjustment. These works would place him in direct relation to concrete poetry, but they are never addressed by him or by his critics, and they have not been published beyond a limited edition of thirty-six loose-leaf binders.

13 He received only one response, in 1974, which he published in his book *For Publication* (1975).

14 The title "Poem" was dropped for its publication in *Art & Language* 1:1 in 1969 (Graham, *Dan* 96).

15 Note that, besides Piper, these are the artists that Kosuth refers to as the concrete poets who are turning to theater in Lippard's *Six Years* ...

Chapter 5

1 McLuhan was a critic of print media and its ordering effects, but he nevertheless continued to write books about space, though while concurrently producing films, sound recordings, and television programs to distribute his ideas. His books after *Understanding Media* were, however, examples of books written *against* the idea of the book, and made use of many of the graphic techniques implemented by concrete poetry. For an exhaustive and convincing treatment of McLuhan as book-artist, see chapter 5 of Richard Cavell's *McLuhan in Space: A Cultural Geography*.

2 (*Os meios de comunicação como extensões do homem*. São Paulo: Cultrix, 1969).

3 For a critique of both Harvey's and Jameson's approaches to postmodernist space, particularly in regard to feminist cultural practice and theory, see Rosalyn Deutsche's *Evictions: Art and Spatial Politics*.

4 See Max Bense's discussion of an advertisement for Dubonnet in comparison to a poem by Eugen Gomringer in chapter 1 (19).

5 I am assuming Goldsmith wrote this tweet, though it is likely somebody else affiliated with UbuWeb has access to the Twitter account. Twelve minutes before this tweet, Goldsmith tweeted an announcement of Primary Information's re-issue of Wiliams's anthology from his personal account (Goldsmith [kg_ubu]).

6 This is sometimes not an issue, especially if the poem exists *as* photograph, like in the case of some of Kitasono Katué's "Plastic Poems."

7 *Poesia visiva* is at times difficult to distinguish from concrete poetry, but by the former I mean those works that generally do not engage with the page or the appearance of printed language *as* material, but which consist of language printed *onto* material. These are not discrete categories with consistent rules. While photographs may sometimes be used to document concrete poems that could not easily be represented otherwise, photography is almost always an integral part of the circulation of *poesia visiva*. Julien Blaine's "Breuvage épandu" is an example of what I would consider *poesia visiva*, more than as concrete poetry (see fig. 5.9).

8 I realize that claiming Bory and the other anthologists, in their placement of concrete poetry within the lineage of visual literature stretching back to ancient times, are operating ahistorically may sound paradoxical, but, as I argue in my introductory chapter under the concept of the "historical mode," the extraction of concrete poetry from its geo-historical context in order to connect it to the formal experiments of "writing" does the exact opposite of *historicizing* it. By making it common to all time, it makes it specific to no time.

REFERENCES

Acconci, Vito. 2006. *Language to Cover a Page: The Early Writings of Vito Acconci*. Edited by Craig Dworkin. Cambridge, MA: MIT Press.

– 2006. "Page/Pages: Reading the First Page of *The New York Times*, Saturday, June 21, 1969." In *Language to Cover a Page: The Early Writings of Vito Acconci*, edited by Craig Dworkin, 125. Cambridge, MA: MIT Press.

Alberro, Alexander. 2003. *Conceptual Art and the Politics of Publicity*. Cambridge, MA: MIT Press.

– 2000. "Reconsidering Conceptual Art, 1966–77." In Alberro and Stimson 2000, xvi–xxxvii.

– 1998. "Structure as Content: Dan Graham's Schema (March 1996) and the Emergence of Conceptual Art." In *Dan Graham*, edited by Gloria Moure, 21–9. Barcelona, Spain: Fundaciõ Antoni Tàpies.

Alberro, Alexander, and Blake Stimson, eds. 2000. *Conceptual Art: A Critical Anthology*. Cambridge, MA: MIT Press.

Alberro, Alexander, and Sabeth Buchmann, eds. 2006. *Art after Conceptual Art*. Cambridge, MA: MIT Press.

Anderson, Benedict. 1983. *Imagined Communities: Reflections on the Origin and Spread of Nationalism*. London: Verso.

Andre, Carl, 2005. "Green." In *Cuts: Texts 1959–2004*, edited by James Meyer, 195. Cambridge, MA: MIT Press.

Andre, Carl and Hollis Frampton. 1981. *12 Dialogues: 1962–1963*. Edited by
  Benjamin H. Buchloh. Halifax: Press of the Nova Scotia College of Art and
  Design.
Appadurai, Arjun. 2000. "Grassroots Globalization and the Research
  Imagination." *Public Culture* 12 (1): 1–19.
– 1996. *Modernity at Large: Cultural Dimensions of Globalization*. Minneapolis:
  University of Minnesota Press.
Arendt, Hannah. 1993. "The Conquest of Space and the Stature of Man." In
  Between Past and Future, 265–82. New York: Penguin Books.
Azeredo, Ronaldo. 2006. "Velocidade." In *Concreta '56: a raiz da forma*, edited
  by Lorenzo Mammì, João Bandeira, André Stolarski, and Carolina Soares,
  171. São Paulo: Museo de Arte Moderna de São Paulo. Exhibition catalogue.
Bann, Stephen, ed. 1967. *Concrete Poetry: An International Anthology*. London:
  London Magazine Editions.
– 2010. Unpublished interview with Stephen Bann. By Anna Katharina
  Schaffner. 18 November 2010. Canterbury, UK. N. pag.
Barthes, Roland. 1967. "The Death of the Author." Translated by Richard
  Howard. *Aspen* 5–6: n. pag.
Bayard, Caroline. 1989. *The New Poetics in Canada and Quebec: From
  Concretism to Post-Modernism*. Toronto: University of Toronto Press.
Beniger, James R. 1986. *The Control Revolution: Technological and Economics
  Origins of the Information Society*. Cambridge, MA: Harvard University
  Press.
Benjamin, Walter. 1968. "On Some Motifs in Baudelaire." In *Illuminations:
  Essays and Reflections*, translated by Harry Zohn, 155–200. New York:
  Schoken Books.
Bense, Max. 1968. "Concrete Poetry." In Solt 1968, 73.
– 1971. "The Projects of Generative Aesthetics." In *Cybernetics, Art, and Ideas*,
  edited by Jasia Reichardt, 57–60. Greenwich, CT: New York Graphic
  Society, Ltd.
– 1968. "Statistical Text." In Solt 1968, 122.
Bill, Max. 1993. "The Mathematical Way of Thinking in the Visual Art of
  Our Time." In *The Visual Mind: Art and Mathematics*, edited by Michele
  Emmer, 5–9. Cambridge, MA: MIT Press.
Blaine, Julien. 1968. "Breuvage épandu." In Bory 1968, 46–9.
Bohn, Willard. 1986. *The Aesthetics of Visual Poetry, 1914–28*. Cambridge, UK:
  Cambridge University Press.
Bory, Jean François, ed. 1968. *Once Again: Concrete Poetry*. Translated by Lee
  Hildreth. New York: New Directions Press.

Bowcott, Owen. 2008. "Britain Lays Claim to 200,000 sq km of the South Atlantic Seabed." *The Guardian*, 24 May, 17.

Bowler, Berjouhi. 1970. *The Word as Image*. London: Studio Vista.

Brennan, Timothy. 2001. "Cosmopolitanism and Internationalism." *New Left Review* 7 (Jan–Feb): 75–84.

Buchloh, Benjamin. 1990. "Conceptual Art 1962–1969: From the Aesthetic of Administration to the Critique of Institutions." *October* 55 (Winter): 105–43.

Burda, Vladimir. 1968. "Ich." In Bory 1968, 79.

Bürger Peter. 1984. *Theory of the Avant-Garde*. Minneapolis: University of Minnesota Press.

Burkeman, Oliver. 2008. "A Very Cold War Indeed." *The Guardian*, 5 April, 16.

Burnham, Jack. 1968. "System Esthetics." *Artforum* 7 (September): 30–5.

Buschinger, Philippe. 2001. Écriture *et typographie en occident et en extrême orient*. Paris: Université Paris.

Campos, Cid, et al. 2008. *Poesia concreta: o projeto verbivocovisual*. Edited by João Bandeira and Lenora de Barros. São Paulo, BR: Artemeios.

Cavell, Richard. 2002. *McLuhan in Space: A Cultural Geography*. Toronto: University of Toronto Press.

Cheah, Pheng, and Bruce Robbins, eds. 1998. *Cosmopolitics: Thinking and Feeling Beyond the Nation*. Minneapolis: University of Minnesota Press.

Chopin, Henri. 1983. "The Limitations of Lettrisme: An Interview with Henri Chopin." By Nicholas Zurbrugg. In *Lettrisme: Into the Present*. Spec issue of *Visible Language* 17: 57–69.

– 1970. "Poem to Be Read Aloud." In *Anthology of Concretism*, edited by Eugene Wildman, 79. Chicago: The Swallow Press.

– 1968. "Why I Am the Author of Sound Poetry and Free Poetry." In Solt 1968, 80–2.

Clifford, James. 1988. *The Predicament of Culture: Twentieth Century Ethnography, Literature, and Art*. Cambridge, MA: Harvard University Press.

Clüver, Claus. 2000. "Concrete Poetry and the New Performance Arts: Intersemiotic, Intermedia, Intercultural." In *East of West: Cross-Cultural Performance and the Staging of Difference*, edited by Claire Sponsler and Xiaomei Chen, 33–62. New York: Palgrave.

– 2008. "The Noigandres Poets and Concrete Art." *Pós* 1 (May): 114–35.

Collins, Peter. (1959) 2004. *Concrete: The Vision of a New Architecture*. Montreal: McGill-Queen's University Press.

Colón, David. 2003. "'Now what the DEFFIL can that mean!': The Latin

American Roots, Rhetoric, and Resistance of Concrete Poetry." *Journal of Latino-Latin American Studies* 1 (1): 34–45.

Consuegra, David. 2004. *American Type: Design and Designers*. New York: Allworth Press.

Cook, Geoffrey. 1979. "Visual Poetry as a Molting." In Kostelanetz 1979, 141–2.

Cosgrove, Denis. 2001. *Apollo's Eye: A Cartographic Genealogy of the Earth in the Western Imagination*. Baltimore: Johns Hopkins University Press.

– 1994. "Contested Global Visions: One-world, Whole-Earth, and the Apollo Space Photographs." *Annals of the Association of American Geographers* 84 (2): 270–94.

Crommelin, Liesbeth. 1970. "Some Notes on the Exhibition." In *Concrete Poetry?*, edited by Liesbeth Crommelin et. al, n. pag. Amsterdam: Stedelijk Museum. Exhibition catalogue.

Curtay, Jean-Paul. 1983. "Super-Writing 1983 – America 1683." In *Lettrisme: Into the Present*, spec. Issue of *Visible Language* 17: 26–47.

de Campos, Augusto. 1964. *Cidade / city / cité*. Stonypath, UK: Wild Hawthorn Press.

– 1982. "The Concrete Coin of Speech." Translated by Jon M. Tolman. *Poetics Today* 3 (3): 167–76.

– 2006. "Concreto." In *Concreta '56: a raiz da forma*, edited by Lorenzo Mammì, João Bandeira, André Stolarski, and Carolina Soares, 145. São Paulo: Museo de Arte Moderna de São Paulo. Exhibition catalogue.

– 1993. "Entretien avec Augusto de Campos." By Jacques Donguy. In *Poésure et Peintrie: "d'un art, l'autre,"* edited by Bernard Blistène and Véronique Legrand, 372–9. Marseille, FR: Musées de Marseille.

– 1966–67. "LUXO LIXO." *Invenção: Revista de arte de vanguarda* 5: 55–6.

– 2008. "Olho por Olho." In Cid Campos et al 2008, 54.

– 1968. "sem um numero." In Solt 1968, 95.

de Campos, Augusto, Haroldo de Campos, and Décio Pignatari. (1958) 2008. "Pilot Plan for Concrete Poetry." Translated by Augusto de Campos, Haroldo de Campos, and Décio Pignatari. In Cid Campos et al. 2008, 90, 92.

de Campos, Haroldo. 1966–67. "ALEA I – VARIAÇÕES SEMÂNTICAS." *Invenção: Revista de arte de vanguarda* 5 (December–January): 32–3.

– 1968. "ALEA I – SEMANTIC VARIATIONS." In Solt 1968, 105–6.

– 2007. "The Informational Temperature of the Text." In *Novas: Selected Writings*, edited by Antonio Sergio Bessa and Odile Cisneros, 223–34. Evanston, IL: Northwestern University Press.

Dencker, Klaus Peter. 1972. *Text-Bilder: Visuelle Poesie international*. Koln, DE: Verlag M. DuMont Schauberg.

Deutsche, Rosalyn. 1996. *Evictions: Art and Spatial Politics.* Cambridge, MA: MIT Press.

"Dire Drama on the Death of the World." 1959. *LIFE* magazine, 30 November, 93–6.

Döhl, Reinhold. 1970. "Some Remarks on Concrete Poetry." In *Concrete Poetry?*, n. pag. Amsterdam: Stedelijk Museum.

Dos Passos, John. 1959. "Foreword." In *Doorway to Brasilia*, by Aloísio Magalhães and Eugene Feldman, n. pag. Philadelphia: Falcon Press.

Drucker, Johanna. 1998. *Figuring the Word: Essays on Books, Writing, and Visual Poetics.* New York: Granary Books.

– 2006. "Interactive, Algorithmic, Networked: Aesthetics of New Media Art." In *At a Distance: Precursors to Art and Activism on the Internet*, edited by Annmarie Chandler and Norie Neumark, 34–59. Cambridge, MA: MIT Press.

– 2009. *Speclab: Digital Aesthetics and Speculative Computing.* Chicago: University of Chicago Press.

– 1994. *The Visible Word: Experimental Typography and Modern Art.* Chicago: University of Chicago Press.

Dworkin, Craig. 2006. "Introduction: Delay in Verse." In *Language to Cover a Page: The Early Writings of Vito Acconci*, edited by Craig Dworkin, x–xviii. Cambridge, MA: MIT Press.

Essary, Loris. 1979. "On Language and Visual Language." In Kostelanetz 1979, 93–102.

Fahlström, Öyvind. 1968. "Hätila Ragulpr Pä Fätskliane Manifesto for Concrete Poetry." Solt, 1968, 74–8.

Fenollosa, Ernest, and Ezra Pound. 2008. *The Chinese Written Character as a Medium for Poetry: A Critical Edition.* Edited by Haun Saussy, Jonathan Stalling, and Lucas Klein. New York: Fordham University Press.

Fernbach-Flarsheim, Carl. 1968. "PØEM 1." In Solt 1968, 246.

– 1968. [untitled poem]. In Solt 1968, 248.

Finlay, Ian Hamilton. 1967. "Au Pair Girl." In Bann 1967, 151.

– 1967. "Homage to Malevich." In Bann 1967, 141.

– 1968. "Letter to Pierre Garnier, September 17th, 1963." In Solt 1968, 84.

– 1968. "Purse Sein." In Solt 1968, 208.

Flanner, Janet [Genêt]. 1961. "Letter from Paris." *The New Yorker*, 25 November, 150–4.

Foster, Hal, Rosalind Krauss, Yve-Alain Bois, and Benjamin H. Buchloh. 2004. *Art Since 1900: Modernism, Antimodernism, Postmodernism.* London: Thames and Hudson.

Frank, Joseph. 1982. "Spatial Form in Modern Literature." In *The Avant-Garde Tradition in Writing*, edited by Richard Kostelanetz, 43–77. Buffalo, NY: Prometheus Books.

Fraser, Valerie. 2000. *Building the New World: Studies in the Modern Architecture of Latin America, 1930–1960*. London: Verso.

"Free Zone Urged in Outer Space." 1957. *New York Times*, 10 October, 20.

Gappmayr, Heinz. 1970. "Zeichen." In *Concrete Poetry?*, edited by Liesbeth Crommelin et al. 62. Amsterdam: Stedelijk Museum. Exhibition catalogue.

Garnier, Pierre and Ilse Garnier. 1968. "Texte pour une architecture." In Solt 1968, 163.

Garnier, Pierre. 1963. "Position I du Mouvement International." Unpublished pamphlet.

– 1968. "Position I of the International Movement." In Solt 1968, 78–80.

Goldsmith, Kenneth. "Being Boring." Accessed 21 May 2010. www.epc.buffalo.edu.

– 2008. "Curation 2.0: Context is the New Content." In Cid Campos et al. 2008, 194–202.

– "From (Command) Line to (Iconic) Constellation." Accessed 30 October 2009. Ubuweb.com.

Goldsmith, Kenneth (ubuweb). 2013. "Just so ya know, UbuWeb was founded, based on, and inspired by that anthology of concrete poetry. It's still the fuel that runs the site." 12 December, 6:16 p.m. Tweet.

Goldsmith, Kenneth (kg_ubu). 2013. "The coolest holiday gift: An Anthology of Concrete Poetry (1967) reprint for $28. Wow: primaryinformation.org/projects/antho…." 12 December, 6:02 p.m. Tweet.

Gomringer, Eugen. 1968. *The Book of Hours and Constellations*. Edited and translated by Jerome Rothenberg. New York: Something Else Press.

– 1968. "Concrete Poetry." In Solt 1968, 67–8.

– 1968. "From Line to Constellation." In Solt 1968, 67.

– 1968. "The Poem as a Functional Object." In Solt 1968, 69–70.

– 2011. Unpublished interview with Eugen Gomringer. By Annette Gilbert. Translated by Carolyne Hauf and Annette Gilbert. N. pag.

– 1967. "Wind." In Bann 1967, 37.

Graham, Dan. 2001. *Dan Graham: Works 1965–2000*. Edited by Marianne Brouwer. Düsseldorf: Richter Verlag.

– 2001. "Figurative." In Graham, *Works* 2001, 95.

– 1975. *For Publication*. Los Angeles: Otis Art Institute of Los Angeles County.

– 2001. "Homes for America." In Graham, *Works* 2001, 103.

– 2000. "My Works for Magazine Pages: 'A History of Conceptual Art.'" In Alberro and Stimson 2000, 418–22.

– 1967. "Poem, March 1966." *Aspen* 5–6: n. pag.

Grossberg, Lawrence. 1997. "The Formation(s) of Cultural Studies: An American in Birmingham." In *Bringing it All Back Home: Essays on Cultural Studies* by Lawrence Grossberg, 195–233. Durham, NC: Duke University Press.

Grünewald, José Lino. 1967. "Preto." In Williams 1967, n. pag.

Guilbaut, Serge and Manuel J. Borja-Villel, eds. 2007. *Be-Bomb: The Transatlantic War of Images and all that Jazz, 1946–1956*. Barcelona and Madrid: Museu d'Art Contemporani de Barcelona and Museo Nacional Centro de Arte Reina Sofía.

Guillén, Mauro F. 2006. *The Taylorized Beauty of the Mechanical: Scientific Management and the Rise of Modernist Architecture*. Princeton, NJ: Princeton University Press.

Gumpel, Liselotte. 1976. *"Concrete" Poetry from East and West Germany: The Language of Exemplarism and Experimentalism*. London: Yale University Press.

Harrison, Charles. 2001. *Essays on Art & Language*. Cambridge, MA: MIT Press.

Harte, Tim. 2004. "Vasily Kamensky's *Tango with Cows*: A Modernist Map of Moscow." *The Slavic and East European Journal* 48 (Winter): 545–66.

Harvey, David. 1989. *The Condition of Postmodernity: An Enquiry into the Origins of Cultural Change*. Oxford: Basil Blackwell.

– 2000. "Cosmopolitanism and the Banality of Geographical Evils." *Public Culture* 12 (2): 529–64.

– 2000. *Spaces of Hope*. Berkeley: University of California Press.

Hayles, N. Katherine. 1999. *How We Became Posthuman: Virtual Bodies in Cybernetics, Literature, and Informatics*. Chicago: University of Chicago Press.

Helvetica. 2007. Directed by Gary Hustwit. Film. VEER.

Higgins, Dick. 1972. "[Letter to Sarenco]." *Lotta Poetica* 15–16 (August–September): n. pag.

– 1987. *Pattern Poetry: Guide to an Unknown Literature*. Albany: SUNY Press.

Hiršal, Josef and Bohumila Grögerová. 1968. "Developer (Vývoj I)." In Solt 1968, 146.

– 1968. *Job-boj*. Prague: Československý spisovatel.

– 1967. "Manifest." In Williams 1967, n. pag.

– 1970. "The Old / New (from the book of JOB:BOJ)." In *Anthology of Concretism*, edited by Eugene Wildman, 124–6. Chicago: The Swallow Press.

Hobsbawm, Eric. 1994. *The Age of Extremes: A History of the World, 1914–1991.* New York: Vintage.

Holford, William. 1957. "Brasília: A New Capital City for Brazil." *Architectural Review* 122: 394–402.

Holston, James. 1989. *The Modernist City: An Anthropological Critique of Brasília.* Chicago: University of Chicago Press.

Jacobs, Jane. 1993. *The Death and Life of Great American Cities.* New York: Modern Library.

Jameson, Fredric. 1984. "The Politics of Theory: Ideological Positions in the Postmodernism Debate." *New German Critique* 33 (Autumn): 53–65.

– 1984. "Postmodernism, or the Cultural Logic of Late Capitalism." *New Left Review* 1 (July–August): 53–92.

– 2010. "Postmodernism Revisited." Public Lecture at Simon Fraser University, Vancouver, BC, 11 March.

– 1998. "Preface." In *The Cultures of Globalization*, edited by Fredric Jameson and Masao Miyoshi, xi–xvii. Durham, NC: Duke University Press.

Johnson, Richard. 1986–87. "What is Cultural Studies Anyway?" *Social Text* 16 (Winter): 38–80.

Katz, Cindi. 2001. "On the Grounds of Globalization: A Topography for Feminist Political Engagement." *Signs: Journal of Women in Culture and Society* 26 (4): 1213–34.

Kittler, Friedrich. 1990. *Discourse Networks 1800/1900.* Translated by Michael Metteer and Chris Cullens. Palo Alto, CA: Stanford University Press.

– 1999. *Gramophone, Film, Typewriter.* Stanford, CA: Stanford University Press.

Klonsky, Milton, ed. 1975. *Speaking Pictures: A Gallery of Pictorial Poetry from the Sixteenth Century to the Present.* New York: Harmony Books.

Knowles, Allison. 1968. "Poem." In Bory 1968, 96.

Kostelanetz, Richard. 1970. *Imaged Words & Worded Images.* New York: Outerbridge & Denstfrey, 1970.

– 1970. "Introduction." *Imaged Words & Worded Images*, n. pag. New York: Outerbridge & Denstfrey.

– ed. 1979. *Visual Literature Criticism: A New Collection.* Carbondale: Southern Illinois University Press.

Kosuth, Joseph. 1970. Untitled statement. In *Information*, edited by Kynaston McShine, 69. New York: Museum of Modern Art. Exhibition catalogue.

Kotz, Liz. 2007. *Words to be Looked At: Language in 1960s Art.* Cambridge, MA: MIT Press.

Krauss, Rosalind. 1979. "Sculpture in the Exapanded Field." *October* 8 (Spring): 30–44.

Kristal, Efraín. 2002. "Considering Coldly: A Response to Franco Moretti." *New Left Review* 15: 61–74.

Kubrick, Stanley, dir. 1964. *Dr Strangelove, or: How I Learned to Stop Worrying and Love the Bomb*. 2001, DVD. Burbank, CA: Columbia TriStar Home Video.

Langer, Susanne K. 1957. *Problems of Art: Ten Philosophical Lectures*. New York: Scribner's.

Le Corbusier. (1933) 1966. *The Radiant City: Elements of a Doctrine of Urbanism to be Used as the Basis of Our Machine-Age Civilization*. Translated by Pamela Knight, Eleanor Levieux, and Derek Coltman. New York: Orion Press.

– (1923) 1986. *Towards a New Architecture*. Translated by Frederick Etchells. New York: Dover Publications.

LeWitt, Sol. 2000. "Paragraphs on Conceptual Art." In Alberro and Stimson 2000, 12–16.

Lippard, Lucy, ed. 1997. *Six Years: The Dematerialization of the Art Object from 1966 to 1972: A Cross-Reference Book of Information on Some Esthetic Boundaries: Consisting of a Bibliography into Which Are Inserted a Fragmented Text, Art Words, Documents, Interview, and Symposia, Arranged Chronologically and Focused on So-Called Conceptual or Information or Idea Art with Mentions of Such Vaguely Designated Areas as Minimal, Anti-form, Systems, Earth, or Process Art, Occurring Now in the Americas, Europe, England, Australia, and Asia (with Occasional Political Overtones, Edited and Annotated by Lucy R. Lippard)*. Berkeley: University of California Press.

Loxley, Simon. 2006. *Type: The Secret History of Letters*. London: I.B. Tauris.

Magalhães, Aloísio, and Eugene Feldman. 1959. *Doorway to Brasilia*. Philadelphia: Falcon Press. N. pag.

Malraux, André. 1949. *The Psychology of Art: Museum without Walls*. Translated by Stuart Gilbert. New York: Pantheon Books.

Mammí, Lorenzo. 2006. "Concret '56: The Toot of Form." In *Concreta '56: a raiz da forma*, 22–50. São Paulo, BR: Museo de Arte Moderna de São Paulo.

Marx, Karl, and Friedrich Engels. 2008. *Manifesto of the Communist Party*. Utrecht, NL: Open Source Socialist Publishing.

Marx, William, ed. 2008. *Les Arrière-gardes au XXe siècle*. Paris: Presses Universitaires de France.

Massin. 1970. *Letter and Image*. Translated by Caroline Hillier and Vivienne Menkes. New York: Van Nostrand Reinhold Company.

Mayer, Hansjörg. 1967. "USA." In Williams 1967, n. pag.

McCaffery, Steve. 1973. *Carnival: The First Panel: 1967–70*. Toronto: Coach House Press. N. pag.

– 1970. *Transitions to the Beast*. Toronto: Ganglia Press. N. pag.

McCaffery, Steve and bpNichol. 1992. *Rational Geomancy: The Kids of the Book Machine: The Collected Research Reports of the Toronto Research Group, 1973–1982*. Vancouver: Talonbooks.

McCullough, Kathleen. 1989. *An Annotated International Bibliography, with an Index of Poets and Poems*. Troy, NY: The Whitston Publishing Company.

McLuhan, Marshall. 1967. *Verbi-Voco-Visual Explorations*. New York: Something Else Press.

McLuhan, Marshall, and Quentin Fiore. 1967. *The Medium is the Massage: An Inventory of Effects*. New York: Bantam Books.

McQuaid, Kim. 2007. "Sputnik Reconsidered: Image and Reality in the Early Space Age." *Canadian Review of American Studies / Revue canadienne d'études américaines* 37 (3): 371–401.

McShine, Kynaston. 1970. *Information*. New York: Museum of Modern Art.

Meyer, James. 2005. "Introduction: Carl Andre, Writer." In *Cuts: Texts 1959–2004*, edited by James Meyer, 1–25. Cambridge, MA: MIT Press.

Mon, Franz. 1968. "From *et 2*." In Solt 1968, 125.

– 2012. "Letters Sounds Syllables Words: The Beginnings of Concrete and Visual Literature in the German Speaking World." In *Poesie - Konkret / Poetry - Concrete: Schriftenreihe für Künstlerpublikationen*, edited by Anne Thurman-Jajes, 196–202. Bremen: Salon Verlag.

Moretti, Franco. 2000. "Conjectures on World Literature." *New Left Review* 1: 54–68.

– 2003. "More Conjectures." *New Left Review* 20: 73–81.

Ngai, Sianne. 2005. *Ugly Feelings*. Cambridge, MA: Harvard University Press.

Nichol, bp. 1968. "Blues." In Solt 1968, 216.

Nova: Sputnik Declassified. 2008. USA: WGBH Boston. Video recording.

O'Brian, John. 2015. *Camera Atomica*. Toronto: Art Gallery of Ontario.

O'Doherty, Brian. 1999. *Inside the White Cube: The Ideology of the Gallery Space*. Berkeley: University of California Press.

Olson, Charles. 1997. *Collected Prose*. Ed. Donald Allen and Benjamin Friedlander. Berkeley: University of California Press.

"The Pause that Arouses." 1950. *Time*, 13 March, 33. Electronic.

Perloff, Marjorie. 1991. *Radical Artifice: Writing Poetry in the Age of Media*. Chicago: University of Chicago Press.

– 2010. *Unoriginal Genius: Poetry by Other Means in the New Century*. Chicago: University of Chicago Press.

– 2007. "Writing as Re-Writing: Concrete Poetry as Arrière-Garde."
   CiberLetras 17 (July). Accessed 18 January 2010. http://www.lehman.cuny.
   edu/ciberletras/v17/perloff.htm.

Perrone, Charles A. 1996. *Seven Faces: Brazilian Poetry Since Modernism.*
   Durham, NC: Duke University Press.

Pignatari, Décio. 1968. "Beba Coca Cola." In Solt 1968, 108.

– 1966–67. "Cr$isto é a solução." *Invenção: Revista de arte de vanguarda* 5:
   78–9.

– 1966–67. "Disenformio [advertisement]." *Invenção: Revista de arte de vanguarda* 5: 52.

– 1993. "Entretien avec Décio Pignatari." By Jacques Donguy. In *Poésure et
   Peintrie: "d'un art, l'autre,"* 450–7. Marseille, FR: Musées de Marseille.

– 1968. "LIFE." In Solt 1968, 108.

– "New Poetry: Concrete." 2008. In Cid Campos et al. 2008, 85–8.

– "Semiotic Poem." 1964. *Invenção: Revista de arte de vanguarda* 4: 84.

Poggioli, Renato. 1968. *The Theory of the Avant-Garde.* Translated by Gerald
   Fitzgerald. Cambridge, MA: Belknap Press.

Prendergast, Christopher. 2001. "Negotiating World Literature." *New Left
   Review* 8: 100–21.

Price, Leah. 2000. *The History of the Anthology and the Rise of the Novel: From
   Richardson to George Eliot.* Cambridge: Cambridge University Press.

Ramírez, Mari Carmen. 2000. "Blueprint Circuits: Conceptual Art and Politics
   in Latin America." In Alberro and Stimson 2000, 550–62.

Read, Justin. 2005. "Alternative Functions: Oscar Niemeyer and the Poetics of
   Modernity." *MODERNISM/modernity* 12 (2): 253–72.

Redfield, Peter. 2002. "The Half-Life of Empire in Outer Space." *Social Studies
   of Science* 32 (5–6): 791–825.

Reichardt, Jasia, ed. 1968. *Cybernetic Serendipity: The Computer and the Arts.*
   London: Studio International.

– ed. 1971. *Cybernetics, Art, and Ideas.* Greenwich, CT: New York Graphic
   Society, Ltd.

– 1965. "Between Poetry and Painting." In *Between Poetry and Painting,* curated by Jasia Reichardt, 9. London: ICA. Exhibition catalogue.

– "Cybernetics, Art, and Ideas." 1971. In *Cybernetics, Art, and Ideas,* edited by
   Jasia Reichardt, 11–17. Greenwich, CT: New York Graphic Society.

Rose, Kenneth. 2001. *One Nation Underground: The Fallout Shelter in
   American Culture.* New York: New York University Press.

Roth, Dieter. 1967. "Some Variations on 4⁴." In Williams 1967, n. pag.

Rühm, Gerhard. 1969. "Jetzt." In *Concrete Poetry: An Exhibition in Four*

Parts, edited by Alvin Balkind, n. pag. Vancouver: The Fine Arts Gallery, University of British Columbia.

– 2012. "A Personal Perspective on Concrete Poetry." In *Poesie - Konkret / Poetry - Concrete: Schriftenreihe für Künstlerpublikationen*, edited by Anne Thurman-Jajes, 220–6.

– 2011. Unpublished interview with Gerhard Rühm. By Friedrich Block. March 2011. N. pag.

Sarenco. 1971. "Poesia visiva e conceptual art / un plagio ben organizzato." *Lotta Poetica* 1 (June): 12–13.

– 1971. "Poesia visiva e conceptual art / un plagio ben organizzato." *Lotta Poetica* 3 (August): 12.

– 1971. "Poesia visiva e conceptual art / un plagio ben organizzato." *Lotta Poetica* 7 (December): 16.

– 1972. "Poesia visiva e conceptual art / un plagio ben organizzato." *Lotta Poetica* 9 (February): 12.

– 1973. "Poetical Licence." *Lotta Poetica* 23–4 (April–May): 12.

Saussure, Ferdinand de. 1986. *Course in General Linguistics*. Translated by Roy Harris. Peru, IL: Open Court Classics.

Saussy, Haun. 2008. "Fenollosa Compounded: A Discrimination." In *The Chinese Written Character as a Medium for Poetry: A Critical Edition*, edited by Haun Saussy, Jonathan Stalling, and Lucas Klein, 1–40. New York: Fordham University Press.

Schnapp, Jeffrey T., and Adam Michaels. 2012. *The Electric Information Age Book: McLuhan/Agel/Fiore and the Experimental Paperback*. New York: Princeton Architectural Press.

Schimmel, Paul, Nicholas Cullinan, Astrid Handa-Gagnard, Shōichi Hirai, Sarah-Neel Smith, and Robert Storr. 2012. *Destroy the Picture: Painting the Void, 1949–1962*. Los Angeles: Museum of Contemporary Art.

Scobie, Stephen. 1997. *Earthquakes and Explorations: Language and Painting from Cubism to Concrete Poetry*. Toronto: University of Toronto Press.

– 1979. "A Homage and an Alphabet: Two Recent Works by Ian Hamilton Finlay." In Kostelanetz 1979, 107–13.

– 1969. "Instructions for Computer Poem 3 – Night and Day." *Concrete Poetry: An Exhibition in Four Parts*, edited by Alvin Balkind, n. pag. Vancouver: The Fine Arts Gallery, University of British Columbia.

Scott, James C. 1998. *Seeing Like a State: How Certain Schemes to Improve the Human Condition Have Failed*. New Haven, CT: Yale University Press.

Seaman, David. 1981. *Concrete Poetry in France*. Ann Arbor: University of Michigan Press.

Shanken, Edward A. 2002. "Art in the Information Age: Technology and Conceptual Art." *Leonardo* 35 (4): 433–8.

– 2002. "Cybernetics and Art: Cultural Convergence in the 1960s." In *From Energy to Information: Representation in Science and Technology, Art, and Literature*, edited by Bruce Clarke and Linda Dalrymple Henderson, 255–77. Stanford, CA: Stanford University Press.

– 1998. "The House that Jack Built: Jack Burnham's Concept of Software as a Metaphor for Art." *Leonardo Electronic Almanac* 6 (November). Accessed 30 October 2009. http://mitpress.mit.edu/e-journals/LEA/ARTICLES/jack.html.

Shannon, Claude and Warren Weaver. 1963. *The Mathematical Theory of Communication*. Urbana: University of Illinois Press.

Sharkey, John. 1970. "$ Kill." In *Concrete Poetry?*, edited by Liesbeth Crommelin et al., 96. Amsterdam: Stedelijk Museum.

Siegelaub, Seth. 2001. "Seth Siegelaub: April 17, 1969." Interview by Patricia Norvell. In *Recording Conceptual Art: Early Interviews with Barry, Huebler, Kaltenbach, LeWitt, Morris, Oppenheim, Siegelaub, Smithson, and Weiner by Patricia Norvell*, edited by Alexander Alberrro and Patricia Norvell, 31–55. Berkeley: University of California Press.

Singh, Simon. 1999. *The Code Book: The Science of Secrecy from Ancient Egypt to Quantum Cryptography*. New York: Anchor Books.

Sington, David, dir. 2007. *In the Shadow of the Moon*. UK / USA: Discovery Films. Video recording.

Smithson, Robert. 1996. *Robert Smithson: The Collected Writings*. Edited by Jack Flam. Berkeley: University of California Press.

Sladen, Mark. 2009. "Poor. Old. Tired. Horse.: Room One." *Roland* 2 (June–August): 4.

Solt, Mary Ellen, ed. 1968. *Concrete Poetry: A World View*. Bloomington: Indiana University Press.

– 1996. "Concrete Steps to an Anthology." In *Experimental, Visual, Concrete: Avant-Garde Poetry since the 1960s*, edited by K. David Jackson, Eric Vos, and Johanna Drucker, 347–51. Atlanta: Rodopi.

– 1968. "Moonshot Sonnet." In Solt 1968, 242.

Spatola, Adriano. 2008. *Toward Total Poetry*. Translated by Brendan W. Hennessey and Guy Bennet. Los Angeles: Otis Books / Seismicity Editions.

Spivak, Gayatri Chakravorty. 1998. "Cultural Talks in the Hot Peace." In *Cosmopolitics: Thinking and Feeling Beyond the Nation*, edited by Pheng Cheah and Bruce Robbins, 329–48. Minneapolis: University of Minnesota Press.

– *Death of a Discipline*. 2003. New York: Columbia University Press.

Stefans, Brian Kim. 2000. "The Dreamlife of Letters." www.arras.net.
Accessed 15 May 2010.

Stein, Gertrude. (1938) 1959. *Picasso*. Boston: Beacon Press.

Thomkins, Andre. 1967. "Dogmat-Mot." In Williams 1967, n. pag.

– "Dogmat-Mot." 1970. In *Concrete Poetry?*, edited by Liesbeth Crommelin
et. al, 56. Amsterdam: Stedelijk Museum.

Tullett, Barrie, ed. 2014. *Typewriter Art: A Modern Anthology*. London:
Laurence King Publishing.

Venturi, Robert, Denise Scott Brown, and Steven Izenour. (1972) 1977.
Learning From Las Vegas: The Forgotten Symbolism of Architectural Form.
Cambridge, MA: MIT Press.

Vree, Paul de. 1971. "Lotta Poetica." *Lotta Poetica* 1 (June): 2.

Wall, Irwin M. 2007. "Hollywood's Imperialism and Coca-Colanization." In
Be-Bomb: The Transatlantic War of Images and All That Jazz: 1946–1956,
edited by Serge Guilbaut and Manuel J. Borja-Villel, 65–75. Barcelona
and Madrid: Museu d'Art Contemporani de Barcelona and Museo
Nacional Centro de Arte Reina Sofía.

Wall, Jeffery. 1969. "Vancouver." *Artforum* 7 (Summer): 70–1.

Wallace, Ian. 1969. "Literature – Transparent and Opaque." In *Concrete
Poetry: An Exhibition in Four Parts*, edited by Alvin Balkind, n. pag.
Vancouver: The Fine Arts Gallery, University of British Columbia.

Wallerstein, Immanuel. 2004. *World-Systems Analysis: An Introduction*.
Durham, NC: Duke University Press.

Walther-Bense, Elizabeth. 1996. The Relations of Haroldo de Campos to
German Concretist Poets, in Particular Max Bense." In *Experimental,
Visual, Concrete: Avant-Garde Poetry since the 1960s*, edited by Kenneth
David Jackson, Eric Vos, Johanna Drucker, 353–66. Amsterdam: Rodopi.

Weaver, Mike. 1966. "Concrete Poetry." *The Lugano Review* 5–6: 100–25.

Whittaker, Sir Edmund. 1958. *From Euclid to Eddington: A Study of
Conceptions of the External World*. New York: Dover Publications, Inc.

Wiener, Norbert. 1954. *The Human Use of Human Beings: Cybernetics and
Society*. Boston: Houghton Mifflin.

Wildman, Eugene, ed. 1970. *Anthology of Concretism*. Chicago: The Swallow
Press.

– 1970. "Afterword." In *Anthology of Concretism*, edited by Eugene Wildman,
161–5. Chicago: The Swallow Press.

Williams, Emmett, ed. 1967. *An Anthology of Concrete Poetry*. New York:
Something Else Press.

Witkins, Richard. 1961. "Ranger Takes Close-up Moon Photos Revealing Craters Only 3 Feet Wide; Data Gained on Landing Site for Man." *New York Times*, 1 August, 1, 8.

Wood, Robin MacKinnon and Margaret Masterman. 1968. "Computer Poetry From CLRU." In *Cybernetic Serendipity: The Computer and the Arts*, edited by Jasia Reichardt, 55. London: Studio International.

INDEX